BUSINESS/SCIENCE/TECHNOLOGY DIVISION
CHICAGO PUBLIC LIBRARY
400 SOUTH STATE STREET
CHICAGO, IL 60605

W9-ABC-994

Chicago Public Library

Form 178 rev. 11-00

UNITED STATES ENTREPRENEURS AND THE COMPANIES THEY BUILT

UNITED STATES ENTREPRENEURS AND THE COMPANIES THEY BUILT

An Index to Biographies in Collected Works

WAHIB NASRALLAH

Z 7164 .C81 N237 2003b
Nasrallah, Wahib, 1945-
United States entrepreneurs
and the companies they

Bibliographies and Indexes in Economics and Economic History,
Number 20

Greenwood Press
Westport, Connecticut • London

Library of Congress Cataloging in Publication Data

Nasrallah, Wahib, 1945–
    United States entrepreneurs and the companies they built : an index to biographies
in collected works / Wahib Nasrallah.
        p. cm.—(Bibliographies and indexes in economics and economic history, ISSN
    0749–1786 ; no. 20)
    Includes bibliographical references and index.
    ISBN 0–313–32332–1 (alk. paper)
    1. Businesspeople—United States—Biography--Indexes. 2. Businesswomen—United
States—Biography—Indexes. 3. Executives—United States—Biography—Indexes. 4. Women
executives—United States—Biography—Indexes. 5. Entrepreneurship—United
States—History—Indexes. 6. Corporations—United States—History—Indexes. 7. Business
enterprises—United States—History—Indexes. I. Title. II. Series.
Z7164.C81N237   2003
[HC102.5.A2]
016.338092'273--dc22   2003057991

British Library Cataloguing in Publication Data is available.

Copyright © 2003 by Wahib Nasrallah

All rights reserved. No portion of this book may be
reproduced, by any process or technique, without the
express written consent of the publisher.

Library of Congress Catalog Card Number: 2003057991
ISBN: 0–313–32332–1
ISSN: 0749–1786

First published in 2003

Greenwood Press, 88 Post Road West, Westport, CT 06881
An imprint of Greenwood Publishing Group, Inc.
www.greenwood.com

Printed in the United States of America

The paper used in this book complies with the
Permanent Paper Standard issued by the National
Information Standards Organization (Z39.48–1984).

10 9 8 7 6 5 4 3 2 1

RO3025 89168

BUSINESS/SCIENCE/TECHNOLOGY DIVISION
CHICAGO PUBLIC LIBRARY
400 SOUTH STATE STREET
CHICAGO, IL 60605

CONTENTS

INTRODUCTION

A large number of executive biographies are published in collected works. These works are very rich with stories of entrepreneurs who shaped the history of American enterprise. In addition they provide portraits of innovators from a variety of ethnic backgrounds. A number of these collected works are devoted to women entrepreneurs who formed very successful companies with familiar names. Most of these works include 10-20 biographies, some include more. The biographies vary in size but are commonly 3-10 pages long.

Very few of these works are analyzed—less than 5%. Since the majority of works are not, easy access to these biographies is practically impossible. In addition, business indexing and abstracting services do not include these works in their coverage. There is a wealth of information contained in these works, but most of them are collecting dust in major libraries due to the lack of indexing.

Until now, there has been no index that identifies where these executive biographies are to be found. This index provides a complete bibliographic entry under the name of the executive, pointing to the collected work, and the page numbers, where the biography can be found.

This book identifies and indexes over 120 biographical collected works. The number of executive biographies indexed is approximately 1,700.

Since every attempt has been made to make this work as comprehensive as possible, no limit was placed on the dates the collected works were published. As a result the earliest collected work included was published in 1893 and the latest in 2001.

The book is in three parts: The main index arranged by entrepreneur's name, an appendix listing all the collected works, and an index by corporation.

THE INDEX

ABBEY, JOHN

Suarez, Ruth. "John Abbey: Ichiban, 'Keeping His Soul in Blues'." In *Superstar Entrepreneurs of Small and Large Businesses Reveal Their Secrets*, 111-116. Piscataway, N.J.: Research and Education Association, 1998.

ABELL, ROSLYN

Koppel, Mara. "The Physics of Trading—Roslyn Abell." In *Women of the Pits: Shattering the Glass Ceiling in Financial Markets*, 141-152. Chicago, Ill.: Dearborn Financial Publishers, 1998.

ABERCROMBIE, JOSEPHINE

Sheehy, Sandy. "Josephine Abercrombie: The Pugilists' Pygmalion." In *Texas Big Rich; Exploits, Eccentricities, And Fabulous Fortunes Won and Lost*, 68-75. New York, N.Y.: Morrow, 1990.

ACEVEDO, RAYDEAN

Alexander, Shoshana. "Raydean Acevedo: Research Management Consultants, Inc. (RMCI), Golden, Colorado." In *Women's Ventures, Women's Visions: 29 Inspiring Stories From Women Who Started*

Their Own Businesses, 175-180. Freedom, Calif.: The Crossing Press, 1997.

ACKERLY, LEONE

Gray, Bob, ed. "A Self-Maid Success Story." In *How Entrepreneurs Make Business Profits: A Study of Personal Success Stories From Cordovan Business Journals*, 77-82. Houston, Tex.: Cordovan Press, 1982.

ADDINGTON, LARRY C.

Aronoff, Craig E., and John L. Ward. "Larry C. Addington." In *Contemporary Entrepreneurs*, 5-11. Detroit, Mich.: Omnigraphics, Inc., 1992.

ADELSON, SHELDON

Silver, A. David. "Sheldon Adelson." In *Entrepreneurial Megabucks: The 100 Greatest Entrepreneurs of the Last 25 Years*, 131-133. New York, N.Y.: Wiley, 1985.

ADONI, JAY

Kingston, Brett. "Jay Adoni of Admos Shoe Corporation." In *The Dynamos: Who Are They Anyway?*, 105-110. New York, N.Y: Wiley, 1987.

ALDRICH, WINTHROP W.

Hillyer, William Hurd. "Winthrop W. Aldrich." In *America's Fifty Foremost Business Leaders,* ed. B. C. Forbes, 3-10. New York, N.Y.: B.C. Forbes, 1948.

ALEXANDER, BILL

Woodard, Michael D. "G O Furniture Manufacturing Company—Bill Alexander." In *Black Entrepreneurs in America: Stories of Struggle and Success*, 199-212. New Brunswick, N.J.: Rutgers University Press, 1997.

ALEXANDER, TODD B.

Mitchell, Niki Butler. "Ciao, Baby!: Todd B. Alexander, Managing Director, Vendemmia, Inc." In *The New Color of Success: Twenty Young Black Millionaires Tell You How They're Making it*, 69-80. Rocklin, Calif.: Prima Publishing, 2000.

ALGER, HORATIO

Davis, William. "Horatio Alger, 1834-99: Creator of the American Dream." *The Innovators: The Essential Guide to Business Thinkers, Achievers and Entrepreneurs*, 16-19. New York, N.Y.: AMACOM, 1987.

Gunther, Max, "Horatio Alger." In *The Very, Very Rich and How They Got That Way*, ed. Max Gunther, 43-48. Chicago, Ill.: The Playboy Press, 1972.

ALLEN, HERBERT

Auletta, Ken. "The Consigliere: Herbert Allen, Matchmaker." In *The Highwaymen; Warriors of the Information Superhighway*, 160-179. New York, N.Y.: Random House, 1997.

ALLEN, MARTIN A.

Silver, A. David. "Martin A. Allen." In *Entrepreneurial Megabucks: The 100 Greatest Entrepreneurs of the Last 25 Years*, 134-136. New York, N.Y.: Wiley, 1985.

ALLEN, ROSCOE

Harris, Wendy Beech. "Roscoe Allen, Roscoe Allen Company: The Other Mr. Peanut." In *Against All Odds: Ten Entrepreneurs Who Followed Their Hearts and Found Success*, 143-161. New York, N.Y.: Wiley, 2001.

ALLRED, CAROL GERBER

Mikaelian, A. "Carol Gerber Allred." In *Women Who Mean Business: Success Stories of Women Over Forty*, 78-82. New York, N.Y.: William Morrow & Co., 1999.

ALLS, KATHY

Alls, Kathy. "Step Out for Success." In *Success Secrets: How Eighteen Everyday Women Became Fortune Builders and Famous Speakers*, 129-148. Glendora, Calif.: Royal CBS Publishing, 1978.

ALLYN, STANLEY C.

Sisson, Herbert Gay. "Stanley C. Allyn." In *America's Fifty Foremost Business Leaders*, ed. B. C. Forbes, 11-22. New York, N.Y.: B.C. Forbes, 1948.

ALPERT, MARTIN

Silver, A. David. "Martin Alpert." In *Entrepreneurial Megabucks: The 100 Greatest Entrepreneurs of the Last 25 Years*, 137-139. New York, N.Y.: Wiley, 1985.

ALVES, STEPHEN

Mitchell, Niki Butler. "Designing Man: Stephen Alves, President and CEO, Alves Contracting Company, Ltd." In *The New Color of Success: Twenty Young Black Millionaires Tell You How They're Making it*, 155-167. Rocklin, Calif.: Prima Publishing, 2000.

AMDAHL, GENE

Slater, Robert. "Gene Amdahl: Mainframe Designer Par Excellence." In *Portraits in Silicon*, 184-193. Cambridge, Mass.: MIT Press, 1987.

AMOS, DANIEL P.

Pottker, Jan. "AFLAC (American Family Corporation): Insuring the Succession." In *Born to Power: Heirs to America's Leading Businesses*, 128-135. New York, N.Y.: Barron's, 1992.

AMOS, JAMES H. JR

Oster, Merrill J. "Franchising Your Future." In *The Entrepreneur's Creed: The Principles & Passions of 20 Successful Entrepreneurs*, 100-109. Nashville, Tenn.: Broadman & Holman Publishers, 2001.

ANDERSON, J. REID

Silver, A. David. "J. Reid Anderson." In *Entrepreneurial Megabucks: The 100 Greatest Entrepreneurs of the Last 25 Years*, 140-142. New York, N.Y.: Wiley, 1985.

ANDERSON, SUSAN L.

Mikaelian, A. "Susan L. Anderson." In *Women Who Mean Business: Success Stories of Women Over Forty*, 180-184. New York, N.Y.: William Morrow & Co., 1999.

ANDROS, DAVID

Elfstrand, Rhonda. "Dr. David Andros, D.D.S.: Doctor of Implantology." In *The Story Behind the Success: Learning From Pittsburgh Professionals*, 4-17 Pittsburgh, Penn.: Steel Publishing Partners, 1996.

ANGELOU, MAYA

Liberman, Gail, and Alan Lavine. "Maya Angelou: Poetry and Novels Earn Millions." In *Rags to Riches: Motivating Stories of How Ordinary People Achieved Extraordinary Wealth!*, 184-194. Chicago, Ill.: Dearborn, 2000.

ARDEN, ELIZABETH

"The Big Business of Beauty: The Feminine Struggle for Equal Rights Early in the 2oth Century Set the Stage for Elizabeth Arden's Blossoming Career in Beauty." In *The 50 Great Pioneers of American Industry*. By the Editors of News Front and Year, 182-185. Maplewood, N.J.: C.S. Hammond, 1964.

Davis, William. "Elizabeth Arden, 1884-1966: The Women Who Made Make-Up Respectable." In *The Innovators: The Essential Guide to Business Thinkers, Achievers and Entrepreneurs*, 19-22. New York, N.Y.: AMACOM, 1987.

ARISON, MICKY

Pottker, Jan. "Carnival Cruise Lines, Inc.: Low Rollers Put Wind in Sales." In *Born to Power: Heirs to America's Leading Businesses*, 28-33. New York, N.Y.: Barron's, 1992.

ARMOUR, JONATHAN OGDEN

Darby, Edwin. "Armour." In *The Fortune Builders*, 1-15. Garden City, N.Y.: Doubleday and Company, Inc., 1986.

ARMOUR, PHILIP DANFORTH

Burnley, James. "Philip Danforth Armour: The Meat King of America." In *Millionaires and Kings of Enterprise; The Marvellous Careers of Some Americans Who by Pluck, Foresight, And Energy Have Made Themselves Masters in the Fields of Industry and Finance*, 30-41. Philadelphia, Penn.: J. B. Lippincott, 1901.

Klepper, Michael M., and Robert Gunther. "Philip Danforth Armour (1832-1901): Pork-Barrel Profits." In *The Wealthy 100 : From Benjamin Franklin to Bill Gates—A Ranking of the Richest Americans, Past and Present*, 123-125. Secaucus, N.J. : Carol Pub. Group, 1996.

"Philip Danforth Armour." In *A Dozen Roads to Success: Being Graphic Sketches of Twelve of the Most Prominent Business Men of America*,

And Showing How They Became Millionaires, 46-57. Philadelphia, Penn.: Girard Pub. Co., 1894.

Stoddard, William Osborn. "Philip Danforth Armour— Organization." In *Men of Business,* 197-211. New York, N.Y.: Scribner's Sons, 1893. 317 p.

ARMOUR, WAYNE

Wallace, Robert L. "Wayne Armour: President and CEO, OFO Technologies, Inc." In *Black Wealth: Your Road to Small Business Success,* 104-109. New York, N.Y.: Wiley, 2000.

ARMSTRONG, KIM

"Kim Armstrong." In *Women Achievers: A Series of Dialogues from the Womanagement Process,* 51-61. New York, N.Y.: American Telephone and Telegraph Co., 1997.

ARMSTRONG, THOMAS M.

Cleary, David Powers. "Armstrong Floors, Let the Buyer Have Faith." In *Great American Brands: The Success Formulas That Made Them Famous,* 1-6. New York, N.Y: Fairchild Publications, 1981.

ARNOLD, JANIE

Lassen, Ali. "Janie Arnold: Salesperson, Schauer Printing." In *The Secret of Their Success: Women Entrepreneurs Reveal How They Made It,* 191-194. Carlsbad, Calif.: Ali Lassen Success System, 1990.

ARNOLD, STANLEY

Uris, Auren. "Stanley Arnold—Idea Man, Incorporated." In *The Executive Breakthrough; 21 Roads to the Top,* 317-336. Garden City, N.Y.: Doubleday, 1967.

ARNONI, BOB

Elfstrand, Rhonda. "Bob Arnoni: The Arnoni Group." In *The Story Behind the Success: Learning From Pittsburgh Professionals*, 18-29. Pittsburgh, Penn.: Steel Publishing Partners, 1996.

ARRETT, DEBRA J.

Mikaelian, A. "Debra J. Arrett." In *Women Who Mean Business: Success Stories of Women Over Forty*, 103-107. New York, N.Y.: William Morrow & Co., 1999.

ARTHUR, JACQUIE

White, Jane. "Jacquie Arthur of M/A-Com: Staying on Track After Being Derailed." In *A Few Good Women: Breaking the Barriers to Top Management*, 125-133. Englewood Cliffs, N.J.: Prentice Hall, 1992.

ARTIS, WILLIE

Wallace, Robert L. "Willie Artis: Founder, Genessee Packaging, Flint, Michigan." In *Black Wealth: Your Road to Small Business Success*, 135-144. New York, N.Y.: Wiley, 2000.

ASH, MARY KAY

Brands, H. W. "Every Women a Queen: Mary Kay Ash." In *Masters of Enterprise: Giants of American Business from John Jacob Astor and J.P. Morgan to Bill Gates and Oprah Winfrey*, 246-255. New York, N.Y.: Free Press, 1999.

Gross, Daniel, and the Editors of Forbes Magazine. "Mary Kay Ash and Her Corporate Culture for Women." In *Forbes Greatest Business Stories of All Time*, 232-245. New York, N.Y.: Wiley, 1996.

Landrum, Gene N. "Mary Kay Ash—A Confident Charismatic." In *Profiles of Female Genius: Thirteen Creative Women Who Changed the World*, 170-186. Amherst, N.Y.: Prometheus Books, 1994.

MacPhee, William. "Mary Kay Ash of Mary Kay Cosmetics." In *Rare Breed: The Entrepreneur, An American Culture*, 21-36. Chicago, Ill.: Probus Publishing Company, 1987.

Sheehy, Sandy. "Mary Kay Ash: Eyeliner and Inspiration." In *Texas Big Rich; Exploits, Eccentricities, And Fabulous Fortunes Won and Lost*, 184-196. New York, N.Y.: Morrow, 1990.

Shook, Robert L. "Mary Kay Ash." In *The Entrepreneurs: Twelve Who Took Risks and Succeeded*, 103-114. New York, N.Y: Harper & Row, 1980.

Silver, A. David. "Mary Kay Ash." In *Entrepreneurial Megabucks: The 100 Greatest Entrepreneurs of the Last 25 Years*, 143-145. New York, N.Y.: Wiley, 1985.

Sobel, Robert, and David B. Sicilia. "Mary Kay Ash: The Pink Cadillac Approach." In *The Entrepreneurs: An American Adventure*, 38-41. Boston, Mass.: Houghton Mifflin Company, 1986.

Taylor, Russel R. "Mary Kay Ash: 'You Can Do It'." In *Exceptional Entrepreneurial Women*, 65-71. New York, N.Y: Quorum Books, 1988.

ASHHURST, CARMEN

Enkelis, Liane, and Karen Olsen. "Carmen Ashhurst: President & Chief Operating Officer, Rush Communications." In *On Our Own Terms: Portraits of Women Business Leaders* , 82-91. San Francisco, Calif.: Berrett-Koehler, 1995.

ASHTON, ALAN C.

Aronoff, Craig E., and John L. Ward. "Alan C. Ashton; Bruce W. Bastian." In *Contemporary Entrepreneurs*, 12-17. Detroit, Mich.: Omnigraphics, Inc., 1992.

ASPINWALL, WILLIAM H.

Klepper, Michael M., and Robert Gunther. "William H. Aspinwall (1807-1875): Spanned the Isthmus of Panama." In *The Wealthy 100 : From Benjamin Franklin to Bill Gates—A Ranking of the Richest Americans, Past and Present,* 236-238. Secaucus, N.J. : Carol Pub. Group, 1996.

THE ASTOR FAMILY

Otten, Alan L. "The Astors." In *American Dynasties Today,* 97-128. Homewood, Ill.: Dow Jones-Irwin, 1990.

Brands, H. W. "Growing Up with the Country: John Jacob Astor." In *Masters of Enterprise: Giants of American Business from John Jacob Astor and J.P. Morgan to Bill Gates and Oprah Winfrey,* 1-11. New York, N.Y.: Free Press, 1999.

Burnley, James. "Kings of Finance and Fortune: The Astors and Vanderbilts." In *Millionaires and Kings of Enterprise; The Marvellous Careers of Some Americans Who by Pluck, Foresight, And Energy Have Made Themselves Masters in the Fields of Industry and Finance,* 490-508. Philadelphia, Penn.: J. B. Lippincott, 1901.

Diamond, Sigmond. "John Jacob Astor." In *The Reputation of the American Businessman,* 23-52. Cambridge, Mass.: Harvard University Press, 1955.

Folsom, Burton W. "John Jacob Astor and the Fur Trade: Testing the Role of Government." In *Empire Builders: How Michigan Entrepreneurs Helped Make America Great,* 9-30. Traverse City, Mich.: Rhodes & Easton, 1998.

Klepper, Michael M., and Robert Gunther. "John Jacob Astor (1763-1848): From Seven Flutes to An Empire in Fur and Real Estate." In *The Wealthy 100 : From Benjamin Franklin to Bill Gates—A Ranking of the Richest Americans, Past and Present,* 18-25. Secaucus, N.J. : Carol Pub. Group, 1996.

Oglesby, Richard E. "John Jacob Astor, '...A Better Businessman Than the Best of Them'." In *Business Entrepreneurs in the West,* ed. Ted C. Hinckley, 8-14. Manhattan, Kans.: Sunflower University Press, 1986.

Stoddard, William Osborn. "John Jacob Astor—Romance." In *Men of Business*, 9-30. New York, N.Y.: Scribner's Sons, 1893. 317 p.

ATKINS, MICHELE

Elfstrand, Rhonda. "Michele Atkins, CFRE: Make-A-Wish Foundation of Western Pennsylvania." In *The Story Behind the Success: Learning From Pittsburgh Professionals*, 30-47. Pittsburgh, Penn.: Steel Publishing Partners, 1996.

AUGUSTINE, LIZABETH J.

Augustine, Lizabeth J. "Nurses: An Unsophisticated Market?" In *How I Became a Nurse Entrepreneur: Tales from 50 Nurses in Business*, 169-179. Petaluma, Calif.: National Nurses in Business Association, 1991.

AVIS, WARREN

Davis, William. "Avis Warren, b. 1917: 'We're Number Two, We Try Harder'." In *The Innovators: The Essential Guide to Business Thinkers, Achievers and Entrepreneurs*, 26-29. New York, N.Y.: AMACOM, 1987.

AXELROD, JANET

Kao, John J. "Janet Axelrod." In *The Entrepreneur*, 32-45. Englewood Cliffs, New Jersey: Prentice Hall, 1991.

AYER, FRANCIS WAYLAND

"Architects of 'Mad Avenue': F.W. Ayer and J. Walter Thompson Found Advertising in Chaos and Turned It into a Respectable, Billion Dollar Business." In *The 50 Great Pioneers of American Industry*. By the Editors of News Front and Year, 68-71. Maplewood, N.J.: C.S. Hammond, 1964.

BACA, JACQUELINE

Oster, Merrill J. "¡LA FAMILIA BUENA!." In *The Entrepreneur's Creed: The Principles & Passions of 20 Successful Entrepreneurs*, 172-181. Nashville, Tenn.: Broadman & Holman Publishers, 2001.

BAIRD, JACQUELINE

Rich-McCoy, Lois. "Synergy and Swimsuits: Gillian Mitchell and Jacqueline Baird." In *Millionairess: Self-Made Women of America*, 23-48. New York, N.Y.: Harper & Row, 1978.

BAJAJ, KAVELLE

Enkelis, Liane, and Karen Olsen. "Kavelle Bajaj: President, I-Net." In *On Our Own Terms: Portraits of Women Business Leaders*, 112-123. San Francisco, Calif.: Berrett-Koehler, 1995.

BAKER, GEORGE F.

Klepper, Michael M., and Robert Gunther. "George F. Baker (1840-1931): The Sphinx of Wall Street." In *The Wealthy 100: From Benjamin Franklin to Bill Gates—A Ranking of the Richest Americans, Past and Present,* 202-204. Secaucus, N.J.: Carol Pub. Group, 1996.

BAKER, GEORGE THEODORE

Hopkins, George E. "Fortunate in His Enemies: George T. Baker, National Airlines, And Federal Regulators." In *Airline Executives and Federal Regulation: Case Studies in American Enterprise from the Airmail Era to the Dawn of the Jet Age*, ed. W. David Lewis, 213-241. Columbus, Ohio: Ohio State University Press, 2000.

BAKER, L. M. (BUD)

Wendel, Charles B. "Preserving Tradition While Focusing on the Future: L. M. 'Bud' Baker Jr., President and CEO, Wachovia Corporation." In *The New Financiers*, 15-34. Chicago, Ill.: Irwin Professional Pub., 1996.

BAKER, MARY M.

Baker, Mary M. "Chicken Soup and What?" In *How I Became a Nurse Entrepreneur: Tales from 50 Nurses in Business*, 7-11. Petaluma, Calif.: National Nurses in Business Association, 1991.

BAKKEN, EARL

Pine, Carol, and Susan Mundale. "Earl Bakken; Sparks of Life." In *Self-Made: The Stories of 12 Minnesota Entrepreneurs*, 39-54. Minneapolis, Minn.: Dorn Books, 1982.

BALDUCCI FAMILY

Buchholz, Barbara B., and Margaret Crane. "Grace's Marketplace, New York, NY." In *Corporate Blood Lines: The Future of the Family Firm*, 43-59. New York, N.Y: Carol Publishing Group, 1989.

BALDWIN, MATTHIAS W.

Burnley, James. "American Locomotive Kings: The Baldwin Firm." In *Millionaires and Kings of Enterprise; The Marvellous Careers of Some Americans Who by Pluck, Foresight, And Energy Have Made Themselves Masters in the Fields of Industry and Finance*, 349-360. Philadelphia, Penn.: J. B. Lippincott, 1901.

BALLIET, LETSON

Burnley, James. "The Story of 'Corduroy Bill': (Letson Balliet)." In *Millionaires and Kings of Enterprise; The Marvellous Careers of Some Americans Who by Pluck, Foresight, And Energy Have Made Themselves Masters in the Fields of Industry and Finance*, 188-199. Philadelphia, Penn.: J. B. Lippincott, 1901.

BALLIN, GENE

Levitt, Mortimer. "Gene Ballin: 'A True Entrepreneur Invents His Own Opportunities'." In *How to Start Your Own Business Without Losing Your Shirt; Secrets of Seventeen Successful Entrepreneurs*, 133-141. New York, N.Y: Atheneum, 1988.

BALTER, NEIL

Aronoff, Craig E., and John L. Ward. "Neil Balter." In *Contemporary Entrepreneurs*, 18-23. Detroit, Mich.: Omnigraphics, Inc., 1992.

BANTRY, BRIAN

Gardner, Ralph. "Brian Bantry." In *Young, Gifted, and Rich: The Secrets of America's Most Successful Entrepreneurs*, 117-129. New York, N.Y.: Wallaby Books, 1984.

BARBER, OHIO C.

Burnley, James. "Ohio C. Barber: The Match King." In *Millionaires and Kings of Enterprise; The Marvellous Careers of Some Americans Who by Pluck, Foresight, And Energy Have Made Themselves Masters in the Fields of Industry and Finance*, 232-239. Philadelphia, Penn.: J. B. Lippincott, 1901.

BARDAHL, OLE

Gray, Bob, ed. "A Legend in Lubricants." In *How Entrepreneurs Make Business Profits: A Study of Personal Success Stories From Cordovan Business Journals*, 110-115. Houston, Tex.: Cordovan Press, 1982.

BARDEN, DON H.

Dingle, Derek T. "Don H. Barden: The Barden Companies, 'The Player'." In *Black Enterprise Titans of the B.E. 100s: Black CEOs Who Redefined and Conquered American Business*, 213-230. New York, N.Y.: Wiley, 1999.

BARKSDALE, JIM

Price, Christopher. "Jim Barksdale—Netscape 'Proof That Adult Supervision Works'." In *The Internet Entrepreneurs: Business Rules Are Good: Break Them*, 50-63. London, Eng.: FT.com, 2000.

BARNARD, CHESTER I.

Wren, Daniel A., and Ronald G. Greenwood. "Chester I. Barnard." In *Management Innovators: The People and Ideas That Have Shaped Modern Business*, 163-169. New York, N.Y.: Oxford University Press, 1998.

BARNUM, PHINEAS T.

"The Prince of Humbugs: Phineas T. Barnum Exposed a Staid and Sober World to the Joys of Light-Hearted Fun and Entertainment." In *The 50 Great Pioneers of American Industry*. By the Editors of News Front and Year, 22-26. Maplewood, N.J.: C.S. Hammond, 1964.

BAROWSKY, JACOB L.

Fucini, Joseph J., and Suzy Fucini. "Jacob L. Barowsky, Adell Chemical Company (LESTOIL): 'Television Showed Us the Way'." In *Experience Inc.; Men and Women Who Founded Famous Companies After the Age of 40*, 47-52. New York, N.Y: Free Press, 1987.

BARTLETT, ART

Shook, Carrie, and Robert L. Shook. "Century 21 International: Franchising the Real Estate Industry." In *Franchising: The Business Strategy That Changed the World*, 23-48. Englewood Cliffs, NJ: Prentice Hall, 1993.

BARTLETT, DONALD

Hillkirk, John, and Gary Jacobson. "Bartlett and Steele: The Pulitzer Touch." In *Grit, Guts, And Genius: True Tales of Megasuccess: Who Made Them Happen and How They Did It*, 51-63. Boston, Mass.: Houghton Mifflin, 1990.

BARTON, BRUCE

Pile, Robert B. "Bruce Barton: Advertising Genius." In *Top Entrepreneurs and Their Businesses*, 66-79. Minneapolis, Minn.: The Oliver Press, Inc., 1993.

BARTZ, CAROL

Enkelis, Liane, and Karen Olsen. "Carol Bartz: President, Chief Executive Officer, and Chairman of the Board, Autodesk, Inc." In *On Our Own Terms: Portraits of Women Business Leaders*, 144-153. San Francisco, Calif.: Berrett-Koehler, 1995.

BASS BROTHERS

Sheehy, Sandy. "The Bass Brothers: Fort Worth's Baby Boom Billionaires." In *Texas Big Rich; Exploits, Eccentricities, And Fabulous Fortunes Won and Lost*, 256-276. New York, N.Y.: Morrow, 1990.

BASTIAN, BRUCE W.

Aronoff, Craig E., and John L. Ward. "Alan C. Ashton; Bruce W. Bastian." In *Contemporary Entrepreneurs*, 12-17. Detroit, Mich.: Omnigraphics, Inc., 1992.

BASZILE, BARRY

Gray, Bob, ed. "The Metal Moonlighter." In *How Entrepreneurs Make Business Profits: A Study of Personal Success Stories From Cordovan Business Journals*, 163-168. Houston, Tex.: Cordovan Press, 1982.

BATSON, PAUL

Gray, Bob, ed. "Man of a Thousand Faces." In *How Entrepreneurs Make Business Profits: A Study of Personal Success Stories From Cordovan Business Journals*, 155-158. Houston, Tex.: Cordovan Press, 1982.

BAUMANN, BOB

Suarez, Ruth. "Bob Baumann: Around Your Neck, 'A Custom-Made Business'." In *Superstar Entrepreneurs of Small and Large Businesses Reveal Their Secrets*, 147-152. Piscataway, N.J.: Research and Education Association, 1998.

BEALS, VAUGHN

Gross, Daniel, and the Editors of Forbes Magazine. "The Turnaround at Harley-Davidson." In *Forbes Greatest Business Stories of All Time*, 298-312. New York, N.Y.: Wiley, 1996.

BEAN, LEON LEONWOOD

Pile, Robert B. "L. L. Bean: The Outdoorsman Who Hated Wet Feet." In *Top Entrepreneurs and Their Businesses*, 28-43. Minneapolis, Minn.: The Oliver Press, Inc., 1993.

BEAUVAIS, EDWARD R.

Aronoff, Craig E., and John L. Ward. "Edward R. Beauvais." In *Contemporary Entrepreneurs*, 24-30. Detroit, Mich.: Omnigraphics, Inc., 1992.

BEAVER, DON

Hillkirk, John, and Gary Jacobson. "New Pig: The 'Oink' Factor of Success." In *Grit, Guts, And Genius: True Tales of Megasuccess: Who Made Them Happen and How They Did It*, 20-23. Boston, Mass.: Houghton Mifflin, 1990.

BECHTEL, STEPHEN D.

Bechtel, Stephen D. "Reflections on Success." In *The Power of Boldness: Ten Master Builders of American Industry Tell Their Success Stories*, ed. Elkan Blout, 169-188. Washington, D.C.: Joseph Henry Press, 1996.

BECHTOLSHEIM, ANDREAS

Kingston, Brett. "Andreas Bechtolsheim, Vinod Khosla, Bill Joy, and Scott McNealy of the SUN Microsystems Team." In *The Dynamos: Who Are They Anyway?*, 49-60. New York, N.Y.: Wiley, 1987.

BECK, ROBERT A.

Shook, Robert L. "Robert A. Beck: The Prudential Insurance Company of America." In *The Chief Executive Officers: Men Who Run Big Business in America*, 7-32. New York, N.Y.: Harper & Row, 1981.

BECKMANN, BARBARA

Alexander, Shoshana. "Barbara Beckmann: Barbara Beckmann Designs, Inc., San Francisco, California." In *Women's Ventures, Women's Visions: 29 Inspiring Stories From Women Who Started Their Own Businesses*, 55-60. Freedom, Calif.: The Crossing Press, 1997.

BEDKE, JANELLE

Zientara, Marguerite. "Janelle Bedke: Catching Up with the Times." In *Women, Technology & Power: Ten Stars and the History They Made*, 201-209. New York, N.Y.: AMACOM, American Management Association, 1987.

Zientara, Marguerite. "Janelle Bedke: Ready to Take a Risk." In *Women, Technology & Power: Ten Stars and the History They Made*, 69-72. New York, N.Y.: AMACOM, American Management Association, 1987.

Zientara, Marguerite. "Janelle Bedke: 'The Power of Simplicity'." In *Women, Technology & Power: Ten Stars and the History They Made*, 134-137. New York, N.Y.: AMACOM, American Management Association, 1987.

BEDOWITZ, STEVEN D.

Aronoff, Craig E., and John L. Ward. "Steven D. Bedowitz." In *Contemporary Entrepreneurs*, 31-35. Detroit, Mich.: Omnigraphics, Inc., 1992.

BEECH, OLIVE ANN

Jeffrey, Laura S. "Olive Ann Beech: First Lady of Aviation." In *Great American Businesswomen*, 26-35. Springfield, N.J.: Enslow Publishers, Inc., 1996.

BELL, ALEXANDER GRAHAM

Barnett, Lincoln. "The Voice Heard Round the World." In *Great Stories of American Businessmen*, From *American Heritage, The Magazine of History*, 158-169. New York, N.Y.: American Heritage Publishing Co., 1954.

Wren, Daniel A., and Ronald G. Greenwood. "Alexander Graham Bell." In *Management Innovators: The People and Ideas That Have Shaped Modern Business*, 98-104. New York, N.Y.: Oxford University Press, 1998.

BELL, GORDON

Slater, Robert. "Gordon Bell: Launching the Age of the Minicomputer." In *Portraits in Silicon*, 206-215. Cambridge, Mass.: MIT Press, 1987.

BELL, MELVYN

MacPhee, William. "Melvyn Bell of Environmental Systems Company." In *Rare Breed: The Entrepreneur, An American Culture*, 39-46. Chicago, Ill.: Probus Publishing Company, 1987.

BELLEFLEUR, SHEILA

Lyons, Mary. "Sheila Bellefleur: Casco Bay Movers Dance Co.: Casco Bay Movers Dance Studio, Founder, 'It's a Big Deal'." In *Maine's Achieving Women: Conversations with Entrepreneurs*, 73-84. Old Orchard Beach, ME: Lilac River Press, 1999.

BELMONT, AUGUST

Klepper, Michael M., and Robert Gunther. "August Belmont (1816-1890): Belmont Stakes." In *The Wealthy 100 : From Benjamin Franklin to*

Bill Gates—A Ranking of the Richest Americans, Past and Present, 291-293. Secaucus, N.J. : Carol Pub. Group, 1996.

BENNETT, JAMES GORDON

Burnley, James. "James Gordon Bennett: The Newspaper King." In *Millionaires and Kings of Enterprise; The Marvellous Careers of Some Americans Who by Pluck, Foresight, And Energy Have Made Themselves Masters in the Fields of Industry and Finance,* 390-399. Philadelphia, Penn.: J. B. Lippincott, 1901.

BENTON, WILLIAM

Gunther, Max, "William Benten: One-Hundred-Fifty Million Dollars." In *The Very, Very Rich and How They Got That Way,* ed. Max Gunther, 20-28. Chicago, Ill.: The Playboy Press, 1972.

BENZIGER, MICHAEL

Aronoff, Craig E., and John L. Ward. "Michael Benziger." In *Contemporary Entrepreneurs,* 36-41. Detroit, Mich.: Omnigraphics, Inc., 1992.

Buchholz, Barbara B., and Margaret Crane. "Glen Ellen Winery, Glen Ellen, CA." In *Corporate Blood Lines: The Future of the Family Firm,* 245-266. New York, N.Y: Carol Publishing Group, 1989.

BEREN, JASHUA

Kingston, Brett. "Jashua Beren of CCT, Inc." In *The Dynamos: Who Are They Anyway?,* 207-215. New York, N.Y: Wiley, 1987.

BERG, ANN

Koppel, Mara. "The Art of a Trader—Ann Berg." In *Women of the Pits: Shattering the Glass Ceiling in Financial Markets,* 81-90. Chicago, Ill.: Dearborn Financial Publishers, 1998.

BERGHOFF, BARBARA

Mikaelian, A. "Barbara Berghoff." In *Women Who Mean Business: Success Stories of Women Over Forty*, 93-97. New York, N.Y.: William Morrow & Co., 1999.

BERKOW, RACINE

Suarez, Ruth. "Racine Berkow: Racine Berkow Associates, 'The Art of Business'." In *Superstar Entrepreneurs of Small and Large Businesses Reveal Their Secrets*, 117-121. Piscataway, N.J.: Research and Education Association, 1998.

BERNBACH, WILLIAM

Millman, Nancy. In *Emperors of Adland; Inside the Advertising Revolution*, 65-77. New York, N.Y.: Warner Books, 1988.

BERNBAUM, GLENN

Levitt, Mortimer. "Glenn Bernbaum: Snob Appeal Made Mortimer's the Playpen for the Rich and Famous." In *How to Start Your Own Business Without Losing Your Shirt; Secrets of Seventeen Successful Entrepreneurs*, 105-112. New York, N.Y: Atheneum, 1988.

BERNS, CHARLES A.

Uris, Auren. "Charles A. Berns—How '21' Became a Famous Number." In *The Executive Breakthrough; 21 Roads to the Top*, 73-81. Garden City, N.Y.: Doubleday, 1967.

BERTHOIN, LINDA ANDRULIS

Mikaelian, A. "Linda Andrulis Berthoin." In *Women Who Mean Business: Success Stories of Women Over Forty*, 215-218. New York, N.Y.: William Morrow & Co., 1999.

BEST, CONNIE

Kingston, Brett. "Sophia Collier and Connie Best of American Natural Beverage Corporation." In *The Dynamos: Who Are They Anyway?*, 85-89. New York, N.Y: Wiley, 1987.

BEZOS, JEFF

Mariotti, Steve, and Mike Caslin. "Jeff Bezos: Amazon.Com." In *The Very Very Rich: How They Got That Way and How You Can, Too!*, 7-10. Franklin Lakes, NJ: Career Press, 2000.

Price, Christopher. "Jeff Bezos—Amazon 'Building the Net's Biggest Brand'." In *The Internet Entrepreneurs: Business Rules Are Good: Break Them*, 64-77. London, Eng.: FT.com, 2000.

BIANCO, JOSEPH J.

Mamis, Robert A. "Muscling In; Joseph J. Bianco, Founder of American DreamCar Inc., Is Betting That America Is Ready for $20,000 Reconditioned Mustangs and GTOs." In *Anatomy of a Start-Up: Why Some New Businesses Succeed and Others Fail: 27 Real-Life Case Studies,* ed. Elizabeth K. Longsworth, 229-237. Boston, Mass.: Inc. Publishing, 1991.

BIBBEY, KATHRYN L.

Mikaelian, A. "Kathryn L. Bibbey." In *Women Who Mean Business: Success Stories of Women Over Forty*, 335-339. New York, N.Y.: William Morrow & Co., 1999.

BIDEZ, MARTHA WARREN

Mikaelian, A. "Martha Warren Bidez, Ph.D." In *Women Who Mean Business: Success Stories of Women Over Forty*, 1-5. New York, N.Y.: William Morrow & Co., 1999.

BIGGERS, JOHN D.

Bell, Laurence. "John D. Biggers." In *America's Fifty Foremost Business Leaders,* ed. B. C. Forbes, 23-32. New York, N.Y.: B.C. Forbes, 1948.

BING, DAVID

Aronoff, Craig E., and John L. Ward. "David Bing." In *Contemporary Entrepreneurs*, 42-46. Detroit, Mich.: Omnigraphics, Inc., 1992.

BINION, LORAINE

White, Jane. "Loraine Binion of Levi Strauss & Co.: The Double Disadvantage: Dealing with Sex and Race Discrimination." In *A Few Good Women: Breaking the Barriers to Top Management,* 89-95. Englewood Cliffs, N.J.: Prentice Hall, 1992.

BIONDI, FRANK J.

Auletta, Ken. "Portrait of a Software Giant: Viacom." In *The Highwaymen; Warriors of the Information Superhighway*, 99-135. New York, N.Y.: Random House, 1997.

BIRCHFIELD, ELIZABETH "CHRIS"

Lyons, Mary. "Elizabeth 'Chris' Birchfield: The Bag Lady, President, 'I Like Mass and Big'." In *Maine's Achieving Women: Conversations with Entrepreneurs*, 7-17. Old Orchard Beach, ME: Lilac River Press, 1999.

BIRDSEYE, CLARENCE

Cleary, David Powers. "Birds Eye Frozen Foods; You've Got a Great Idea— If You Can Make It Work." In *Great American Brands: The Success Formulas That Made Them Famous*, 7-12. New York, N.Y: Fairchild Publications, 1981.

BIRNBACH, LISA

Gardner, Ralph. "Lisa Birnbach." In *Young, Gifted, and Rich: The Secrets of America's Most Successful Entrepreneurs*, 25-38. New York, N.Y.:

Wallaby Books, 1984.

BISSELL, ANNA

Cleary, David Powers. "Bissell Carpet Sweepers; To Live Up to Our Ideals, We Must Keep Clean." In *Great American Brands: The Success Formulas That Made Them Famous*, 13-18. New York, N.Y: Fairchild Publications, 1981.

BISSELL, MELVILLE R.

Cleary, David Powers. "Bissell Carpet Sweepers; To Live Up to Our Ideals, We Must Keep Clean." In *Great American Brands: The Success Formulas That Made Them Famous*, 13-18. New York, N.Y: Fairchild Publications, 1981.

BIXLER, PHILIP MITMAN

Buchholz, Barbara B., and Margaret Crane. "Bixler's, Easton, PA." In *Corporate Blood Lines: The Future of the Family Firm*, 78-91. New York, N.Y.: Carol Publishing Group, 1989.

BLACK, H. S.

Burnley, James. "H. S. Black: The American 'Sky-Scraper' King." In *Millionaires and Kings of Enterprise; The Marvellous Careers of Some Americans Who by Pluck, Foresight, And Energy Have Made Themselves Masters in the Fields of Industry and Finance*, 361-367. Philadelphia, Penn.: J. B. Lippincott, 1901.

BLACK, S. DUNCAN

Cleary, David Powers. "Black & Decker Power Tools; No Idea Is Worth Anything Unless You Have the Guts to Back It Up. In *Great American Brands: The Success Formulas That Made Them Famous*, 19-23. New York, N.Y: Fairchild Publications, 1981.

BLAIR, JOHN I.

Klepper, Michael M., and Robert Gunther. "John I. Blair (1802-1899): 40,000 Miles Per Year." In *The Wealthy 100 : From Benjamin Franklin to Bill Gates—A Ranking of the Richest Americans, Past and Present*, 85-87. Secaucus, N.J. : Carol Pub. Group, 1996.

BLISS, CORNELIUS N.

Burnley, James. "Cornelius N. Bliss: A Merchant Prince and Statesman." In *Millionaires and Kings of Enterprise; The Marvellous Careers of Some Americans Who by Pluck, Foresight, And Energy Have Made Themselves Masters in the Fields of Industry and Finance*, 368-375. Philadelphia, Penn.: J. B. Lippincott, 1901.

BLOCK, HENRY W.

Goldwasser, Thomas. "H&R Block: Helping People with Taxing Issues." In *Family Pride; Profiles of Five of America's Best-Run Family Businesses*, 125-162. New York, N.Y.: Dodd, Mead and Company, 1986.

Shook, Carrie, and Robert L. Shook. "H&R Block: Turning Taxes into Profit." In *Franchising: The Business Strategy That Changed the World*, 1-22. Englewood Cliffs, NJ: Prentice Hall, 1993.

Silver, A. David. "Henry Wollman Block; Richard A. Block." In *Entrepreneurial Megabucks: The 100 Greatest Entrepreneurs of the Last 25 Years*, 146-149. New York, N.Y.: Wiley, 1985.

BLOCK, RICHARD A.

Silver, A. David. "Henry Wollman Block; Richard A. Block." In *Entrepreneurial Megabucks: The 100 Greatest Entrepreneurs of the Last 25 Years*, 146-149. New York, N.Y.: Wiley, 1985.

BLOCK, THOMAS M.

Pottker, Jan. "H&R Block, Inc.: New Kid on the Block." In *Born to Power: Heirs to America's Leading Businesses*, 108-119. New York, N.Y.: Barron's, 1992.

BLODEE, LEIF

Case, John. "Hot Seats; Building Eurostyle Chairs for the Corporate Elite." In *Anatomy of a Start-Up: Why Some New Businesses Succeed and Others Fail: 27 Real-Life Case Studies,* ed. Elizabeth K. Longsworth, 191-200. Boston, Mass.: Inc. Publishing, 1991.

BLOOMBERG, MICHAEL

Smith, Roy C. "The Bloomberg." In *Wealth Creators: The Rise of Today's Rich and Super-Rich*, 38-43. New York, N.Y.: Truman Talley, 2001.

BLOUGH, ROGER M.

"Recasting a Basic Industry: Roger M. Blough." In *Lessons of Leadership: 21 Executives Speak Out on Creating, Developing and Managing Success*. Presented by the editors of Nation's Business, 216-225. Garden City, N.Y.: Doubleday, 1968.

BLOUNT, WINTON M.

Silver, A. David. "Winton Malcom Blount." In *Entrepreneurial Megabucks: The 100 Greatest Entrepreneurs of the Last 25 Years*, 150-152. New York, N.Y.: Wiley, 1985.

BLOUT, ELKAN

Blout, Elkan. "Polaroid: Dreams to Reality." In *The Power of Boldness: Ten Master Builders of American Industry Tell Their Success Stories*, ed. Elkan Blout, 61-76. Washington, D.C.: Joseph Henry Press, 1996.

BLUE, BILL

Murphy, Linda. "Larry Piland and Bill Blue: Datel Systems, Inc." In *Computer Entrepreneurs: People Who Built Successful Businesses Around Computers*, 57-64. San Diego, Calif.: Computer Publishing Enterprises, 1990.

BLUHDORN, CHARLES

Sobel, Robert. "Charles Bluhdorn: The Manipulator." In *The Rise and Fall of the Conglomerate Kings*, 101-126. New York, N.Y.: Stein and Day, 1984.

BLUMKIN, ROSE

Silver, A. David. "Rose Blumkin." In *Entrepreneurial Megabucks: The 100 Greatest Entrepreneurs of the Last 25 Years*, 153-155. New York, N.Y.: Wiley, 1985.

BOEHM, HELEN F.

MacPhee, William. "Helen F. Boehm of the Boehm Porcelain Studios." In *Rare Breed: The Entrepreneur, An American Culture*, 49-65. Chicago, Ill.: Probus Publishing Company, 1987.

BOEHM, RON

Gray, Bob, ed. "The Man Who Beat the Mail." In *How Entrepreneurs Make Business Profits: A Study of Personal Success Stories From Cordovan Business Journals*, 15-21. Houston, Tex.: Cordovan Press, 1982.

BOEING, BILL

"Flying the Mails: Early Air Mail Routes Blazed Trail for Today's Commercial Airlines; First Private Air Mail Contractor Was William Boeing, Aircraft Manufacturer and Airline Magnate-To-Be." In *The 50 Great Pioneers of American Industry*. By the Editors of News Front and Year, 186-195. Maplewood, N.J.: C.S. Hammond, 1964.

BOESKY, IVAN

Davis, William. "Ivan Boesky, b.1937: 'The Pied Piper of Arbitrage'." In *The Innovators: The Essential Guide to Business Thinkers, Achievers and Entrepreneurs*, 43-47. New York, N.Y.: AMACOM, 1987.

BOGEN, LAUREN

Suarez, Ruth. "Lauren Bogen: Lauren Bogen, 'Wearing Down the Competition'." In *Superstar Entrepreneurs of Small and Large Businesses Reveal Their Secrets*, 153-156. Piscataway, N.J.: Research and Education Association, 1998.

BOHANNON, ROBERT H.

Wendel, Charles B. "Generating Profits by Selecting Underserved Niches: Robert H. Bohannon, President & CEO, Travelers Express Company." In *The New Financiers*, 35-54. Chicago, Ill.: Irwin Professional Pub., 1996.

BOLDT, GEORGE C.

Burnley, James. "George C. Boldt: The King of Hotel-Keepers." In *Millionaires and Kings of Enterprise; The Marvellous Careers of Some Americans Who by Pluck, Foresight, And Energy Have Made Themselves Masters in the Fields of Industry and Finance*, 285-288. Philadelphia, Penn.: J. B. Lippincott, 1901.

BOLLENBACH, STEPHEN

Kadlec, Daniel J. "Stephen Bollenbach: Treasurer for Hire." In *Masters of the Universe; Winning Strategies of America's Greatest Deal Makers*, 101-132. New York, N.Y.: HarperBusiness, 1999.

BONDOC, VICTORIA

Suarez, Ruth. "Victoria Bondoc: Gemini Industries, 'A Detour From the Corporate Food Chain'." In *Superstar Entrepreneurs of Small and Large Businesses Reveal Their Secrets*, 23-28. Piscataway, N.J.: Research and Education Association, 1998.

BOOKER, EFFIE

Harris, Wendy Beech. "Effie Booker, Cabana Car Wash: The Queen of Car Washes." In *Against All Odds: Ten Entrepreneurs Who Followed Their Hearts and Found Success*, 21-46. New York, N.Y.: Wiley, 2001.

BOOZ, EDWIN G.

Davis, William. "Edwin G. Booz, 1887-1951: Father of Modern Management Consukting." In *The Innovators: The Essential Guide to Business Thinkers, Achievers and Entrepreneurs*, 52-55. New York, N.Y.: AMACOM, 1987.

BORDEN, GAIL

"Miracle Man of Milk: Gail Borden's Invention of Pure, Spoilage-Free Condensed Milk Opened a Mass Market for Dairy Products, Launched Today's $10 Billion Dairying Industry." In *The 50 Great Pioneers of American Industry*. By the Editors of News Front and Year, 45-47. Maplewood, N.J.: C.S. Hammond, 1964.

BORLAND, RUSSELL

Tsang, Cheryl D. "Russell Borland: 'The Author', 1980-1997." In *Microsoft First Generation: The Success Secrets of the Visionaries Who Launched a Technology Empire*, 69-86. New York, N.Y.: Wiley, 2000.

BOSTIC, STEVEN R.

Aronoff, Craig E., and John L. Ward. "Steven R. Bostic." In *Contemporary Entrepreneurs*, 47-53. Detroit, Mich.: Omnigraphics, Inc., 1992.

BOUCHARD, MICHELINE

Mikaelian, A. "Micheline Bouchard, P. Eng., CM." In *Women Who Mean Business: Success Stories of Women Over Forty*, 345-350. New York, N.Y.: William Morrow & Co., 1999.

BOUCHER, CONSTANCE

Rich-McCoy, Lois. "The Klingsborg Connection: Constance Boucher." In *Millionairess: Self-Made Women of America*, 73-95. New York, N.Y.: Harper & Row, 1978.

BOWSER, HAMILTON SR.

Woodard, Michael D. "Evanbow Construction—Hamilton Bowser Sr." In *Black Entrepreneurs in America: Stories of Struggle and Success*, 80-98. New Brunswick, N.J.: Rutgers University Press, 1977.

BOWSER, YVETTE LEE

Mitchell, Niki Butler. "A New Day: Yvette Lee Bowser, President and CEO, SisterLee Productions." In *The New Color of Success: Twenty Young Black Millionaires Tell You How They're Making it*, 1-13. Rocklin, Calif.: Prima Publishing, 2000.

BOYER, HERBERT W.

Silver, A. David. "Robert A. Swanson; Herbert W. Boyer." In *Entrepreneurial Megabucks: The 100 Greatest Entrepreneurs of the Last 25 Years*, 413-416. New York, N.Y.: Wiley, 1985.

BRADFORD, LAURA K.

Mikaelian, A. "Laura K. Bradford." In *Women Who Mean Business: Success Stories of Women Over Forty*, 46-49. New York, N.Y.: William Morrow & Co., 1999.

BRADLEE, BENJAMINE C.

Cose, Ellis. "The Underdog." In *The Press*, 27-119. New York, N.Y.: Morrow, 1989.

BRADLEY, JOHN

Oster, Merrill J. "Mastering Your Craft." In *The Entrepreneur's Creed: The Principles & Passions of 20 Successful Entrepreneurs*, 76-87. Nashville, Tenn.: Broadman & Holman Publishers, 2001.

BRADLEY, MELODY K.

Mikaelian, A. "Melody K. Bradley." In *Women Who Mean Business: Success Stories of Women Over Forty*, 175-179. New York, N.Y.: William Morrow & Co., 1999.

BRADY, ANTHONY N.

Klepper, Michael M., and Robert Gunther. "Anthony N. Brady (1843-1913): The Great Consolidator." In *The Wealthy 100 : From Benjamin Franklin to Bill Gates—A Ranking of the Richest Americans, Past and Present,* 210-212. Secaucus, N.J. : Carol Pub. Group, 1996.

BRAMWELL, ELIZABETH

Herera, Sue. "Elizabeth Bramwell: Bramwell Capital Management." In *Women of the Street: Making It on Wall Street—The World's Toughest Business,* 47-58. New York, N.Y.: Wiley, 1997.

BRANSON, RICHARD

Mariotti, Steve, and Mike Caslin. "Richard Branson: Virgin Group, LTD." In *The Very Very Rich: How They Got That Way and How You Can, Too!,* 11-16. Franklin Lakes, NJ: Career Press, 2000.

BRAVO, ROSE MARIE

Mikaelian, A. "Rose Marie Bravo." In *Women Who Mean Business: Success Stories of Women Over Forty*, 224-228. New York, N.Y.: William Morrow & Co., 1999.

BREECH, ERNEST R.

"Reviving the Giants: Ernest R. Breech." In *Lessons of Leadership: 21*

Executives Speak Out on Creating, Developing and Managing Success. Presented by the editors of Nation's Business, 169-183. Garden City, N.Y.: Doubleday, 1968.

BREMYER, JAYNE

Bremyer, Jayne. "Soaring with the Stars." In *Success Secrets: How Eighteen Everyday Women Became Fortune Builders and Famous Speakers*, 189-202. Glendora, Calif.: Royal CBS Publishing, 1978.

BRICE, JULIE

Kingston, Brett. "Julie Brice of I Can't Believe It's Yogurt." In *The Dynamos: Who Are They Anyway?*, 91-94. New York, N.Y.: Wiley, 1987.

BRICKLIN, DANIEL

Slater, Robert. "Daniel Bricklin: The Spreadsheet Pioneer Who Invented VisiCalc." In *Portraits in Silicon*, 284-294. Cambridge, Mass.: MIT Press, 1987.

BRIGHT, H. R. "BUM"

Sheehy, Sandy. "H. R. 'Bum' Bright: Cowboys and Capitalism." In *Texas Big Rich; Exploits, Eccentricities, And Fabulous Fortunes Won and Lost*, 145-153. New York, N.Y.: Morrow, 1990.

BRINKLEY, CHRISTIE

Gardner, Ralph. "Christie Brinkley." In *Young, Gifted, and Rich: The Secrets of America's Most Successful Entrepreneurs*, 105-115. New York, N.Y.: Wallaby Books, 1984.

BRITTIN, LEWIS

Pile, Robert B. "Lewis Brittin: The Connecticut Colonel and His Flying Dream." In *Top Entrepreneurs and Their Businesses*, 12-27. Minneapolis, Minn.: The Oliver Press, Inc., 1993.

BRITZ, JEFFREY

Kingston, Brett. "Jeffrey Britz of First Realty Reserve." In *The Dynamos: Who Are They Anyway?*, 165-170. New York, N.Y.: Wiley, 1987.

BROADER, SHELLEY

Pestrak, Debra. "Shelley Broader: Vice-President, Perishable Merchandising—Hannaford Brothers." In *Playing with the Big Boys: Success Stories of the Most Powerful Women in Business*, 187-202. Carlsbad, CA: SUN Publications, 2001.

BRODIE, JULIAN

Levitt, Mortimer. "Julian Brodie: Expert Counseling for the New Retiree Market, At Wholesale." In *How to Start Your Own Business Without Losing Your Shirt; Secrets of Seventeen Successful Entrepreneurs*, 69-76. New York, N.Y: Atheneum, 1988.

BRODIE, RICHARD

Tsang, Cheryl D. "Richard Brodie: 'The Dilettante', 1981-1994." In *Microsoft First Generation: The Success Secrets of the Visionaries Who Launched a Technology Empire*, 47-68. New York, N.Y.: Wiley, 2000.

BRONFMAN, EDGAR JR.

Auletta, Ken. "No Longer the Son of: Seagram's Edgar Bronfman Jr." In *The Highwaymen; Warriors of the Information Superhighway*, 136-159. New York, N.Y.: Random House, 1997.

BROOKS, PETER CHARDON

Klepper, Michael M., and Robert Gunther. "Peter Chardon Brooks (1767-1849): Wealthiest Man in New England." In *The Wealthy 100 : From Benjamin Franklin to Bill Gates—A Ranking of the Richest Americans, Past and Present*, 322-324. Secaucus, N.J. : Carol Pub. Group, 1996.

BROOKS, SHEILA

Mitchell, Niki Butler. "Calling the Shots: Sheila Brooks: President and CEO, SRB Productions, Inc." In *The New Color of Success: Twenty Young Black Millionaires Tell You How They're Making it*, 131-143. Rocklin, Calif.: Prima Publishing, 2000.

BROSSEAU, BILL

Gray, Bob, ed. "Stumbling Into the Oil Patch." In *How Entrepreneurs Make Business Profits: A Study of Personal Success Stories From Cordovan Business Journals*, 102-106. Houston, Tex.: Cordovan Press, 1982.

BROWN, CARL

Mitchell, Niki Butler. "For Us, By Us: J. Alexander Martin, Vice President and Head Designer; Daymond John, President and CEO; Carl Brown, Co-Founder; Keith Perrin, Co-Founder, FUBU." In *The New Color of Success: Twenty Young Black Millionaires Tell You How They're Making it*, 29-42. Rocklin, Calif.: Prima Publishing, 2000.

BROWN, CHARLES L.

Shook, Robert L. "Charles L. Brown: American Telephone and Telegraph Company." In *The Chief Executive Officers: Men Who Run Big Business in America*, 33-52. New York, N.Y.: Harper & Row, 1981.

BROWN, DEAVER

"Deaver Brown, General Sound of Boston." In *Profiles in Success: How Six Entrepreneurs Have Prospered in a Tough Business Environment*, 36-45. By the editors of *Managing*. New York, N.Y.: HBJ Newsletters, 1981.

BROWN FAMILY

Pottker, Jan. "Brown-Forman Corporation: Southern Discomfort." In *Born to Power: Heirs to America's Leading Businesses*, 390-394. New York, N.Y.: Barron's, 1992.

BROWN, LEWIS H.

Shannon, Homer H. "Lewis H. Brown." In *America's Fifty Foremost Business Leaders,* ed. B. C. Forbes, 33-42. New York, N.Y.: B.C. Forbes, 1948.

BROWN, PATRIKA

Shook, Robert L. "The Erotic Baker." In *Why Didn't I Think of That,* 66-83. New York, N.Y.: New American Library, 1982.

BROWNE, HARRY

King, Norman. "Harry Browne." In *The Money Messiah$,* 190-192. New York, N.Y.: Coward-McCann, 1983.

BROYHILL, JAMES EDGAR

Aronoff, Craig E., and John L. Ward. "James Edgar Broyhill." In *Contemporary Entrepreneurs,* 54-58. Detroit, Mich.: Omnigraphics, Inc., 1992.

BRUCE, CAROLYN

Bruce, Carolyn. "Could It Work Here?" In *How I Became a Nurse Entrepreneur: Tales from 50 Nurses in Business,* 243-248. Petaluma, Calif.: National Nurses in Business Association, 1991.

BRUGGERE, THOMAS H.

Aronoff, Craig E., and John L. Ward. "Thomas H. Bruggere." In *Contemporary Entrepreneurs,* 59-65. Detroit, Mich.: Omnigraphics, Inc., 1992.

BRUNSON, DOROTHY

Enkelis, Liane, and Karen Olsen. "Dorothy Brunson: President and Chief Executive Officer, Brunson Communications." In *On Our Own Terms: Portraits of Women Business Leaders* , 40-49. San Francisco, Calif.: Berrett-Koehler, 1995.

Taylor, Russel R. "Dorothy Brunson; Revolutionary of Radio." In *Exceptional Entrepreneurial Women*, 103-109. New York, N.Y: Quorum Books, 1988.

BRYANT, JOHN

Mitchell, Niki Butler. "Keeping Hope Alive: John Bryant, Chairman and CEO, Operation HOPE and Bryant Group Companies, Inc.." In *The New Color of Success: Twenty Young Black Millionaires Tell You How They're Making it*, 15-27. Rocklin, Calif.: Prima Publishing, 2000.

BUCHANAN, JUDY KOCH

Enkelis, Liane, and Karen Olsen. "Judy Koch Buchanan: President, RSP Manufacturing." In *On Our Own Terms: Portraits of Women Business Leaders* , 18-27. San Francisco, Calif.: Berrett-Koehler, 1995.

BUCHWALD, ALEXANDER

Gray, Bob, ed. "Paying Through the Teeth." In *How Entrepreneurs Make Business Profits: A Study of Personal Success Stories From Cordovan Business Journals*, 71-76. Houston, Tex.: Cordovan Press, 1982.

BUCKMAN, PAMELA M.

Buckman, Pamela M. "A Roller Coaster Ride into Business." In *How I Became a Nurse Entrepreneur: Tales from 50 Nurses in Business*, 65-70. Petaluma, Calif.: National Nurses in Business Association, 1991.

BUFFETT, WARREN E.

Klepper, Michael M., and Robert Gunther. "Warren Buffett (1930-): The Sage of Omaha." In *The Wealthy 100 : From Benjamin Franklin to Bill Gates—A Ranking of the Richest Americans, Past and Present*, 148-152. Secaucus, N.J. : Carol Pub. Group, 1996.

Silver, A. David. "Warren E. Buffett." In *Entrepreneurial Megabucks: The 100 Greatest Entrepreneurs of the Last 25 Years*, 156-159. New York, N.Y.: Wiley, 1985.

Smith, Roy C. "The Sage of Omaha." In *Wealth Creators: The Rise of Today's Rich and Super-Rich*, 140-146. New York, N.Y.: Truman Talley, 2001.

Train, John. "Warren Buffett: A Share in a Business." In *The Money Masters*, 1-41. New York, N.Y.: Harper & Row, 1980.

Train, John. "Warren Buffett: A Share in a Business." In *Money Masters of Our Time*, 14-51. New York, N.Y.: HarperBusiness, 2000.

BUFFORD, TAKASHI

Mitchell, Niki Butler. "Hollywood Shuffle: Takashi Bufford, President and CEO, Kid, I Love It But You'll Never Get It Made, Not in This Town." In *The New Color of Success: Twenty Young Black Millionaires Tell You How They're Making it*, 81-94. Rocklin, Calif.: Prima Publishing, 2000.

BUFORD, BOB

Oster, Merrill J. "Beyond Success to Significance." In *The Entrepreneur's Creed: The Principles & Passions of 20 Successful Entrepreneurs*, 14-25. Nashville, Tenn.: Broadman & Holman Publishers, 2001.

BUNTING, GEORGE AVERY

Goldwasser, Thomas. "Hallmark: Caring Enough to Send the Very Best." In *Family Pride; Profiles of Five of America's Best-Run Family Businesses*, 45-84. New York, N.Y.: Dodd, Mead and Company, 1986.

BURBANK, LUTHER

McSherry, Ronald T. "Luther Burbank: The Plant Wizard of California." In *Nine American Self-Made Men and Their Secrets to Success*, 26-29. Denver, Colo.: U.S.A. Publishing, 1983.

BURCH, LAUREL

Alexander, Shoshana. "Laurel Burch: Laurel Burch Design Studio, Inc., San Francisco, California." In *Women's Ventures, Women's Visions: 29 Inspiring Stories From Women Who Started Their Own Businesses*, 27-34. Freedom, Calif.: The Crossing Press, 1997.

BURKHARD, GENE

Gray, Bob, ed. "The Overseer of Underwear." In *How Entrepreneurs Make Business Profits: A Study of Personal Success Stories From Cordovan Business Journals*, 144-149. Houston, Tex.: Cordovan Press, 1982.

BURNS, LESLIE HENNER

Koppel, Mara. "Family Business—Leslie Henner Burns." In *Women of the Pits: Shattering the Glass Ceiling in Financial Markets*, 29-34. Chicago, Ill.: Dearborn Financial Publishers, 1998.

BURNS, URSULA

Pestrak, Debra. "Ursula Burns: Senior Corporate Vice-President and Vice-President Worldwide Manufacturing Operations, Xerox." In *Playing with the Big Boys: Success Stories of the Most Powerful Women in Business*, 163-184. Carlsbad, CA: SUN Publications, 2001.

BURR, DONALD C.

Aronoff, Craig E., and John L. Ward. "Donald C. Burr." In *Contemporary Entrepreneurs*, 66-74. Detroit, Mich.: Omnigraphics, Inc., 1992.

Silver, A. David. "Donald C. Burr." In *Entrepreneurial Megabucks: The 100 Greatest Entrepreneurs of the Last 25 Years*, 160-162. New York, N.Y.: Wiley, 1985.

BURRELL, THOMAS J.

Mariotti, Steve, and Mike Caslin. "Thomas J. Burrell: Burrell Communications Group." In *The Very Very Rich: How They Got That*

Way and How You Can, Too!, 17-22. Franklin Lakes, NJ: Career Press, 2000.

BUSCH, ADOLPHUS

Cleary, David Powers. "Budweiser Beer; Making Friends Is Our Business." In *Great American Brands: The Success Formulas That Made Them Famous*, 24-35. New York, N.Y: Fairchild Publications, 1981.

Klepper, Michael M., and Robert Gunther. "Adolphus Busch (1839-1913): The Baron of Beer." In *The Wealthy 100 : From Benjamin Franklin to Bill Gates—A Ranking of the Richest Americans, Past and Present*, 213-215. Secaucus, N.J. : Carol Pub. Group, 1996.

BUSCH, ARLENE

Koppel, Mara. "Global Trader—Arlene Busch." In *Women of the Pits: Shattering the Glass Ceiling in Financial Markets*, 43-48. Chicago, Ill.: Dearborn Financial Publishers, 1998.

Koppel, Robert. "Lady Luck: Arlene Busch." In *Bulls, Bears, And Millionaires: War Stories of Trading Life*, 139-148. Chicago, Ill.: Dearborn Financial Publishers, 1997.

BUSH, JOHN A.

Cleary, David Powers. "Buster Brown Shoes; Kids of Six Today Are Smarter Than They Used to Be at Twelve." In *Great American Brands: The Success Formulas That Made Them Famous*, 36-39. New York, N.Y: Fairchild Publications, 1981.

BUSHNELL, NOLAN

Landrum, Gene N. "Nolan Bushnell—Confident." In *Profiles of Genius: Thirteen Creative Men Who Changed the World*, 106-120. Buffalo, N.Y.: Prometheus Books, 1993.

Slater, Robert. "Nolan Bushnell: Captain Pong, Leader of the Video Game Revolution." In *Portraits in Silicon*, 296-307. Cambridge, Mass.: MIT Press, 1987.

BUTCHER, JACOB F.

Adams, James Ring. "The Butcher Revels." In *The Big Fix: Inside the S&L Scandal: How an Unholy Alliance of Politics and Money Destroyed America's Banking System*, 87-124. New York, N.Y: Wiley, 1990.

BUTLER, MICHAEL

Pottker, Jan. "Theatrical and Motion Picture Production: From Heir to Hair, Michael Butler, Producer—Heir to Butler Paper, Butler Aviation." In *Born to Power: Heirs to America's Leading Businesses*, 458-463. New York, N.Y.: Barron's, 1992.

BUTTS, PAT

Gray, Bob, ed. "Growing Big in Graphic Arts." In *How Entrepreneurs Make Business Profits: A Study of Personal Success Stories From Cordovan Business Journals*, 22-26. Houston, Tex.: Cordovan Press, 1982.

BUYNISKI, VICTORIA B.

Aronoff, Craig E., and John L. Ward. "Victoria B. Buyniski." In *Contemporary Entrepreneurs*, 75-80. Detroit, Mich.: Omnigraphics, Inc., 1992.

THE CABOT FAMILY

Bulkeley, William. "The Cabots." In *American Dynasties Today,* 1-44. Homewood, Ill.: Dow Jones-Irwin, 1990.

Cabot, Thomas D. "A Short History of Cabot Corporation." In *The Power of Boldness: Ten Master Builders of American Industry Tell Their Success Stories.*, ed. Elkan Blout, 135-158. Washington, D.C.: Joseph Henry Press, 1996.

Pottker, Jan. "Cabot Corporation: Ink Black Profits Color This Family." In *Born to Power: Heirs to America's Leading Businesses*, 328-330. New York, N.Y.: Barron's, 1992.

Train, John. "Paul Cabot: All the Damn Facts." In *Money Masters of Our Time*, 81-91. New York, N.Y.: HarperBusiness, 2000.

Train, John. "Paul Cabot: The Realist." In *The Money Masters*, 42-56. New York, N.Y.: Harper & Row, 1980.

CADE, JOHN

Kingston, Brett. "John Cade of Cade Industries/EDAC Technologies." In *The Dynamos: Who Are They Anyway?*, 189-194. New York, N.Y: Wiley, 1987.

CADET, MELISSA

White, Jane. "Melissa Cadet of River West Developments: Finding Success Outside the Fortune 500." In *A Few Good Women: Breaking the Barriers to Top Management*, 113-124. Englewood Cliffs, N.J.: Prentice Hall, 1992.

CAIN, HERMAN

Oster, Merrill J. "Food for Thought." In *The Entrepreneur's Creed: The Principles & Passions of 20 Successful Entrepreneurs*, 56-65. Nashville, Tenn.: Broadman & Holman Publishers, 2001.

CALANO, JAMES

Kingston, Brett. "James Calano and Jeff Salzman of Careertrack." In *The Dynamos: Who Are They Anyway?*, 97-100. New York, N.Y: Wiley, 1987.

CALLAWAY, ELY R.

Ericksen, Gregory K. "Ely R. Callaway: Callaway Golf Co., 'Find a Way to Make It Better'." In *What's Luck Got to Do with It; Twelve Entrepreneurs Reveal the Secrets Behind Their Success*, 81-98. New York, N.Y.: Wiley, 1997.

CAMERON, LINDA

Lassen, Ali. "Linda Cameron, Family Therapist." In *The Secret of Their Success: Women Entrepreneurs Reveal How They Made It*, 83-88. Carlsbad, Calif.: Ali Lassen Success System, 1990.

CAMPBELL, PHYLLIS J.

Mikaelian, A. "Phyllis J. Campbell." In *Women Who Mean Business: Success Stories of Women Over Forty*, 320-324. New York, N.Y.: William Morrow & Co., 1999.

CANION, JOSEPH R.

Aronoff, Craig E., and John L. Ward. "Joseph R. Canion." In *Contemporary Entrepreneurs*, 81-86. Detroit, Mich.: Omnigraphics, Inc., 1992.

CAPE, RONALD E.

Silver, A. David. "Ronald E. Cape." In *Entrepreneurial Megabucks: The 100 Greatest Entrepreneurs of the Last 25 Years*, 163-166. New York, N.Y.: Wiley, 1985.

CARDELLO, SHEENA

Elfstrand, Rhonda. "Sheena Cardello: The S. C. Cardello Company." In *The Story Behind the Success: Learning From Pittsburgh Professionals*, 48-60. Pittsburgh, Penn.: Steel Publishing Partners, 1996.

CARDIN, FREDERICK A.

Hopkins, Michael S. "The Perfect Business?" In *Anatomy of a Start-Up: Why Some New Businesses Succeed and Others Fail: 27 Real-Life Case Studies,* ed. Elizabeth K. Longsworth, 135-146. Boston, Mass.: Inc. Publishing, 1991.

CARLSON, CURTIS L.

Pine, Carol, and Susan Mundale. "Curt Carlson: Stamped in Gold." In *Self-Made: The Stories of 12 Minnesota Entrepreneurs*, 209-223. Minneapolis, Minn.: Dorn Books, 1982.

Silver, A. David. "Curtis L. Carlson." In *Entrepreneurial Megabucks: The 100 Greatest Entrepreneurs of the Last 25 Years*, 167-170. New York, N.Y.: Wiley, 1985.

CARNEGIE, ANDREW

Brands, H. W. "Auld Lang Syne: Andrew Carnegie." In *Masters of Enterprise: Giants of American Business from John Jacob Astor and J.P. Morgan to Bill Gates and Oprah Winfrey*, 50-63. New York, N.Y.: Free Press, 1999.

Burnley, James. "Andrew Carnegie: America's Greatest Ironmaster." In *Millionaires and Kings of Enterprise; The Marvellous Careers of Some Americans Who by Pluck, Foresight, And Energy Have Made Themselves Masters in the Fields of Industry and Finance*, 1-16. Philadelphia, Penn.: J. B. Lippincott, 1901.

Davis, William. "Andrew Carnegie, 1835-1919: The Steelmaster Philanthropist." In *The Innovators: The Essential Guide to Business Thinkers, Achievers and Entrepreneurs*, 66-70. New York, N.Y.: AMACOM, 1987.

Heilbroner, Robert L. "Epitaph for the Steel Master." In *Great Stories of American Businessmen*, From *American Heritage, The Magazine of History*, 248-259. New York, N.Y.: American Heritage Publishing Co., 1954.

Hughes, Jonathan. "Carnegie and the American Steel Industry." In *The Vital Few: The Entrepreneur and American Economic Progress*, 220-273. Expanded Edition, New York, N.Y.: Oxford University Press, 1986.

Klepper, Michael M., and Robert Gunther. "Andrew Carnegie (1835-1919): Man of Steel." In *The Wealthy 100 : From Benjamin Franklin to Bill*

Gates—A Ranking of the Richest Americans, Past and Present, 29-33 Secaucus, N.J. : Carol Pub. Group, 1996.

Livesay, Harold C. "The Star-Spangled Scotchman: Andrew Carnegie." In *American Made: Men Who Shaped the American Economy*, 86-125. Boston, Mass.: Little, Brown, 1979.

McSherry, Ronald T. "Andrew Carnegie: The Steel King." In *Nine American Self-Made Men and Their Secrets to Success*, 53-60. Denver, Colo.: U.S.A. Publishing, 1983.

Wren, Daniel A., and Ronald G. Greenwood. "Andrew Carnegie." In *Management Innovators: The People and Ideas That Have Shaped Modern Business*, 33-41. New York, N.Y.: Oxford University Press, 1998.

CARNEY BROTHERS

Shook, Carrie, and Robert L. Shook. "Pizza Hut: Franchising America's Favorite Pizza." In *Franchising: The Business Strategy That Changed the World*, 167-196. Englewood Cliffs, NJ: Prentice Hall, 1993.

Silver, A. David. "Frank L. Carney." In *Entrepreneurial Megabucks: The 100 Greatest Entrepreneurs of the Last 25 Years*, 171-173. New York, N.Y.: Wiley, 1985.

CARPENTER, CANDICE

Mariotti, Steve, and Mike Caslin. "Candice Carpenter, iVillage: 'Success is About Creating Value'." In *The Very Very Rich: How They Got That Way and How You Can, Too!*, 23-26. Franklin Lakes, NJ: Career Press, 2000.

Price, Christopher. "Candice Carpenter, Nancy Evans—iVillage 'A Different Vision of Net Success'." In *The Internet Entrepreneurs: Business Rules Are Good: Break Them*, 160-174. London, Eng.: FT.com, 2000.

Smith, Roy C. "Candy's New American Dream." In *Wealth Creators: The Rise of Today's Rich and Super-Rich*, 82-89. New York, N.Y.: Truman Talley, 2001.

CARPENTER, WALTER S. JR.

Farrar, Larston D. "Walter S. Carpenter Jr." In *America's Fifty Foremost Business Leaders,* ed. B. C. Forbes, 43-52. New York, N.Y.: B.C. Forbes, 1948.

CARRET, PHILIP

Train, John. "Philip Carret: The Money Mind." In *The New Money Masters : Winning Investment Strategies of Soros, Lynch, Steinhardt, Rogers, Neff, Wanger, Michaelis, Carret,* 50-66. New York, N.Y.: Harper & Row, 1989.

Train, John. "Philip Carret: Think Small." In *Money Masters of Our Time,* 218-226. New York, N.Y.: HarperBusiness, 2000.

CARRIER, WILLIS

"He Beat the Heat: Willis Carrier, Inventor of Mechanical Air Conditioning, Designed World's First Temperature-Humidity Control System for a Brooklyn Printing Plant in 1902, Founded Carrier Corporation in 1914. Today, Air Conditioning is a $4-Billion-Dollar Industry and Has Brought Cool Comfort to Millions of Homes." In *The 50 Great Pioneers of American Industry.* By the Editors of News Front and Year, 134-137. Maplewood, N.J.: C.S. Hammond, 1964.

CARSEY, MARCY

Alexander, Shoshana. "Marcy Carsey: The Carsey-Werner Company, Los Angeles, California." In *Women's Ventures, Women's Visions: 29 Inspiring Stories From Women Who Started Their Own Businesses,* 84-89. Freedom, Calif.: The Crossing Press, 1997.

CARTER, LORRAINE

Harris, Wendy Beech. "Lorraine Carter, Caption Reporters, Inc.: A Woman of Her Word." In *Against All Odds: Ten Entrepreneurs Who Followed Their Hearts and Found Success,* 71-92. New York, N.Y.: Wiley, 2001.

CARVER, ROY J.

Fucini, Joseph J., and Suzy Fucini. "Roy J. Carver, Bandag, Inc.: 'Conceive, Believe, Achieve'." In *Experience Inc.; Men and Women Who Founded Famous Companies After the Age of 40*, 53-58. New York, N.Y: Free Press, 1987.

CASE, STEVE

Jager, Rama Dev, and Rafael Ortiz. "Steve Case: America Online; It's the Customer Stupid." In *In the Company of Giants: Candid Conversations with the Visionaries of the Digital World*, 61-72. New York, N.Y.: McGraw-Hill, 1997.

CASEY, DOUGLAS R.

King, Norman. "Douglas R. Casey." In *The Money Messiah$*, 181-183. New York, N.Y.: Coward-McCann, 1983.

CASTO, MARYLES

Taylor, Russel R. "Maryles Casto: 'Never Say No'." In *Exceptional Entrepreneurial Women*, 73-78. New York, N.Y: Quorum Books, 1988.

CATANIA, MARY LOU

Catania, Mary Lou. "On My Own." In *How I Became a Nurse Entrepreneur: Tales from 50 Nurses in Business*, 285-290. Petaluma, Calif.: National Nurses in Business Association, 1991.

CATHY FAMILY

Oster, Merrill J. "When Life Hands You a Chicken, Make a Sandwich." In *The Entrepreneur's Creed: The Principles & Passions of 20 Successful Entrepreneurs*, 120-131. Nashville, Tenn.: Broadman & Holman Publishers, 2001.

CATO, SID

Hillkirk, John, and Gary Jacobson. "Sid Cato: The Guru of Annual Reports." In *Grit, Guts, And Genius: True Tales of Megasuccess: Who Made Them Happen and How They Did It*, 33-37. Boston, Mass.: Houghton Mifflin, 1990.

CAVAN, DAVID

Oster, Merrill J. "Back from the Brink." In *The Entrepreneur's Creed: The Principles & Passions of 20 Successful Entrepreneurs*, 202-209. Nashville, Tenn.: Broadman & Holman Publishers, 2001.

CHAMBERS, PAM

Mikaelian, A. "Pam Chambers." In *Women Who Mean Business: Success Stories of Women Over Forty*, 74-77. New York, N.Y.: William Morrow & Co., 1999.

CHAMPION, GEORGE

"Preaching What You Practice: George Champion." In *Lessons of Leadership: 21 Executives Speak Out on Creating, Developing and Managing Success*. Presented by the editors of Nation's Business, 237-247. Garden City, N.Y.: Doubleday, 1968.

CHANDLER, OTIS

Coleridge, Nicholas. "A Fistful of Dollars: Otis Chandler and the Los Angeles Times." In *Paper Tigers: The Latest, Greatest Newspaper Tycoons*, 155-178. New York, N.Y.: Carol Publishing Group, 1994.

Cose, Ellis. "The Contender: Times Mirror." In *The Press*, 120-184. New York, N.Y.: Morrow, 1989.

CHAPMAN, LEE M.

Mitchell, Niki Butler. "Mojo Highway Is a Rough Road to Success: Lee M. Chapman III, Chairman and CEO; Curtis J. Lewis II, President and COO, Mojo Highway Brewing Company, LLC." In *The New Color of*

Success: Twenty Young Black Millionaires Tell You How They're Making it, 183-198. Rocklin, Calif.: Prima Publishing, 2000.

CHAPPELL, EMMA C.

Dingle, Derek T. "Emma C. Chappell: United Bank of Philadelphia, 'The People's Banker'." In *Black Enterprise Titans of the B.E. 100s: Black CEOs Who Redefined and Conquered American Business*, 137-154. New York, N.Y.: Wiley, 1999.

Farnham, Alan. "Emma Chappell: Founder of the United Bank of Philadelphia, 'I Had This Awful Inclination to Give Up'." In *Forbes Great Success Stories: Twelve Tales of Victory Wrested from Defeat*, 106-123. New York, N.Y.: Wiley, 2000.

CHARATAN, DEBORAH LEE

Kingston, Brett. "Deborah Lee Charatan of Bach Realty." In *The Dynamos: Who Are They Anyway?*, 153-155. New York, N.Y: Wiley, 1987.

Taylor, Russel R. "Deborah Lee Charatan; She Made Millions Before Age Thirty." In *Exceptional Entrepreneurial Women*, 41-45. New York, N.Y: Quorum Books, 1988.

CHAVIS, EARL

Wallace, Robert L. "Earl Chavis: Founder, Chavis Tool & Company, Lamar, South Carolina." In *Black Wealth: Your Road to Small Business Success*, 52-59. New York, N.Y.: Wiley, 2000.

CHEEK, JOEL O.

Cleary, David Powers. "Maxwell House Coffee; Good to the Last Drop." In *Great American Brands: The Success Formulas That Made Them Famous*, 217-222. New York, N.Y: Fairchild Publications, 1981.

CHENAULT, KENNETH

Clarke, Caroline V. "Kenneth Chenault: CEO, American Express Co." In *Take a Lesson: Today's Black Achievers and How They Made It and*

What They Learned Along the Way, 7-13. New York, N.Y.: Wiley, 2001.

CHENEL, LAURA

Aronoff, Craig E., and John L. Ward. "Laura Chenel." In *Contemporary Entrepreneurs*, 87-94. Detroit, Mich.: Omnigraphics, Inc., 1992.

CHEVALIER, JERRY WILLIAM

Chevalier, Jerry William. "Going for Broke." In *How I Became a Nurse Entrepreneur: Tales from 50 Nurses in Business*, 225-232. Petaluma, Calif.: National Nurses in Business Association, 1991.

CHILDS, GEORGE W.

"George W. Childs." In *A Dozen Roads to Success: Being Graphic Sketches of Twelve of the Most Prominent Business Men of America, And Showing How They Became Millionaires,* 7-16. Philadelphia, Penn.: Girard Pub. Co., 1894.

CHRISTOPHER, DORIS

Ericksen, Gregory K. "Doris Christopher—The Pampered Chef, Ltd., 'The Kitchen Store That Comes to Your Door'." In *Women Entrepreneurs Only: Twelve Women Entrepreneurs Tell The Stories of Their Success*, 109-129. New York, N.Y.: Wiley, 1999.

CLAIBORNE, LIZ

Brands, H. W. "Dress for success: Liz Caliborne." In *Masters of Enterprise: Giants of American Business from John Jacob Astor and J.P. Morgan to Bill Gates and Oprah Winfrey*, 267-274. New York, N.Y.: Free Press, 1999.

Davis, William. "Liz Claiborne, b. 1929: The Executive Women's Dress Designer." In *The Innovators: The Essential Guide to Business Thinkers, Achievers and Entrepreneurs*, 74-77. New York, N.Y.: AMACOM, 1987.

Landrum, Gene N. "Liz Claiborne—Persevering Pioneer." In *Profiles of Female Genius: Thirteen Creative Women Who Changed the World*, 206-222. Amherst, N.Y.: Prometheus Books, 1994.

Mariotti, Steve, and Lorraine Mooney. "Liz Claiborne: The Wizard of the Working Woman's Wardrobe." In *Entrepreneurs in Profile*, 114-117. London: National Foundation for Teaching Entrepreneurship, 1991.

CLARK, CATHERINE

Rich-McCoy, Lois. "Ceres and Chardonnay: Catherine Clark." In *Millionairess: Self-Made Women of America*, 49-72. New York, N.Y.: Harper & Row, 1978.

CLARK, HOWARD

Gross, Daniel, and the Editors of Forbes Magazine. "American Express and the Charge Card." In *Forbes Greatest Business Stories of All Time*, 212-231. New York, N.Y.: Wiley, 1996.

CLARK, JAMES H.

Aronoff, Craig E., and John L. Ward. "James H. Clark." In *Contemporary Entrepreneurs*, 95-100. Detroit, Mich.: Omnigraphics, Inc., 1992.

CLARK, WILLIAM ANDREWS

Burnley, James. "W. A. Clark: The Copper King of Montana." In *Millionaires and Kings of Enterprise; The Marvellous Careers of Some Americans Who by Pluck, Foresight, And Energy Have Made Themselves Masters in the Fields of Industry and Finance*, 42-49. Philadelphia, Penn.: J. B. Lippincott, 1901.

Klepper, Michael M., and Robert Gunther. "William Andrew Clark (1839-1925): Montana Copper King." In *The Wealthy 100 : From Benjamin Franklin to Bill Gates—A Ranking of the Richest Americans, Past and Present,* 159-161. Secaucus, N.J. : Carol Pub. Group, 1996.

CLASH, KEVIN

Clarke, Caroline V. "Kevin Clash: Principal Puppeteer, Jim Henson Company." In *Take a Lesson: Today's Black Achievers and How They Made It and What They Learned Along the Way*, 15-22. New York, N.Y.: Wiley, 2001.

CLEMENT, MARTIN W.

Westbrook, Francis Jr. "Martin W. Clement" In *America's Fifty Foremost Business Leaders,* ed. B. C. Forbes, 53-62. New York, N.Y.: B.C. Forbes, 1948.

COCHRAN, JOHNNIE L.

Clarke, Caroline V. "Johnnie L. Cochran Jr.: Partner, The Cochran Group; Schneider, Kleinick, Weitz, Damashek & Shoot." In *Take a Lesson: Today's Black Achievers and How They Made It and What They Learned Along the Way*, 23-29. New York, N.Y.: Wiley, 2001.

COCHRANE, JOSEPHINE GARIS

Cleary, David Powers. "Kitchenaid Dishwashers; 'If Nobody Else Is Going to Invent a Dishwashing Machine, I'll Do It Myself'." In *Great American Brands: The Success Formulas That Made Them Famous*, 192-196. New York, N.Y: Fairchild Publications, 1981.

COE, THOMAS D.

Uris, Auren. "Thomas D. Coe—The Mom-And-Pop Machine Shop." In *The Executive Breakthrough; 21 Roads to the Top*, 139-149. Garden City, N.Y.: Doubleday, 1967.

COHEN, ABBY JOSEPH

Herera, Sue. "Abby Joseph Cohen: Co-Chair Investment Policy Committee, Goldman Sachs." In *Women of the Street: Making It on Wall Street— The World's Toughest Business*, 59-70. New York, N.Y.: Wiley, 1997.

COHEN, MARK

Murphy, Linda. "Mark Cohen: Pro-Gamer." In *Computer Entrepreneurs: People Who Built Successful Businesses Around Computers*, 119-128. San Diego, Calif.: Computer Publishing Enterprises, 1990.

COHEN, SOLOMON

Koppel, Robert. "Solomon's Mind: Solomon Cohen." In *Bulls, Bears, And Millionaires: War Stories of Trading Life*, 33-46. Chicago, Ill.: Dearborn Financial Publishers, 1997.

COHENOUR, CHERYL R.

Mikaelian, A. "Cheryl R. Cohenour." In *Women Who Mean Business: Success Stories of Women Over Forty*, 252-256. New York, N.Y.: William Morrow & Co., 1999.

COLANGELO, JERRY

Oster, Merrill J. "MVP." In *The Entrepreneur's Creed: The Principles & Passions of 20 Successful Entrepreneurs*, 36-45. Nashville, Tenn.: Broadman & Holman Publishers, 2001.

COLE, IDA

Tsang, Cheryl D. "Ida Cole: 'The Independent', 1984-1990." In *Microsoft First Generation: The Success Secrets of the Visionaries Who Launched a Technology Empire*, 131-148. New York, N.Y.: Wiley, 2000.

COLEMAN, DEBI

Mikaelian, A. "Debi Coleman." In *Women Who Mean Business: Success Stories of Women Over Forty*, 257-261. New York, N.Y.: William Morrow & Co., 1999.

COLES, MICHAEL

Aronoff, Craig E., and John L. Ward. "Michael Coles." In *Contemporary Entrepreneurs*, 101-106. Detroit, Mich.: Omnigraphics, Inc., 1992.

COLLADO, RAPHAEL

Kingston, Brett. "Raphael Collado and Ramon Morales of Protocom Devices." In *The Dynamos: Who Are They Anyway?*, 35-44. New York, N.Y.: Wiley, 1987.

COLLIER, SOPHIA

Kingston, Brett. "Sophia Collier and Connie Best of American Natural Beverage Corporation." In *The Dynamos: Who Are They Anyway?*, 85-89. New York, N.Y: Wiley, 1987.

COLLYER, JOHN L.

Sisson, Herbert Gay. "John L. Collyer." In *America's Fifty Foremost Business Leaders,* ed. B. C. Forbes, 63-72. New York, N.Y.: B.C. Forbes, 1948.

COLT, SAMUEL

Grant, Ellsworth S. "Gunmaker to the World." In *Great Stories of American Businessmen*, From *American Heritage, The Magazine of History*, 81-98. New York, N.Y.: American Heritage Publishing Co., 1954.

Klepper, Michael M., and Robert Gunther. "Samuel Colt (1814-1862): The Gunslinger." In *The Wealthy 100 : From Benjamin Franklin to Bill Gates—A Ranking of the Richest Americans, Past and Present*, 246-248. Secaucus, N.J. : Carol Pub. Group, 1996.

COLTON, DAVID D.

Lewis, Oscar. "Colton: 'I Propose to Stand or Fall with You All...'." In *The Big Four; The Story of Huntington, Stanford, Hopkins, and Crocker, And of the Building of the*

Central Pacific, 283-320. New York, N.Y.: A.A. Knopf, 1938.

COLUMBUS-GREEN, CAROL

Suarez, Ruth. "Carol Columbus-Green: Laracris, Inc. (Dubbed Aubergine), 'No More Tummies'." In *Superstar Entrepreneurs of Small and Large Businesses Reveal Their Secrets*. 175-180. Piscataway, N.J.: Research and Education Association, 1998.

CONNER, FINIS

Aronoff, Craig E., and John L. Ward. "Finis Conner." In *Contemporary Entrepreneurs*, 107-113. Detroit, Mich.: Omnigraphics, Inc., 1992.

CONNORS, MARY JEAN

Mikaelian, A. "Mary Jean Connors." In *Women Who Mean Business: Success Stories of Women Over Forty*, 31-35. New York, N.Y.: William Morrow & Co., 1999.

COOK, MARY JANE

Cook, Mary Jane. "A New Journey at 47." In *Success Secrets: How Eighteen Everyday Women Became Fortune Builders and Famous Speakers*, 263-274. Glendora, Calif.: Royal CBS Publishing, 1978.

COOK, SCOTT

Jager, Rama Dev, and Rafael Ortiz. "Scott Cook: Intuit; It's the Customer, Stupid. Part II." In *In the Company of Giants: Candid Conversations with the Visionaries of the Digital World*, 73-85. New York, N.Y.: McGraw-Hill, 1997.

COOK, THOMAS

"The Man from Cook's: Thomas Cook, Crusading for the Temperance Cause, Accidentally Launched the Multi-Billion Dollar Travel Industry." In *The 50 Great Pioneers of American Industry*. By the Editors of News Front and Year, 30-33. Maplewood, N.J.: C.S. Hammond, 1964.

COOPER, JOEL

Aronoff, Craig E., and John L. Ward. "Joel Cooper; Michael Tomson." In *Contemporary Entrepreneurs*, 114-118. Detroit, Mich.: Omnigraphics, Inc., 1992.

COOPER, PETER

"Peter Cooper." In *A Dozen Roads to Success: Being Graphic Sketches of Twelve of the Most Prominent Business Men of America, And Showing How They Became Millionaires, 152-169. Philadelphia, Penn.: Girard Pub. Co., 1894.*

Stoddard, William Osborn. "Peter Cooper—Invention." In *Men of Business*, 264-280. New York, N.Y.: Scribner's Sons, 1893. 317 p.

COORS, PETER H.

Pottker, Jan. "Adolph Coors Company: Brewing Up a New Culture at Adolph Coors." In *Born to Power: Heirs to America's Leading Businesses*, 144-157. New York, N.Y.: Barron's, 1992.

COPELAND, WAYNE E. JR.

Gilder, George. "A Sad Heart in a Personal Jet." In *The Spirit of Enterprise*, 115-130. New York, N.Y: Simon and Schuster, 1984.

COPPERFIELD, DAVID

Liberman, Gail, and Alan Lavine. "David Copperfield: Makes Millions from Magic Tricks." In *Rags to Riches: Motivating Stories of How Ordinary People Achieved Extraordinary Wealth!*, 140-147. Chicago, Ill.: Dearborn, 2000.

CORNELL, CLARA E.

Cornell, Clara E. "A Wake-Up Call to Action." In *How I Became a Nurse Entrepreneur: Tales from 50 Nurses in Business*, 181-184. Petaluma, Calif.: National Nurses in Business Association, 1991.

CORNELL, EZRA

Wren, Daniel A., and Ronald G. Greenwood. "Ezra Cornell." In *Management Innovators: The People and Ideas That Have Shaped Modern Business*, 94-98. New York, N.Y.: Oxford University Press, 1998.

CORNFELD, BERNARD

Davis, William. "Bernard Cornfeld, b. 1926: The Mutual Funds Wizard." In *The Innovators: The Essential Guide to Business Thinkers, Achievers and Entrepreneurs*, 86-89. New York, N.Y.: AMACOM, 1987.

Gunther, Max, "Bernard Cornfeld: One-Hundred-Fifty Million Dollars." In *The Very, Very Rich and How They Got That Way*, ed. Max Gunther, 74-88. Chicago, Ill.: The Playboy Press, 1972.

CORNFELD, MICHAEL

Kao, John J. "Robert Michael Companies (A)." In *The Entrepreneur*, 110-124. Englewood Cliffs, New Jersey: Prentice Hall, 1991.

CORONA, RAY

Adams, James Ring. "Darkness at Sunshine State." In *The Big Fix: Inside the S&L Scandal: How an Unholy Alliance of Politics and Money Destroyed America's Banking System*, 125-142. New York, N.Y: Wiley, 1990.

COSENTINO, LOUIS

Pine, Carol, and Susan Mundale. "Louis Cosentino; Doing Something Right." In *Self-Made: The Stories of 12 Minnesota Entrepreneurs*, 87-99. Minneapolis, Minn.: Dorn Books, 1982.

COSS, LAWRENCE M.

Wendel, Charles B. "Building a Consumer Franchise: Lawrence M. Coss, Chairman & CEO, Green Tree Financial Corporation." In *The New Financiers*, 55-80. Chicago, Ill.: Irwin Professional Pub., 1996.

COSTELLO, JENNIFER

Koppel, Mara. "New Kid on the Block—Jennifer Costello." In *Women of the Pits: Shattering the Glass Ceiling in Financial Markets*, 153-164. Chicago, Ill.: Dearborn Financial Publishers, 1998.

COTSAKOS, CHRISTOS

Ericksen, Gregory K. "William Porter & Christos Cotsakos—E*TRADE 'Go For It'." In *Net Entrepreneurs Only : 10 Entrepreneurs Tell the Stories of Their Success*, 61-80. New York : John Wiley, 2000.

Price, Christopher. "Christos Cotsakos—E*Trade 'Courage Under Fire'." In *The Internet Entrepreneurs: Business Rules Are Good: Break Them*, 78-95. London, Eng.: FT.com, 2000.

COWAN, HIRAM D.

Gray, Bob, ed. "Powder Ignites a Business." In *How Entrepreneurs Make Business Profits: A Study of Personal Success Stories From Cordovan Business Journals*, 11-14. Houston, Tex.: Cordovan Press, 1982.

COWLES, KRISTI

Alexander, Shoshana. "Kristi Cowles: Pederson Victorian Bed & Breakfast; Singing Wolf Center, Lake Geneva, Wisconsin." In *Women's Ventures, Women's Visions: 29 Inspiring Stories From Women Who Started Their Own Businesses*, 132-138. Freedom, Calif.: The Crossing Press, 1997.

CRABLE, WILLIAM H. "TOBY"

Koppel, Robert. "Tennis Anyone?: William H. 'Toby' Crable." In *Bulls, Bears, And Millionaires: War Stories of Trading Life*, 68-74. Chicago, Ill.: Dearborn Financial Publishers, 1997.

CRAIG, JENNY

Ericksen, Gregory K. "Jenny Craig—Jenny Craig, Inc., 'I've Always Had a Lot of Confidence'." In *Women Entrepreneurs Only: Twelve Women Entrepreneurs Tell The Stories of Their Success*, 23-43. New York, N.Y.: Wiley, 1999.

CRAIN, KEITH

Pottker, Jan. "Crain Communications, Inc.: Shared Power." In *Born to Power: Heirs to America's Leading Businesses*, 58-67. New York, N.Y.: Barron's, 1992.

CRAIN, RANCE

Pottker, Jan. "Crain Communications, Inc.: Shared Power." In *Born to Power: Heirs to America's Leading Businesses*, 58-67. New York, N.Y.: Barron's, 1992.

CRAMP, WILLIAM

Burnley, James. "William Cramp & Sons: The American Shipbuilder Kings." In *Millionaires and Kings of Enterprise; The Marvellous Careers of Some Americans Who by Pluck, Foresight, And Energy Have Made Themselves Masters in the Fields of Industry and Finance*, 329-339. Philadelphia, Penn.: J. B. Lippincott, 1901.

CRANE, BOB

Gray, Bob, ed. "Problem Properties Pay Off." In *How Entrepreneurs Make Business Profits: A Study of Personal Success Stories From Cordovan Business Journals*, 132-138. Houston, Tex.: Cordovan Press, 1982.

CRANE, CHRISTOPHER

Oster, Merrill J. "The Road to an IPO." In *The Entrepreneur's Creed: The Principles & Passions of 20 Successful Entrepreneurs*, 132-141. Nashville, Tenn.: Broadman & Holman Publishers, 2001.

CRANE FAMILY

Pottker, Jan. "Crane & Company, Inc.: Worth the Paper It's Written on." In *Born to Power: Heirs to America's Leading Businesses*, 236-243. New York, N.Y.: Barron's, 1992.

CRAPO, HENRY H.

Folsom, Burton W. "Henry Crapo and William Durant: From Lumber to Carriages to Cars." In *Empire Builders: How Michigan Entrepreneurs Helped Make America Great*, 55-86. Traverse City, Mich.: Rhodes & Easton, 1998.

CRAY, SEYMOUR

Slater, Robert. "Seymour Cray: The Hermit of Chippewa Falls and His 'Simple, Dumb Things'." In *Portraits in Silicon*, 194-204. Cambridge, Mass.: MIT Press, 1987.

CROCKER, CHARLES

Lewis, Oscar. "Crocker: 'Everyone Was Afraid of Me...'." In The Big Four; The Story of Huntington, Stanford, Hopkins, And Crocker, And of the Building of the Central Pacific, 49-123. New York, N.Y.: A.A. Knopf, 1938.

CROW, IMALEE

Crow, Imalee. "Pure, Unadulterated Frustration." In *How I Became a Nurse Entrepreneur: Tales from 50 Nurses in Business*, 135-141. Petaluma, Calif.: National Nurses in Business Association, 1991.

CROW, TRAMMELL

Davis, William. "Trammell Crow, b. 1914: Creator of the Dallas Skyline." In *The Innovators: The Essential Guide to Business Thinkers, Achievers and Entrepreneurs*, 90-92. New York, N.Y.: AMACOM, 1987.

CRUM, BRUCE

Elfstrand, Rhonda. "Bruce Crum; Chris Frank: Adams Development Group." In *The Story Behind the Success: Learning From Pittsburgh Professionals*, 62-73. Pittsburgh, Penn.: Steel Publishing Partners, 1996.

CRUZ, HMBERTO

Liberman, Gail, and Alan Lavine. "Humberto Cruz: Frugal Columnist Saves More Than $1 Million." In *Rags to Riches: Motivating Stories of How Ordinary People Achieved Extraordinary Wealth!*, 148-162. Chicago, Ill.: Dearborn, 2000.

CUBAN, MARK

Ericksen, Gregory K. "Mark Cuban & Todd Wagner—Yahoo Broadcast 'Every Business in the World Is a Potential Customer'." In *Net Entrepreneurs Only : 10 Entrepreneurs Tell the Stories of Their Success*, 185-206. New York : John Wiley, 2000.

CULLEN, MICHEL

Davis, William. "Michael Cullen, 1864-1936: The World's Most Daring Price-Wrecker." In *The Innovators: The Essential Guide to Business Thinkers, Achievers and Entrepreneurs*, 92-95. New York, N.Y.: AMACOM, 1987.

CULPEPPER, BRENDA J.

Mikaelian, A. "Brenda J. Culpepper." In *Women Who Mean Business: Success Stories of Women Over Forty*, 50-54. New York, N.Y.: William Morrow & Co., 1999.

CUMMINGS, NATHAN

Pile, Robert B. "Nathan Cummings: "Nobody Doesn't Like Sara Lee." In *Top Entrepreneurs and Their Businesses*, 80-95. Minneapolis, Minn.: The Oliver Press, Inc., 1993.

CURLEY, JOHN

Cose, Ellis. "The Chains: Gannett and Knight-Ridder." In *The Press*, 281-356. New York, N.Y.: Morrow, 1989.

CURLEY, TOM

Cose, Ellis. "The Chains: Gannett and Knight-Ridder." In *The Press*, 281-356. New York, N.Y.: Morrow, 1989.

CURRY, EUGENE

Wallace, Robert L. "Eugene Curry: Founder, Seven Systems, Inc., Gaithersburg, Maryland." In *Black Wealth: Your Road to Small Business Success*, 110-114. New York, N.Y.: Wiley, 2000.

CURTIS, CYRUS H. K.

"How Magazines Went National: Cyrus H. K. Curtis Led the Turn-Of-The Century Publishing Revolution That Created the Mass Circulation Magazine; S. S. McClure Dramatized Its Power As a National Opinion-Maker." In *The 50 Great Pioneers of American Industry*. By the Editors of News Front and Year, 148-151. Maplewood, N.J.: C.S. Hammond, 1964.

"How Magazines Went National Part 2: McClure and the 'Muckrakers'... Curtis and the Saturday Evening Post... National Magazines and National Advertisers..." In *The 50 Great Pioneers of American Industry*. By the Editors of News Front and Year, 152-155. Maplewood, N.J.: C.S. Hammond, 1964.

Klepper, Michael M., and Robert Gunther. "Cyrus H. K. Curtis (1850-1933): Post Master." In *The Wealthy 100 : From Benjamin Franklin to Bill*

Gates—A Ranking of the Richest Americans, Past and Present, 88-90. Secaucus, N.J. : Carol Pub. Group, 1996.

CUSTIN, MILDRED

Uris, Auren. "Mildred Custin—Bonwit Teller's Best Buy." In *The Executive Breakthrough; 21 Roads to the Top*, 117-124. Garden City, N.Y.: Doubleday, 1967.

DAHL, GARY

Shook, Robert L. "The Pet Rock." In *Why Didn't I Think of That*, 1-18. New York, N.Y.: New American Library, 1982.

DAHLBERG, KEN

Oster, Merrill J. "Where's the Action." In *The Entrepreneur's Creed: The Principles & Passions of 20 Successful Entrepreneurs*, 192-201. Nashville, Tenn.: Broadman & Holman Publishers, 2001.

DALLAS, C. DONALD

Westbrook, Francis Jr. "C. Donald Dallas." In *America's Fifty Foremost Business Leaders,* ed. B. C. Forbes, 73-82. New York, N.Y.: B.C. Forbes, 1948.

DALY, BETTYE

Woodard, Michael D. "MayDay Chemical—Bettye Daly." In *Black Entrepreneurs in America: Stories of Struggle and Success*, 127-142. New Brunswick, N.J.: Rutgers University Press, 1997.

d'ARBELOFF, ALEXANDER V.

Silver, A. David. "Alexander V. d'Arbeloff; Nicholas DeWolf." In *Entrepreneurial Megabucks: The 100 Greatest Entrepreneurs of the Last 25 Years*, 174-177. New York, N.Y.: Wiley, 1985.

DART, DANIEL J.

Kahn, Joseph P. "The Money Game: Can Blackstone Bank Succeed by Focusing on Markets Other Lenders Ignore?" In *Anatomy of a Start-Up: Why Some New Businesses Succeed and Others Fail: 27 Real-Life Case Studies,* ed. Elizabeth K. Longsworth, 31-41. Boston, Mass.: Inc. Publishing, 1991.

DAVIDSON, WILLIAM G.

Gross, Daniel, and the Editors of Forbes Magazine. "The Turnaround at Harley-Davidson." In *Forbes Greatest Business Stories of All Time,* 298-312. New York, N.Y.: Wiley, 1996.

Pottker, Jan. "Harley-Davidson, Inc: The Hog with Attitude." In *Born to Power: Heirs to America's Leading Businesses,* 158-167. New York, N.Y.: Barron's, 1992.

DAVIS, ARTHUR VINING

Klepper, Michael M., and Robert Gunther. "Arthur Vining Davis (1867-1962): The Emperor of Aluminum." In *The Wealthy 100 : From Benjamin Franklin to Bill Gates—A Ranking of the Richest Americans, Past and Present,* 263-265. Secaucus, N.J. : Carol Pub. Group, 1996.

DAVIS, BARBARA LANGFORD

Mikaelian, A. "Barbara Langford Davis." In *Women Who Mean Business: Success Stories of Women Over Forty,* 277-281. New York, N.Y.: William Morrow & Co., 1999.

DAVIS, BOB

Price, Christopher. "Bob Davis—Lycos 'Searching Out the Next Deal'." In *The Internet Entrepreneurs: Business Rules Are Good: Break Them,* 1-16. London, Eng.: FT.com, 2000.

DAVIS, BRETT

Kingston, Brett. "Brett Davis of Stockton Savings Association/Troy and Nichols Mortgage Company." In *The Dynamos: Who Are They Anyway?*, 11-20. New York, N.Y.: Wiley, 1987.

DAVIS, JERRY G.

Buchholz, Barbara B., and Margaret Crane. "Unified Services, Inc., Washington, D.C." In *Corporate Blood Lines: The Future of the Family Firm*, 229-244. New York, N.Y: Carol Publishing Group, 1989.

DAVIS, JOHN

Gardner, Ralph. "John Davis." In *Young, Gifted, and Rich: The Secrets of America's Most Successful Entrepreneurs*, 93-104. New York, N.Y.: Wallaby Books, 1984.

DAVIS, KEVIN

Gray, Bob, ed. "Author Rescues Apartments." In *How Entrepreneurs Make Business Profits: A Study of Personal Success Stories From Cordovan Business Journals*, 122-127. Houston, Tex.: Cordovan Press, 1982.

DAVIS, SUSAN

Alexander, Shoshana. "Susan Davis: Capital Missions Company, West Chicago, Illinois." In *Women's Ventures, Women's Visions: 29 Inspiring Stories From Women Who Started Their Own Businesses*, 119-124. Freedom, Calif.: The Crossing Press, 1997.

DAVIS, T. CULLEN

Sheehy, Sandy. "T. Cullen Davis: Murder and Millions." In *Texas Big Rich; Exploits, Eccentricities, And Fabulous Fortunes Won and Lost*, 239-255. New York, N.Y.: Morrow, 1990.

DAY, BENJAMIN

"The New York Sun: 'Read All About It'." In *The 50 Great Pioneers of American Industry*. By the Editors of News Front and Year, 19-21. Maplewood, N.J.: C.S. Hammond, 1964.

DAY, CECIL B.

Silver, A. David. "Cecil B. Day; Richard C. Kessler." In *Entrepreneurial Megabucks: The 100 Greatest Entrepreneurs of the Last 25 Years*, 178-180. New York, N.Y.: Wiley, 1985.

DAYANI, ELIZABETH

"Built on Quality: Committed to Service." In *How I Became a Nurse Entrepreneur: Tales from 50 Nurses in Business*, 203-209. Petaluma, Calif.: National Nurses in Business Association, 1991.

DAY-JOHNSON, CARY

Lassen, Ali. "Cary Day-Johnson, Director, Mary Kay Cosmetics." In *The Secret of Their Success: Women Entrepreneurs Reveal How They Made It*, 43-47. Carlsbad, Calif.: Ali Lassen Success System, 1990.

DE FOREST, LEE

"Baron of Broadcasting: Lee De Forest's Invention of the Audion Brought Millions Within Reach of the Very Best in Entertainment, Education." In *The 50 Great Pioneers of American Industry*. By the Editors of News Front and Year, 196-199. Maplewood, N.J.: C.S. Hammond, 1964.

DE GOLYER, EVERETTE LEE

Davis, William. "Everette Lee De Golyer, 1886-1956: Father of the Oil Industry." In *The Innovators: The Essential Guide to Business Thinkers, Achievers and Entrepreneurs*, 99-101. New York, N.Y.: AMACOM, 1987.

DE GRAFF, ROBERT F.

Fucini, Joseph J., and Suzy Fucini. "Robert F. De Graff, Pocket Books, Inc.: 'People Would Buy More Books If They Were Cheaper'." In *Experience Inc.; Men and Women Who Founded Famous Companies After the Age of 40*, 129-135. New York, N.Y: Free Press, 1987.

DE LAMAR, J. R.

Burnley, James. "J. R. De Lamar: A Millionaire of Adventure." In *Millionaires and Kings of Enterprise; The Marvellous Careers of Some Americans Who by Pluck, Foresight, And Energy Have Made Themselves Masters in the Fields of Industry and Finance*, 293-296. Philadelphia, Penn.: J. B. Lippincott, 1901.

DE LOREAN, JOHN Z.

Shook, Robert L. "John Z. De Lorean." In *The Entrepreneurs: Twelve Who Took Risks and Succeeded*, 157-171. New York, N.Y: Harper & Row, 1980.

DE LUCA, PETER C.

"Peter C. de Luca, Cardiac Imaging of Boston." In *Profiles in Success: How Six Entrepreneurs Have Prospered in a Tough Business Environment*, 54-63. By the editors of *Managing*. New York, N.Y.: HBJ Newsletters, 1981.

DE VOS, RICHARD

Uris, Auren. "Jay Van Andel and Richard De Vos—Prospecting on the Doorstep." In *The Executive Breakthrough; 21 Roads to the Top*, 381-394. Garden City, N.Y.: Doubleday, 1967.

DECKER, ALONZO G.

Cleary, David Powers. "Black & Decker Power Tools; No Idea Is Worth Anything Unless You Have the Guts to Back It Up." In *Great American Brands: The Success Formulas That Made*

Them Famous, 19-23. New York, N.Y: Fairchild Publications, 1981.

DEDOMINIC, PATTY

Mikaelian, A. "Patty DeDominic." In *Women Who Mean Business: Success Stories of Women Over Forty*, 36-40. New York, N.Y.: William Morrow & Co., 1999.

DEEDS, CORKY

Murphy, Linda. "Corky Deeds: LightSpeed." In *Computer Entrepreneurs: People Who Built Successful Businesses Around Computers*, 65-70. San Diego, Calif.: Computer Publishing Enterprises, 1990.

DELL, MICHAEL

Aronoff, Craig E., and John L. Ward. "Michael Dell." In *Contemporary Entrepreneurs*, 119-125. Detroit, Mich.: Omnigraphics, Inc., 1992.

Jager, Rama Dev, and Rafael Ortiz. "Michael Dell: Dell Computer; Growing Texas Reign." In *In the Company of Giants: Candid Conversations with the Visionaries of the Digital World*, 115-126. New York, N.Y.: McGraw-Hill, 1997.

Koehn, Nancy F. "Michael Dell." In *Brand New: How Entrepreneurs Earned Consumers' Trust from Wedgwood to Dell*, 259-305. Boston, Mass.: Harvard Business School Press, 2001.

DEMAGNUS, ALBERT

Woodard, Michael D. "Computer Management Services, Inc.—Albert and Sharon DeMagnus." In *Black Entrepreneurs in America: Stories of Struggle and Success*, 70-80. New Brunswick, N.J.: Rutgers University Press, 1977.

DEMELLO, TIMOTHY A.

Mamis, Robert A. "Play Money; Currently the Hottest Fad in Town, Wall Street Games Inc. Must Choose Among Three Long-Term Growth

Strategies." In *Anatomy of a Start-Up: Why Some New Businesses Succeed and Others Fail: 27 Real-Life Case Studies,* ed. Elizabeth K. Longsworth, 176-186. Boston, Mass.: Inc. Publishing, 1991.

DEMING, W. EDWARD

Wren, Daniel A., and Ronald G. Greenwood. "W. Edward Deming." In *Management Innovators: The People and Ideas That Have Shaped Modern Business*, 204-213. New York, N.Y.: Oxford University Press, 1998.

DENHART, GUN

Mikaelian, A. "Gun Denhart." In *Women Who Mean Business: Success Stories of Women Over Forty*, 262-266. New York, N.Y.: William Morrow & Co., 1999.

DENTON, EUGENE K.

Uris, Auren. "Eugene K. Denton—A Fortune in Taste." In *The Executive Breakthrough; 21 Roads to the Top*, 101-112. Garden City, N.Y.: Doubleday, 1967.

DEPEW, CHAUNCEY MITCHELL

Stoddard, William Osborn. "Chauncey Mitchell Depew—Growth." In *Men of Business*, 161-181. New York, N.Y.: Scribner's Sons, 1893. 317 p.

DERBY, ELIAS HASKET

Klepper, Michael M., and Robert Gunther. "Elias Hasket Derby (1739-1799): Trailblazer of American Global Commerce." In *The Wealthy 100 : From Benjamin Franklin to Bill Gates—A Ranking of the Richest Americans, Past and Present*, 145-147. Secaucus, N.J. : Carol Pub. Group, 1996.

DESIO, ANTHONY

Aronoff, Craig E., and John L. Ward. "Anthony DeSio." In *Contemporary Entrepreneurs*, 126-132. Detroit, Mich.: Omnigraphics, Inc., 1992.

DEUPREE, RICHARD R.

Sisson, Herbert Gay. "Richard R. Deupree." In *America's Fifty Foremost Business Leaders,* ed. B. C. Forbes, 83-92. New York, N.Y.: B.C. Forbes, 1948.

DEVER, MIKE

Koppel, Robert. "Rocket Man: Mike Dever." In *Bulls, Bears, And Millionaires: War Stories of Trading Life*, 16-32. Chicago, Ill.: Dearborn Financial Publishers, 1997.

DEVINNEY, BETTY

Mikaelian, A. "Betty DeVinney." In *Women Who Mean Business: Success Stories of Women Over Forty*, 286-290. New York, N.Y.: William Morrow & Co., 1999.

DEWOLF, NICHOLAS

Silver, A. David. "Alexander V. d'Arbeloff; Nicholas DeWolf." In *Entrepreneurial Megabucks: The 100 Greatest Entrepreneurs of the Last 25 Years*, 174-177. New York, N.Y.: Wiley, 1985.

DIENST, JOCELYN D.

Mikaelian, A. "Jocelyn D. Dienst." In *Women Who Mean Business: Success Stories of Women Over Forty*, 233-236. New York, N.Y.: William Morrow & Co., 1999.

DILLARD, WILLIAM T.

Buchholz, Barbara B., and Margaret Crane. "Dillard Department Stores Inc., Little Rock, AR." In *Corporate Blood Lines: The Future of the Family Firm*, 60-77. New York, N.Y: Carol Publishing Group, 1989.

DINES, JAMES

King, Norman. "James Dines." In *The Money Messiah$*, 118-147. New York, N.Y.: Coward-McCann, 1983.

DION, C. NORMAN

Silver, A. David. "C. Norman Dion." In *Entrepreneurial Megabucks: The 100 Greatest Entrepreneurs of the Last 25 Years*, 181-183. New York, N.Y.: Wiley, 1985.

DISNEY, WALT

Auletta, Ken. "The Human Factor; Troubles in Disneyland." In *The Highwaymen; Warriors of the Information Superhighway*, 230-247. New York, N.Y.: Random House, 1997.

Brands, H. W. "Fantasy Inc.: Walt Disney." In *Masters of Enterprise: Giants of American Business from John Jacob Astor and J.P. Morgan to Bill Gates and Oprah Winfrey*, 182-194. New York, N.Y.: Free Press, 1999.

Davis, William. "Walt Disney, 1901-66: America's 'Happy Accident'." In *The Innovators: The Essential Guide to Business Thinkers, Achievers and Entrepreneurs*, 106-108. New York, N.Y.: AMACOM, 1987.

Gross, Daniel, and the Editors of Forbes Magazine. "Walt Disney and His Family-Entertainment Empire." In *Forbes Greatest Business Stories of All Time*, 122-141. New York, N.Y.: Wiley, 1996.

Hillkirk, John, and Gary Jacobson. "Disney: New Life for a 12,000-Year-Old Mouse." In *Grit, Guts, And Genius: True Tales of Megasuccess: Who Made Them Happen and How They Did It*, 129-141. Boston, Mass.: Houghton Mifflin, 1990.

Pile, Robert B. "Walt Disney: And a Mouse That Might Have Been Named Mortimer." In *Top Entrepreneurs and Their Businesses*, 44-65. Minneapolis, Minn.: The Oliver Press, Inc., 1993.

DISTELDORF, JANET

Koppel, Mara. "Cash Dance—Janet Disteldorf." In *Women of the Pits: Shattering the Glass Ceiling in Financial Markets*, 117-128. Chicago, Ill.: Dearborn Financial Publishers, 1998.

DODGE BROTHERS

Klepper, Michael M., and Robert Gunther. "John Francis Dodge (1864-1920), and Horace Elgin Dodge (1868-1920): Twin Engines of the Auto Industry." In *The Wealthy 100 : From Benjamin Franklin to Bill Gates—A Ranking of the Richest Americans, Past and Present*, 227-230. Secaucus, N.J. : Carol Pub. Group, 1996.

DOHMEN-RAMIREZ, BERT

King, Norman. "Bert Dohmen-Ramirez." In *The Money Messiah$*, 207-208. New York, N.Y.: Coward-McCann, 1983.

DOLAN, MARION B.

Dolan, Marion B. "What Are You Going to Do with Your Life." In *How I Became a Nurse Entrepreneur: Tales from 50 Nurses in Business*, 37-41. Petaluma, Calif.: National Nurses in Business Association, 1991.

DOLLAR, ROBERT

Klepper, Michael M., and Robert Gunther. "Capt. Robert Dollar (1844-1932): Founded President Lines." In *The Wealthy 100 : From Benjamin Franklin to Bill Gates—A Ranking of the Richest Americans, Past and Present*, 300-302. Secaucus, N.J. : Carol Pub. Group, 1996.

DONOGHUE, WILLIAM

King, Norman. "William Donoghue." In *The Money Messiah$*, 209-213. New York, N.Y.: Coward-McCann, 1983.

DORE, ARTHUR P.

Shook, Robert L. "The Toughman Contest." In *Why Didn't I Think of That*, 146-163. New York, N.Y.: New American Library, 1982.

DORRANCE FAMILY

Cleary, David Powers. "Campbell's Soup; We Blend the Best with Careful Pains in Skillful Combination, And Everything We Make Contains Our Business Reputation." In *Great American Brands: The Success Formulas That Made Them Famous*, 53-59. New York, N.Y: Fairchild Publications, 1981.

Klepper, Michael M., and Robert Gunther. "John T. Dorrance (1873-1930): Sultan of Soup." In *The Wealthy 100 : From Benjamin Franklin to Bill Gates—A Ranking of the Richest Americans, Past and Present*, 217-219. Secaucus, N.J. : Carol Pub. Group, 1996.

Pottker, Jan. "Campbell Soup Company: Simmering the Family Stock at Campbell Soup." In *Born to Power: Heirs to America's Leading Businesses*, 350-359. New York, N.Y.: Barron's, 1992.

DORSEY, EILLEN E.

Wallace, Robert L. "Walter W. Hill Jr. and Eillen E. Dorsey: Founders, ECS Technologies, Baltimore, Maryland." In *Black Wealth: Your Road to Small Business Success*, 60-66. New York, N.Y.: Wiley, 2000.

DOTTS, RICHARD

Silver, A. David. "Richard Dotts." In *Entrepreneurial Megabucks: The 100 Greatest Entrepreneurs of the Last 25 Years*, 184-186. New York, N.Y.: Wiley, 1985.

DOUGLAS, DONALD WILLS

Fadiman, Jeffrey A. "Dreamer of the Drawing Board: Donald Wills Douglas (1892-1981)." In *Business Entrepreneurs in the West*, ed. Ted C. Hinckley, 83-93. Manhattan, Kans.: Sunflower University Press, 1986.

Ryder, David W. "Donald W. Douglas." In *America's Fifty Foremost Business Leaders*, ed. B. C. Forbes, 93-100. New York, N.Y.: B.C. Forbes, 1948.

Sobel, Robert. "Donald Douglas: The Fortunes of War." In *The Entrepreneurs: Explorations Within the American Business Tradition*, 289-340. New York, N.Y.: Weybright and Talley, 1974.

DOW, CHARLES

Davis, William. "Charles Dow, 1854-1920: Creator of the Dow Jones Index." In *The Innovators: The Essential Guide to Business Thinkers, Achievers and Entrepreneurs*, 109-111. New York, N.Y.: AMACOM, 1987.

DOW, HERBERT

Folsom, Burton W. "Herbert Dow and the Liberation of the American Chemical Industry." In *Empire Builders: How Michigan Entrepreneurs Helped Make America Great*, 87-114. Traverse City, Mich.: Rhodes & Easton, 1998.

DOW, WILLARD H.

Dale, Bert. "Willard H. Dow." In *America's Fifty Foremost Business Leaders*, ed. B. C. Forbes, 101-108. New York, N.Y.: B.C. Forbes, 1948.

DOWNEY, JOAN

Downey, Joan. "How to Doughnut-Proof a Nurse." In *How I Became a Nurse Entrepreneur: Tales from 50 Nurses in Business*, 151-157. Petaluma, Calif.: National Nurses in Business Association, 1991.

DRAKE, LINDA C.

Mikaelian, A. "Linda C. Drake." In *Women Who Mean Business: Success Stories of Women Over Forty*, 55-59. New York, N.Y.: William Morrow & Co., 1999.

DRAKE, WILLIS K.

Fucini, Joseph J., and Suzy Fucini. "Willis K. Drake, Data Card Corporation: 'Support Good Ideas with a Solid Corporate Structure'." In *Experience Inc.; Men and Women Who Founded Famous Companies After the Age of 40*, 136-142. New York, N.Y: Free Press, 1987.

DREW, DANIEL

Mountfield, David. "Bandits in the Palace: Gould, Fisk and the Erie." In *The Railway Barons*, 131-158. New York, N.Y.: Norton, 1979.

DRUCKER, PETER F.

Wren, Daniel A., and Ronald G. Greenwood. "Peter F. Drucker." In *Management Innovators: The People and Ideas That Have Shaped Modern Business*, 226-235. New York, N.Y.: Oxford University Press, 1998.

DRYDEN, JOHN F.

"Insurance for Everybody: John F. Dryden Tapped the Mass Market for Life Insurance with Low-Cost, Pay-by-the-Week 'Industrial' Policies." In *The 50 Great Pioneers of American Industry*. By the Editors of News Front and Year, 76-80. Maplewood, N.J.: C.S. Hammond, 1964.

THE DU PONTS

Livesay, Harold C. "The Patriarchal Pioneer: Pierre S. Du Pont." In *American Made: Men Who Shaped the American Economy*, 182-211. Boston, Mass.: Little, Brown, 1979.

Machalaba, Daniel, and Paul R. Martin. "The Du Ponts." In *American Dynasties Today*, 165-198. Homewood, Ill.: Dow Jones-Irwin, 1990.

DUBROF, DAVID

Suarez, Ruth. "David Dubrof: Lettuce Souprise You, 'Today's Special: Sauteed Egos'." In *Superstar Entrepreneurs of Small and Large Businesses Reveal Their Secrets*, 85-88. Piscataway, N.J.: Research and Education Association, 1998.

DUCK, TOM

Fucini, Joseph J., and Suzy Fucini. "Tom Duck, Ugly Duckling Rent-A-Car System, Inc.: 'Some People Just Take a Little Bit Longer Than Others to Get There'." In *Experience Inc.; Men and Women Who Founded Famous Companies After the Age of 40*, 185-191. New York, N.Y: Free Press, 1987.

DUDACK, GAIL M.

Herera, Sue. "Gail M. Dudack: Managing Director and Chief Investment Strategist, UBS Securities, LLC." In *Women of the Street: Making It on Wall Street—The World's Toughest Business*, 99-114. New York, N.Y.: Wiley, 1997.

DUDLEY, JOE L. SR.

Liberman, Gail, and Alan Lavine. "Joe L. Dudley Sr.: From Farmhouse to Hair Care King." In *Rags to Riches: Motivating Stories of How Ordinary People Achieved Extraordinary Wealth!*, 87-99. Chicago, Ill.: Dearborn, 2000.

DUKE, JAMES BUCHANAN

Klepper, Michael M., and Robert Gunther. "James Buchanan Duke (1856-1925): Tobacco Tsar." In *The Wealthy 100 : From Benjamin Franklin to Bill Gates—A Ranking of the Richest Americans, Past and Present*, 181-185. Secaucus, N.J. : Carol Pub. Group, 1996.

Sobel, Robert. "James Buchanan Duke: Opportunism Is the Spur." In *The Entrepreneurs: Explorations Within the American Business Tradition*, 148-194. New York, N.Y.: Weybright and Talley, 1974.

"Sold American: Founder of American Tobacco Co., Buck Duke Was First to Mass-Produce Cigarettes, Sparked Revolution in U.S. Smoking Habits, Laid Foundation for Today's $6.6 Billion U.S. Tobacco Industry." In *The 50 Great Pioneers of American Industry*. By the Editors of News Front and Year, 95-97. Maplewood, N.J.: C.S. Hammond, 1964.

DUKE, RICHARD

Davis, William. "Richard Duke, 1929-1977: The Man Who Invented 'Lawn Care'." In *The Innovators: The Essential Guide to Business Thinkers, Achievers and Entrepreneurs*, 115-117. New York, N.Y.: AMACOM, 1987.

Nayak, P. Ranganath, and John M. Ketteringham. "ChemLawn and Dick Duke's Lonely Battle." In *Breakthroughs!*, 57-84. San Diego, Calif.: Pfeiffer & Company, 1994.

DUNNING, JACK

Murphy, Linda. "Jack Dunning & Ed Stopper: ComputorEdge." In *Computer Entrepreneurs: People Who Built Successful Businesses Around Computers*, 101-110. San Diego, Calif.: Computer Publishing Enterprises, 1990.

DUNKELBARGER, SHIRLEY W.

Dunkelbarger, Shirley W. "Don't Spend Less, Earn More Through Better Speaking." In *Success Secrets: How Eighteen Everyday Women Became Fortune Builders and Famous Speakers*, 237-250. Glendora, Calif.: Royal CBS Publishing, 1978.

DURANT, WILLIAM CRAPO

Folsom, Burton W. "Henry Crapo and William Durant: From Lumber to Carriages to Cars." In *Empire Builders: How Michigan Entrepreneurs Helped Make America Great*, 55-86. Traverse City, Mich.: Rhodes & Easton, 1998.

Wren, Daniel A., and Ronald G. Greenwood. "William C. Durant." In *Management Innovators: The People and Ideas That Have Shaped*

Modern Business, 156-158. New York, N.Y.: Oxford University Press, 1998.

DUTKA, SOLOMON

Uris, Auren. "Solomon Dutka—Profits from Prophecy." In *The Executive Breakthrough; 21 Roads to the Top*, 223-238. Garden City, N.Y.: Doubleday, 1967.

DUTTON, DIANE M.

Mikaelian, A. "Diane M. Dutton." In *Women Who Mean Business: Success Stories of Women Over Forty*, 229-232. New York, N.Y.: William Morrow & Co., 1999.

DWYER, KAREN

Shook, Robert L. "The Erotic Baker." In *Why Didn't I Think of That*, 66-83. New York, N.Y.: New American Library, 1982.

DYCK, BILL

Loewen, Ted. "Bill Dyck: A Little More Room to Operate." In *Entrepreneurs in the Faith Community: Profiles of Mennonites in Business*, ed. Calvin W. Redekop, and Benjamin W. Redekop, 166-180. Scottdale, Penn.: Herald Press, 1996.

DYSON, ESTHER

Zientara, Marguerite. "Esther Dyson: Intellectual Blue Blood." In *Women, Technology & Power: Ten Stars and the History They Made*, 77-82. New York, N.Y.: AMACOM, American Management Association, 1987.

Zientara, Marguerite. "Esther Dyson: Making Sense of It All." In *Women, Technology & Power: Ten Stars and the History They Made*, 155-162. New York, N.Y.: AMACOM, American Management Association, 1987.

Zientara, Marguerite. "Esther Dyson: Skipping a Beat." In *Women, Technology & Power: Ten Stars and the History They Made*, 214-219. New York, N.Y.: AMACOM, American Management Association, 1987.

DZIKO, TRISH MILLINES

Tsang, Cheryl D. "Trish Millines Dziko: 'The Athlete' 1988-1996." In *Microsoft First Generation: The Success Secrets of the Visionaries Who Launched a Technology Empire*, 227-242. New York, N.Y.: Wiley, 2000.

EARLY, CHRISTY

Lassen, Ali. "Christy Early: Owner, Personal Touch Cleaning." In *The Secret of Their Success: Women Entrepreneurs Reveal How They Made It*, 37-40. Carlsbad, Calif.: Ali Lassen Success System, 1990.

EASTMAN, GEORGE

Davis, William. "George Eastman, 1854-1932: 'You Press the Button, We Do the Rest'." In *The Innovators: The Essential Guide to Business Thinkers, Achievers and Entrepreneurs*, 117-120. New York, N.Y.: AMACOM, 1987.

"He Clicked the Shutter for Billions of Snapshots: George Eastman Invented Film, Low-Priced Camera, Created $2-Billion-A-Year Industry, Turned Whole U.S. into Nation of Camera Fans." In *The 50 Great Pioneers of American Industry*. By the Editors of News Front and Year, 119-122. Maplewood, N.J.: C.S. Hammond, 1964.

Klepper, Michael M., and Robert Gunther. "George Eastman (1854-1932): A Million-Dollar Smile." In *The Wealthy 100 : From Benjamin Franklin to Bill Gates—A Ranking of the Richest Americans, Past and Present*, 163-165. Secaucus, N.J. : Carol Pub. Group, 1996.

McSherry, Ronald T. "George Eastman: The Kodak King." In *Nine American Self-Made Men and Their Secrets to Success*, 31-39. Denver, Colo.: U.S.A. Publishing, 1983.

ECKERT, JOHN P.

"Computers Come of Age: Electronic Data Processing, Miracle of Modern Technology, Was Spawned in Basement of University of Pennsylvania's Moore School of Engineering." In *The 50 Great Pioneers of American Industry*. By the Editors of News Front and Year, 200-203. Maplewood, N.J.: C.S. Hammond, 1964.

EDELMAN, LOUISE

Aronoff, Craig E., and John L. Ward. "Samuel Edelman; Louise Edelman." In *Contemporary Entrepreneurs*, 133-138. Detroit, Mich.: Omnigraphics, Inc., 1992.

EDELMAN, SAMUEL

Aronoff, Craig E., and John L. Ward. "Samuel Edelman; Louise Edelman." In *Contemporary Entrepreneurs*, 133-138. Detroit, Mich.: Omnigraphics, Inc., 1992.

EDISON, THOMAS ALVA

Burnley, James. "Edison—'The Wizard': The Story of America's Greatest Inventor." In *Millionaires and Kings of Enterprise; The Marvellous Careers of Some Americans Who by Pluck, Foresight, And Energy Have Made Themselves Masters in the Fields of Industry and Finance*, 161-174. Philadelphia, Penn.: J. B. Lippincott, 1901.

Davis, William. "Thomas A. Edison, 1847-1931: The Innovator-Entrepreneur." In *The Innovators: The Essential Guide to Business Thinkers, Achievers and Entrepreneurs*, 121-124. New York, N.Y.: AMACOM, 1987.

"Let There Be Light: Edison's Incandescent Lamp Lit Up World." In *The 50 Great Pioneers of American Industry*. By the Editors of News Front and Year, 64-67. Maplewood, N.J.: C.S. Hammond, 1964.

Livesay, Harold C. "The Most Useful American: Thomas A. Edison." In *American Made: Men Who Shaped the American Economy*, 126-156. Boston, Mass.: Little, Brown, 1979.

Wren, Daniel A., and Ronald G. Greenwood. "Thomas Alva Edison." In *Management Innovators: The People and Ideas That Have Shaped Modern Business*, 16-24. New York, N.Y.: Oxford University Press, 1998.

EDMARK, TOMIMA

Suarez, Ruth. "Tomima Edmark: TopsyTail, 'The Idea Is Just the Beginning'." In *Superstar Entrepreneurs of Small and Large Businesses Reveal Their Secrets*, 157-161. Piscataway, N.J.: Research and Education Association, 1998.

EICHENFIELD, SAMUEL L.

Wendel, Charles B. "Exploiting Corporate Flexibility and Discipline: Samuel L. Eichenfield, Chairman, President, & CEO, The FINOVA Group Inc." In *The New Financiers*, 81-106. Chicago, Ill.: Irwin Professional Pub., 1996.

EISNER (RICHARD A.) & COMPANY

White, Jane. "Linda Wroblewski of Richard Eisner & Co.: 'Someday You're Going to Be Partner." In *A Few Good Women: Breaking the Barriers to Top Management*, 135-142. Englewood Cliffs, N.J.: Prentice Hall, 1992.

ELKINS, WILLIAM LUKENS

Burnley, James. "William Lukens Elkins: The Philadelphia Millionaire." In *Millionaires and Kings of Enterprise; The Marvellous Careers of Some Americans Who by Pluck, Foresight, And Energy Have Made Themselves Masters in the Fields of Industry and Finance*, 247-250. Philadelphia, Penn.: J. B. Lippincott, 1901.

ELLIS, CARLENE

White, Jane. "Carlene Ellis of Intel Corporation: 'I Don't Buy This Women-As-Victim Bull'." In *A Few Good Women: Breaking the Barriers to Top Management*, 159-169. Englewood Cliffs, N.J.: Prentice Hall, 1992.

ELLISON, LAWRENCE J.

Farnham, Alan. "Larry Ellison: Founder and CEO of Oracle, 'When We Hit the Wall, We Hit It Very, Very Hard'." In *Forbes Great Success Stories: Twelve Tales of Victory Wrested from Defeat*, 44-63. New York, N.Y.: Wiley, 2000.

Klepper, Michael M., and Robert Gunther. "Lawrence J. Ellison (1944-): A Software Samurai." In *The Wealthy 100: From Benjamin Franklin to Bill Gates—A Ranking of the Richest Americans, Past and Present*, 316-318. Secaucus, N.J. : Carol Pub. Group, 1996.

ELOWITCH, ANNETTE

Lyons, Mary. "Annette Elowitch: Barridoff Galleries, Co-Owner, 'I Want It to Continue Just Like This'." In *Maine's Achieving Women: Conversations with Entrepreneurs*, 113-119. Old Orchard Beach, ME: Lilac River Press, 1999.

ELYACHAR FAMILY

Buchholz, Barbara B., and Margaret Crane. "Elyachar Real Estate, New York, N.Y. and Sarasota, FL." In *Corporate Blood Lines: The Future of the Family Firm*, 193-211. New York, N.Y: Carol Publishing Group, 1989.

ENGEL, BRUCE L.

Aronoff, Craig E., and John L. Ward. "Bruce L. Engel." In *Contemporary Entrepreneurs*, 139-145. Detroit, Mich.: Omnigraphics, Inc., 1992.

ERICKSON, BEVERLY F.

Mikaelian, A. "Beverly F. Erickson." In *Women Who Mean Business: Success Stories of Women Over Forty*, 151-155. New York, N.Y.: William Morrow & Co., 1999.

ERLICH, LINDA

Suarez, Ruth. "Linda Erlich: Quality Mailing & Fulfillment Services, Inc., 'An Undemocratic Household'." In *Superstar Entrepreneurs of Small and Large Businesses Reveal Their Secrets*, 5-8. Piscataway, N.J.: Research and Education Association, 1998.

ESKIN, GERALD

Hillkirk, John, and Gary Jacobson. "Information Resources: A Revolution in Marketing." In *Grit, Guts, And Genius: True Tales of Megasuccess: Who Made Them Happen and How They Did It*, 186-196. Boston, Mass.: Houghton Mifflin, 1990.

ESSMAN, PANSY ELLEN

Essman, Pansy Ellen. "What You Can Imagine Is Yours." In *Success Secrets: How Eighteen Everyday Women Became Fortune Builders and Famous Speakers*, 31-42. Glendora, Calif.: Royal CBS Publishing, 1978.

ESTY, JANET M.

Rich-McCoy, Lois. "Medical Mousetrap: Janet M. Esty." In *Millionairess: Self-Made Women of America*, 127-151. New York, N.Y.: Harper & Row, 1978.

EUBANKS, GORDON

Jager, Rama Dev, and Rafael Ortiz. "Gordon Eubanks: Symantec; Brands and Bands." In *In the Company of Giants: Candid Conversations with the Visionaries of the Digital World*, 45-59. New York, N.Y.: McGraw-Hill, 1997.

EVANS, LESLIE

Lyons, Mary. "Leslie Evans: Leslie Evans Design, Principal, 'It's Cool to Do Something That You Really Love'." In *Maine's Achieving Women: Conversations with Entrepreneurs*, 133-139. Old Orchard Beach, ME: Lilac River Press, 1999.

EVANS, NANCY

Price, Christopher. "Candice Carpenter, Nancy Evans—iVillage 'A Different Vision of Net Success'." In *The Internet Entrepreneurs: Business Rules Are Good: Break Them*, 160-174. London, Eng.: FT.com, 2000.

Smith, Roy C. "Candy's New American Dream." In *Wealth Creators: The Rise of Today's Rich and Super-Rich*, 82-89. New York, N.Y.: Truman Talley, 2001.

EVANS, NEIL

Tsang, Cheryl D. "Neil Evans: 'The Professor' 1983-1994." In *Microsoft First Generation: The Success Secrets of the Visionaries Who Launched a Technology Empire*, 87-112. New York, N.Y.: Wiley, 2000.

EVINRUDE, BESS

Cleary, David Powers. "Evinrude Outboard Motors; I'll Take Care of Your Books, Ole." In *Great American Brands: The Success Formulas That Made Them Famous*, 80-86. New York, N.Y: Fairchild Publications, 1981.

EVINRUDE, OLE

Cleary, David Powers. "Evinrude Outboard Motors; I'll Take Care of Your Books, Ole." In *Great American Brands: The Success Formulas That Made Them Famous*, 80-86. New York, N.Y: Fairchild Publications, 1981.

"He Launched the Outboard Motor: Today's Multi-Billion-Dollar Recreational Boating Industry Was Born in 1909, When Ole Evinrude Developed the First Practical Outboard Motor." In *The 50 Great Pioneers of American Industry*. By the Editors of News Front and Year, 172-174. Maplewood, N.J.: C.S. Hammond, 1964.

FABER, KAREN SCHMIDT

Liberman, Gail, and Alan Lavine. "Timothy B. and Karen Schmidt Faber:

Couple Creates and Sells Personnel Business." In *Rags to Riches: Motivating Stories of How Ordinary People Achieved Extraordinary Wealth!*, 195-206. Chicago, Ill.: Dearborn, 2000.

FABER, TIMOTHY B.

Liberman, Gail, and Alan Lavine. "Timothy B. and Karen Schmidt Faber: Couple Creates and Sells Personnel Business." In *Rags to Riches: Motivating Stories of How Ordinary People Achieved Extraordinary Wealth!*, 195-206. Chicago, Ill.: Dearborn, 2000.

FAIRLESS, BENJAMINE F.

Hillyer, William Hurd. "Benjamine F. Fairless." In *America's Fifty Foremost Business Leaders,* ed. B. C. Forbes, 109-118. New York, N.Y.: B.C. Forbes, 1948.

FARAH FAMILY

Pottker, Jan. "Farah, Inc.: No Family and No Company." In *Born to Power: Heirs to America's Leading Businesses*, 370-375. New York, N.Y.: Barron's, 1992.

FARLEY, WILLIAM FRANCIS

Silver, A. David. "William Francis Farley." In *Entrepreneurial Megabucks: The 100 Greatest Entrepreneurs of the Last 25 Years*, 187-189. New York, N.Y.: Wiley, 1985.

FARR, MEL SR.

Dingle, Derek T. "Mel Farr Sr.: Mel Farr Automotive Group, Inc., 'The Superstar'." In *Black Enterprise Titans of the B.E. 100s: Black CEOs Who Redefined and Conquered American Business*, 115-136. New York, N.Y.: Wiley, 1999.

FARRELL, MARY

Herera, Sue. "Mary Farrell: Managing Director, PaineWebber." In *Women of the Street: Making It on Wall Street—The World's Toughest Business*, 1-14. New York, N.Y.: Wiley, 1997.

Pestrak, Debra. "Mary Farrell: Managing Director, Senior Investment Strategist and Member of the Policy Committee for PaineWebber, Inc." In *Playing with the Big Boys: Success Stories of the Most Powerful Women in Business*, 141-160. Carlsbad, CA: SUN Publications, 2001.

FARRELL, NELDA

Lassen, Ali. "Nelda Farrell: Owner, Shannon's Cleaning Service." In *The Secret of Their Success: Women Entrepreneurs Reveal How They Made It*, 175-180. Carlsbad, Calif.: Ali Lassen Success System, 1990.

FATJO, TOM J. JR.

Silver, A. David. "Tom J. Fatjo Jr." In *Entrepreneurial Megabucks: The 100 Greatest Entrepreneurs of the Last 25 Years*, 190-195. New York, N.Y.: Wiley, 1985.

FAUNCE, NANCY

White, Jane. "Nancy Faunce of Eastman Kodak: Breaking Ground in a Male-Dominated Field." In *A Few Good Women: Breaking the Barriers to Top Management*, 77-88. Englewood Cliffs, N.J.: Prentice Hall, 1992.

FEDER, CHRISTINE

Gray, Bob, ed. "The Art of Specialty Selling." In *How Entrepreneurs Make Business Profits: A Study of Personal Success Stories From Cordovan Business Journals*, 90-95. Houston, Tex.: Cordovan Press, 1982.

FELD, KENNETH J.

Pottker, Jan. "Ringling Bros. and Barnum & Baily Combined Shows, Inc.: Flying Without a Net." In *Born to Power: Heirs to America's Leading Businesses*, 98-107. New York, N.Y.: Barron's, 1992.

FERMI, ENRICO

"Birth of the Atomic Age: Italian-Born Physicist Enrico Fermi Unleashed the Atom's Mighty Fury and Discovered the World's Newest Energy Source." In *The 50 Great Pioneers of American Industry*. By the Editors of News Front and Year, 204-207. Maplewood, N.J.: C.S. Hammond, 1964.

FERRIS, RICHARD J.

Shook, Robert L. "Richard J. Ferris: UAL, Inc." In *The Chief Executive Officers: Men Who Run Big Business in America*, 53-76. New York, N.Y.: Harper & Row, 1981.

FERTEL, RUTH

Ericksen, Gregory K. "Ruth Fertel—Ruth's Chris Steak House, 'Treat Others the Way You Want to Be Treated'." In *Women Entrepreneurs Only: Twelve Women Entrepreneurs Tell The Stories of Their Success*, 45-65 New York, N.Y.: Wiley, 1999.

FETTER, LIZ

Pestrak, Debra. "Liz Fetter: President and Chief Executive Officer, NorthPoint Communications." In *Playing with the Big Boys: Success Stories of the Most Powerful Women in Business*, 121-138. Carlsbad, CA: SUN Publications, 2001.

FEUERSTEIN, AARON

Farnham, Alan. "Aaron Feuerstein: CEO and Owner of Malden Mills, 'Did You Ever Read the Book of Job?'." In *Forbes Great Success Stories: Twelve Tales of Victory Wrested from Defeat*, 2-23. New York, N.Y.: Wiley, 2000.

FEY, GRACE

Herera, Sue. "Grace Fey: Executive Vice President and Director, Frontier Capital Management." In *Women of the Street: Making It on Wall Street—The World's Toughest Business*, 115-126. New York, N.Y.: Wiley, 1997.

FICHTNER, CHIP

Gardner, Ralph. "Chip Fichtner." In *Young, Gifted, and Rich: The Secrets of America's Most Successful Entrepreneurs*, 39-51. New York, N.Y.: Wallaby Books, 1984.

FICKLING, WILLIAM ARTHUR

Silver, A. David. "William Arthur Fickling." In *Entrepreneurial Megabucks: The 100 Greatest Entrepreneurs of the Last 25 Years*, 196-198. New York, N.Y.: Wiley, 1985.

FIELD, CYRUS WEST

Stoddard, William Osborn. "Cyrus West Field—Tenacity." In *Men of Business*, 131-160. New York, N.Y.: Scribner's Sons, 1893. 317 p.

FIELD, MARSHALL

Darby, Edwin. "Field." In *The Fortune Builders*, 17-94. Garden City, N.Y.: Doubleday and Company, Inc., 1986.

Klepper, Michael M., and Robert Gunther. "Marshall Field (1834-1906): Field of Dreams." In *The Wealthy 100 : From Benjamin Franklin to Bill Gates—A Ranking of the Richest Americans, Past and Present*, 49-51. Secaucus, N.J. : Carol Pub. Group, 1996.

Koehn, Nancy F. "Marshall Field, 1834-1906." In *Brand New: How Entrepreneurs Earned Consumers' Trust from Wedgwood to Dell*, 93-133. Boston, Mass.: Harvard Business School Press, 2001.

"Marshall Field." In *A Dozen Roads to Success: Being Graphic Sketches of Twelve of the Most Prominent Business Men of America, And*

Showing How They Became Millionaires, 90-101. Philadelphia, Penn.: Girard Pub. Co., 1894.

Polos, Nicholas. "Marshall Field—The 'Merchant Prince'—And Robert E. Wood—The 'Soldier Merchant'." In *Business Entrepreneurs in the West*, ed. Ted C. Hinckley, 28-38. Manhattan, Kans.: Sunflower University Press, 1986.

Stoddard, William Osborn. "Marshall Field—Business Principles." In *Men of Business*, 281-294. New York, N.Y.: Scribner's Sons, 1893. 317 p.

FIELD, MARSHALL V

Pottker, Jan. "Field Corporation: Fields of Conquest." In *Born to Power: Heirs to America's Leading Businesses*, 280-296. New York, N.Y.: Barron's, 1992.

FIELD, TED

Pottker, Jan. "Interscope Communications, Interscope Records: If the Glass Slipper Fits..." In *Born to Power: Heirs to America's Leading Businesses*, 410-416. New York, N.Y.: Barron's, 1992.

FIELDS, DEBBIE

Aronoff, Craig E., and John L. Ward. "Debbie Fields." In *Contemporary Entrepreneurs*, 146-152. Detroit, Mich.: Omnigraphics, Inc., 1992.

Jeffrey, Laura S. "Debbie Fields: Sweet Smell, and Taste, of Success." In *Great American Businesswomen*, 92-101. Springfield, N.J.: Enslow Publishers, Inc., 1996.

Mariotti, Steve, and Mike Caslin. "Debbie Fields, Mrs. Fields' Original Cookies, Inc.: Good Enough Never Is" In *The Very Very Rich: How They Got That Way and How You Can, Too!*, 27-33. Franklin Lakes, NJ: Career Press, 2000.

Silver, A. David. "Debbie Fields." In *Entrepreneurial Megabucks: The 100 Greatest Entrepreneurs of the Last 25 Years*, 199-201. New York, N.Y.: Wiley, 1985.

Gardner, Ralph. "Debbie Fields." In *Young, Gifted, and Rich: The Secrets of America's Most Successful Entrepreneurs*, 79-91. New York, N.Y.: Wallaby Books, 1984.

FINEGOLD, ARYEH

Silver, A. David. "Aryeh Finegold." In *Entrepreneurial Megabucks: The 100 Greatest Entrepreneurs of the Last 25 Years*, 202-204. New York, N.Y.: Wiley, 1985.

FINNEGAN, MARY

Lyons, Mary. "Mary Finnegan: Finnegan & Associates, Inc., Founder, 'Not Being Intimidated Is So Important for Women'." In *Maine's Achieving Women: Conversations with Entrepreneurs*, 39-51. Old Orchard Beach, ME: Lilac River Press, 1999.

FIRESTONE FAMILY

Bell, Laurence. "Harvey S. Firestone." In *America's Fifty Foremost Business Leaders,* ed. B. C. Forbes, 119-128. New York, N.Y.: B.C. Forbes, 1948.

Buchholz, Barbara B., and Margaret Crane. "The Firestone Vineyard, Los Olivos, CA." In *Corporate Blood Lines: The Future of the Family Firm*, 111-126. New York, N.Y: Carol Publishing Group, 1989.

FISHER, CARL G.

Davis, William. "Carl Fisher, 1874-1939: The Magic City of the Sunshine State." In *The Innovators: The Essential Guide to Business Thinkers, Achievers and Entrepreneurs*, 128-133. New York, N.Y.: AMACOM, 1987.

FISHER, PHILIP

Train, John. "Philip Fisher: Investment Engineer." In *The Money Masters*, 57-81. New York, N.Y.: Harper & Row, 1980.

Train, John. "Philip Fisher: The Cutting Edge." In *Money Masters of Our*

Time, 92-107. New York, N.Y.: HarperBusiness, 2000.

FISK, JIM

Mountfield, David. "Bandits in the Palace: Gould, Fisk and the Erie." In *The Railway Barons*, 131-158. New York, N.Y.: Norton, 1979.

FITZPATRICK, EILEEN TABATA

Alexander, Shoshana. "Eileen Tabata Fitzpatrick: Kanojo, Irvine, California." In *Women's Ventures, Women's Visions: 29 Inspiring Stories From Women Who Started Their Own Businesses*, 104-111. Freedom, Calif.: The Crossing Press, 1997.

FLAGLER, HENRY M.

Davis, William. "Henry M. Flagler, 1830-1913: The Man Who Made Florida." In *The Innovators: The Essential Guide to Business Thinkers, Achievers and Entrepreneurs*, 134-137. New York, N.Y.: AMACOM, 1987.

Klepper, Michael M., and Robert Gunther. "Henry M. Flagler (1830-1913): The Ponce de Leon of Florida Resorts." In *The Wealthy 100 : From Benjamin Franklin to Bill Gates—A Ranking of the Richest Americans, Past and Present*, 176-180. Secaucus, N.J. : Carol Pub. Group, 1996.

FLATT, MARY

Shook, Robert L. "Eastern Onion." In *Why Didn't I Think of That*, 84-193. New York, N.Y.: New American Library, 1982.

FLETCHER, CHARLES

Burnley, James. "Charles Fletcher: The Textile King." In *Millionaires and Kings of Enterprise; The Marvellous Careers of Some Americans Who by Pluck, Foresight, And Energy Have Made Themselves Masters in the Fields of Industry and Finance*, 289-292. Philadelphia, Penn.: J. B. Lippincott, 1901.

FLINT, CHARLES RANLETT

Burnley, James. "Charles Ranlett Flint: The Rubber King of America." In *Millionaires and Kings of Enterprise; The Marvellous Careers of Some Americans Who by Pluck, Foresight, And Energy Have Made Themselves Masters in the Fields of Industry and Finance,* 146-160. Philadelphia, Penn.: J. B. Lippincott, 1901.

FOLLETT, MARY PARKER

Wren, Daniel A., and Ronald G. Greenwood. "Mary Parker Follett." In *Management Innovators: The People and Ideas That Have Shaped Modern Business,* 194-198. New York, N.Y.: Oxford University Press, 1998.

FORD, BILL

Pottker, Jan. "Ford Models, Inc.: Children, Meet Your Roommate Kim Basinger." In *Born to Power: Heirs to America's Leading Businesses,* 220-228. New York, N.Y.: Barron's, 1992.

FORD, EILEEN

Jeffrey, Laura S. "Eileen Ford: A Model Career." In *Great American Businesswomen,* 56-63. Springfield, N.J.: Enslow Publishers, Inc., 1996.

THE FORD FAMILY

Apcar, Leonard M. "The Fords." In *American Dynasties Today,* 233-281. Homewood, Ill.: Dow Jones-Irwin, 1990.

Brands, H. W. "The Mechanic of Revolution: Henry Ford." In *Masters of Enterprise: Giants of American Business from John Jacob Astor and J.P. Morgan to Bill Gates and Oprah Winfrey,* 95-106. New York, N.Y.: Free Press, 1999.

Cleary, David Powers. "Ford Cars; Somewhere Along the Line, There's Always Something More. Our Job Is to Find It, Refine It, and Get the Public Accustomed to It." In *Great American Brands: The Success*

Formulas That Made Them Famous, 87-111. New York, N.Y.: Fairchild Publications, 1981.

Davis, William. "Henry Ford, 1863-1947: 'Any Colour They Like…As Long As It's Black'." In *The Innovators: The Essential Guide to Business Thinkers, Achievers and Entrepreneurs*, 137-140. New York, N.Y.: AMACOM, 1987.

Diamond, Sigmond. "Henry Ford." In *The Reputation of the American Businessman*, 142-175. Cambridge, Mass.: Harvard University Press, 1955.

Fanning, Leonard M. "Henry Ford." In *Titans of Business*, 141-172. Philadelphia, Penn.: Lippincott, 1964. 240 p.

Finlay, Bob. "Henry Ford II." In *America's Fifty Foremost Business Leaders*, ed. B. C. Forbes, 129-136. New York, N.Y.: B.C. Forbes, 1948.

Folsom, Burton W. "Henry Ford and the Triumph of the Auto Industry." In *Empire Builders: How Michigan Entrepreneurs Helped Make America Great*, 139-164. Traverse City, Mich.: Rhodes & Easton, 1998.

Gross, Daniel, and the Editors of Forbes Magazine. "Henry Ford and the Model T." In *Forbes Greatest Business Stories of All Time*, 74-89. New York, N.Y.: Wiley, 1996.

"He Made the Fords Roll By: Ford Made First Car in 1896, In 1908 Concentrated on Low-Cost Model T, Sold 15 Million by 1927." In *The 50 Great Pioneers of American Industry*. By the Editors of News Front and Year, 169-171. Maplewood, N.J.: C.S. Hammond, 1964.

Hughes, Jonathan. "Henry Ford and the Automobile Age." In *The Vital Few: The Entrepreneur and American Economic Progress*, 274-355. Expanded Edition, New York, N.Y.: Oxford University Press, 1986.

Klepper, Michael M., and Robert Gunther. "Henry Ford (1863-1947): After Two Failures, Rode the Model T to Fame and Fortune." In *The Wealthy 100 : From Benjamin Franklin to Bill Gates—A Ranking of the*

Richest Americans, Past and Present, 53-59. Secaucus, N.J. : Carol Pub. Group, 1996.

Livesay, Harold C. "Superstar of the Worldwide Car: Henry Ford II." In *American Made: Men Who Shaped the American Economy*, 240-266. Boston, Mass.: Little, Brown, 1979.

Livesay, Harold C. "The Insolent Charioteer: Henry Ford." In *American Made: Men Who Shaped the American Economy*, 158-181. Boston, Mass.: Little, Brown, 1979.

McSherry, Ronald T. "The World's First Billionaire: How Henry Ford Built 15,000,000 Cars." In *Nine American Self-Made Men and Their Secrets to Success*, 62-76. Denver, Colo.: U.S.A. Publishing, 1983.

Mariotti, Steve, and Mike Caslin. "Henry Ford, Ford Motor Company: An Automobile in Front of Every Home." In *The Very Very Rich: How They Got That Way and How You Can, Too!*, 35-40. Franklin Lakes, NJ: Career Press, 2000.

Means, Howard B. "Henry Ford: Building Cars and Markets for Them." In *Money & Power: The History of Business*, 165-183. New York, N.Y.: Wiley, 2001.

Mariotti, Steve, and Lorraine Mooney. "Henry Ford: Pioneer Par Excellence." In *Entrepreneurs in Profile*, 86-90. London: National Foundation for Teaching Entrepreneurship, 1991.

Nevins, Allan. "Henry Ford—A Complex Man." In *Great Stories of American Businessmen*, From *American Heritage, The Magazine of History*, 348-353. New York, N.Y.: American Heritage Publishing Co., 1954.

Wren, Daniel A., and Ronald G. Greenwood. "Henry Ford." In *Management Innovators: The People and Ideas That Have Shaped Modern Business*, 41-49. New York, N.Y.: Oxford University Press, 1998.

FORD, KATIE

Pottker, Jan. "Ford Models, Inc.: Children, Meet Your Roommate Kim Basinger." In *Born to Power: Heirs to America's Leading Businesses*, 220-228. New York, N.Y.: Barron's, 1992.

FOREMAN, JOYCE

Wallace, Robert L. "Joyce Foreman: Founder, Foreman Office Products, Dallas, Texas." In *Black Wealth: Your Road to Small Business Success*, 92-103. New York, N.Y.: Wiley, 2000.

FORSTMANN, TED

Kadlec, Daniel J. "Ted Forstmann: Master of the LBO." In *Masters of the Universe; Winning Strategies of America's Greatest Deal Makers*, 161-190. New York, N.Y.: HarperBusiness, 1999.

FOSTER, SCOTT A.

Koppel, Robert. "Is There an Austrian Magician in the House: Scott A. Foster." In *Bulls, Bears, And Millionaires: War Stories of Trading Life*, 116-128. Chicago, Ill.: Dearborn Financial Publishers, 1997.

FOX, JOHN M.

Uris, Auren. "John M. Fox—$400,000,000 Fruit Cup." In *The Executive Breakthrough; 21 Roads to the Top*, 169-182. Garden City, N.Y.: Doubleday, 1967.

FRAAS, KERRY

Elfstrand, Rhonda. "Kerry Fraas: Attorney at Law." In *The Story Behind the Success: Learning From Pittsburgh Professionals*, 74-87. Pittsburgh, Penn.: Steel Publishing Partners, 1996.

FRANCIS, CLARENCE

Shannon, Homer H. "Clarence Francis." In *America's Fifty Foremost Business Leaders,* ed. B. C. Forbes, 137-146. New York, N.Y.: B.C. Forbes, 1948.

FRANK, CHRIS

Elfstrand, Rhonda. "Bruce Crum, Chris Frank: Adams Development Group." In *The Story Behind the Success: Learning From Pittsburgh Professionals*, 62-73. Pittsburgh, Penn.: Steel Publishing Partners, 1996.

FRANKLIN, ANGELA

Franklin, Angela. "A Day at the White House." In *How I Became a Nurse Entrepreneur: Tales from 50 Nurses in Business*, 267-275. Petaluma, Calif.: National Nurses in Business Association, 1991.

FRANKLIN, BENJAMIN

Klepper, Michael M., and Robert Gunther. "Benjamin Franklin (1706-1790): Lived Usefully and Died Rich." In *The Wealthy 100 : From Benjamin Franklin to Bill Gates—A Ranking of the Richest Americans, Past and Present,* 294-296. Secaucus, N.J. : Carol Pub. Group, 1996.

FRASER, MARGOT

Suarez, Ruth. "Margot Fraser: Birkenstock, 'A World of Change'." In *Superstar Entrepreneurs of Small and Large Businesses Reveal Their Secrets,* 163-166. Piscataway, N.J.: Research and Education Association, 1998.

FRENCH, BRENDA

Suarez, Ruth. "Brenda French: French Rags, 'From Rags to Riches'." In *Superstar Entrepreneurs of Small and Large Businesses Reveal Their Secrets.* 167-173. Piscataway, N.J.: Research and Education Association, 1998.

FRICK, HENRY CLAY

Burnley, James. "H. C. Frick: The Coke King." In *Millionaires and Kings of Enterprise; The Marvellous Careers of Some Americans Who by Pluck, Foresight, And Energy Have Made Themselves Masters in the Fields of Industry and Finance,* 400-406. Philadelphia, Penn.: J. B. Lippincott, 1901.

Klepper, Michael M., and Robert Gunther. "Henry C. Frick (1849-1919): 'I'll See You in Hell'." In *The Wealthy 100 : From Benjamin Franklin to Bill Gates—A Ranking of the Richest Americans, Past and Present,* 106-109. Secaucus, N.J. : Carol Pub. Group, 1996.

FRIESS, FOSTER

Oster, Merrill J. "Billion-Dollar Maxims." In *The Entrepreneur's Creed: The Principles & Passions of 20 Successful Entrepreneurs,* 4-13. Nashville, Tenn.: Broadman & Holman Publishers, 2001.

FRIPP, PATRICIA

Fripp, Patricia. "It Seemed Like a Good Idea at the Time." In *Success Secrets: How Eighteen Everyday Women Became Fortune Builders and Famous Speakers,* 97-112. Glendora, Calif.: Royal CBS Publishing, 1978.

FRIST, THOMAS F. JR.

Silver, A. David. "Thomas F. Frist Sr.; Thomas F. Frist Jr." In *Entrepreneurial Megabucks: The 100 Greatest Entrepreneurs of the Last 25 Years,* 205-207. New York, N.Y.: Wiley, 1985.

FRIST, THOMAS F. SR.

Silver, A. David. "Thomas F. Frist Sr.; Thomas F. Frist Jr." In *Entrepreneurial Megabucks: The 100 Greatest Entrepreneurs of the Last 25 Years,* 205-207. New York, N.Y.: Wiley, 1985.

FRYE, TOD

Gardner, Ralph. "Tod Frye." In *Young, Gifted, and Rich: The Secrets of America's Most Successful Entrepreneurs*, 197-207. New York, N.Y.: Wallaby Books, 1984.

FUDGE, ANN M.

Clarke, Caroline V. "Ann M. Fudge: Executive Vice President, Kraft Foods, Inc.; President, Maxwell House and Post Divisions." In *Take a Lesson: Today's Black Achievers and How They Made It and What They Learned Along the Way*, 31-36. New York, N.Y.: Wiley, 2001.

FULKERSON, KAY A.

Mikaelian, A. "Kay A. Fulkerson." In *Women Who Mean Business: Success Stories of Women Over Forty*, 21-25. New York, N.Y.: William Morrow & Co., 1999.

FULLERTON, VICKIE R.

"Improved Patient Outcome and Cost-Containment." In *How I Became a Nurse Entrepreneur: Tales from 50 Nurses in Business*, 221-224. Petaluma, Calif.: National Nurses in Business Association, 1991.

FULTON, ROBERT

Oster, Merrill J. "Web of Life." In *The Entrepreneur's Creed: The Principles & Passions of 20 Successful Entrepreneurs*, 182-191. Nashville, Tenn.: Broadman & Holman Publishers, 2001.

FUQUA, JOHN BROOKS

Silver, A. David. "John Books Fuqua." In *Entrepreneurial Megabucks: The 100 Greatest Entrepreneurs of the Last 25 Years*, 208-210. New York, N.Y.: Wiley, 1985.

FURST, AUSTIN O.

Aronoff, Craig E., and John L. Ward. "Austin O. Furst Jr." In *Contemporary Entrepreneurs*, 153-158. Detroit, Mich.: Omnigraphics, Inc., 1992.

GABBARD, O. GENE

Aronoff, Craig E., and John L. Ward. "O. Gene Gabbard." In *Contemporary Entrepreneurs*, 159-163. Detroit, Mich.: Omnigraphics, Inc., 1992.

GALBREATH, JOHN W.

Shook, Robert L. "John W. Galbreath." In *The Entrepreneurs: Twelve Who Took Risks and Succeeded*, 1-17. New York, N.Y: Harper & Row, 1980.

GALLAGHER, KATHY

Gardner, Ralph. "Kathy Gallagher." In *Young, Gifted, and Rich: The Secrets of America's Most Successful Entrepreneurs*, 53-64. New York, N.Y.: Wallaby Books, 1984.

GALLUP, PATRICIA

Mikaelian, A. "Patricia Gallup." In *Women Who Mean Business: Success Stories of Women Over Forty*, 205-209. New York, N.Y.: William Morrow & Co., 1999.

GALVIN, ROBERT

Galvin, Robert. "Communication: The Lever of Effectiveness and Productivity." In *The Power of Boldness: Ten Master Builders of American Industry Tell Their Success Stories*, ed. Elkan Blout, 159-168. Washington, D.C.: Joseph Henry Press, 1996.

GAMBLE FAMILY

Cleary, David Powers. "Ivory Soap; 99 44/100% Pure—It Floats." In *Great American Brands: The Success Formulas That*

Made Them Famous, 172-181. New York, N.Y: Fairchild Publications, 1981.

GANNETT, FRANK

Cose, Ellis. "The Chains: Gannett and Knight-Ridder." In *The Press*, 281-356. New York, N.Y.: Morrow, 1989.

GARCIA, ANNA

Mikaelian, A. "Anna Garcia." In *Women Who Mean Business: Success Stories of Women Over Forty*, 41-45. New York, N.Y.: William Morrow & Co., 1999.

GARDNER, KAY

Lyons, Mary. "Kay Gardner: Sea Gnomes Music, 'I've Been Independent my Entire Life'." In *Maine's Achieving Women: Conversations with Entrepreneurs*, 85-94. Old Orchard Beach, ME: Lilac River Press, 1999.

GARRETT, JOHN W.

Klepper, Michael M., and Robert Gunther. "John W. Garrett (1820-1884): The General of the Baltimore & Ohio." In *The Wealthy 100 : From Benjamin Franklin to Bill Gates—A Ranking of the Richest Americans, Past and Present*, 194-196. Secaucus, N.J. : Carol Pub. Group, 1996.

GARRISON, KAREN

Pestrak, Debra. "Karen Garrison: President, Pitney Bowes Management Services." In *Playing with the Big Boys: Success Stories of the Most Powerful Women in Business*, 97-119. Carlsbad, CA: SUN Publications, 2001.

GARSON, BONNIE

"Bonnie Garson." In *Women Achievers: A Series of Dialogues from the Womanagement Process*, 107-119. New York, N.Y.: American

Telephone and Telegraph Co., 1997.

GARZARELLI, ELAINE

Jeffrey, Laura S. "Elaine Garzarelli: The Wizard of Wall Street." In *Great American Businesswomen*, 74-81. Springfield, N.J.: Enslow Publishers, Inc., 1996.

GATES, BILL

Brands, H. W. "Standard Operating Procedures: Bill Gates." In *Masters of Enterprise: Giants of American Business from John Jacob Astor and J.P. Morgan to Bill Gates and Oprah Winfrey*, 315-331. New York, N.Y.: Free Press, 1999.

Davis, William. "Bill Gates, b. 1955: Software's Whiz-Kid." In *The Innovators: The Essential Guide to Business Thinkers, Achievers and Entrepreneurs*, 148-151. New York, N.Y.: AMACOM, 1987.

Gross, Daniel, and the Editors of Forbes Magazine. "William Gates and the Dominance of Microsoft." In *Forbes Greatest Business Stories of All Time*, 334-351. New York, N.Y.: Wiley, 1996.

Jager, Rama Dev, and Rafael Ortiz. "Bill Gates: Microsoft; Running the Panzer Division." In *In the Company of Giants: Candid Conversations with the Visionaries of the Digital World*, 143-160. New York, N.Y.: McGraw-Hill, 1997.

Landrum, Gene N. "William Gates III—Driven." In *Profiles of Genius: Thirteen Creative Men Who Changed the World*, 121-133. Buffalo, N.Y.: Prometheus Books, 1993.

Mariotti, Steve, and Mike Caslin. "Bill Gates, Microsoft, Inc.: The Richest Man in America Who Plans to Give It All Away." In *The Very Very Rich: How They Got That Way and How You Can, Too!*, 41-45. Franklin Lakes, NJ: Career Press, 2000.

Means, Howard B. "Bill Gates and Cyberspace: The Dematerialized Future." In *Money & Power: The History of Business*, 227-245. New York, N.Y.: Wiley, 2001.

Silver, A. David. "William Gates; Paul Allen." In *Entrepreneurial Megabucks: The 100 Greatest Entrepreneurs of the Last 25 Years*, 211-212. New York, N.Y.: Wiley, 1985.

Slater, Robert. "William Gates: Engine of the Small Computer Revolution." In *Portraits in Silicon*, 262-271. Cambridge, Mass.: MIT Press, 1987.

GATES, JOHN W.

Burnley, James. "The Story of John W. Gates: A Steel and Wire Financier." In *Millionaires and Kings of Enterprise; The Marvellous Careers of Some Americans Who by Pluck, Foresight, And Energy Have Made Themselves Masters in the Fields of Industry and Finance*, 441-453. Philadelphia, Penn.: J. B. Lippincott, 1901.

GEFFEN, DAVID

Aronoff, Craig E., and John L. Ward. "David Geffen." In *Contemporary Entrepreneurs*, 164-170. Detroit, Mich.: Omnigraphics, Inc., 1992.

Liberman, Gail, and Alan Lavine. "David Geffen: Brooklyn Slums Spawn Billionaire Record Mogul." In *Rags to Riches: Motivating Stories of How Ordinary People Achieved Extraordinary Wealth!*, 66-76. Chicago, Ill.: Dearborn, 2000.

GEFRE, ROSALIND "SISTER"

Alexander, Shoshana. "Sister Rosalind Gefre: Professional Message Center, School of Professional Message, St. Paul, Min." In *Women's Ventures, Women's Visions: 29 Inspiring Stories From Women Who Started Their Own Businesses*, 35-42. Freedom, Calif.: The Crossing Press, 1997.

GEISSE, JOHN F.

Aronoff, Craig E., and John L. Ward. "John F. Geisse." In *Contemporary Entrepreneurs*, 171-175. Detroit, Mich.: Omnigraphics, Inc., 1992.

GENEEN, HAROLD

Davis, William. "Harold Sydney Geneen, b. 1910: The Michelangelo of Management." In *The Innovators: The Essential Guide to Business Thinkers, Achievers and Entrepreneurs*, 151-155. New York, N.Y.: AMACOM, 1987.

Sobel, Robert. "Harold Geneen: The Master." In *The Rise and Fall of the Conglomerate Kings*, 127-154. New York, N.Y.: Stein and Day, 1984.

GERARD, MONTE MAUPIN

Mikaelian, A. "Monte Maupin Gerard." In *Women Who Mean Business: Success Stories of Women Over Forty*, 98-102. New York, N.Y.: William Morrow & Co., 1999.

GERBER, FAMILY

Cleary, David Powers. "Gerber Baby Foods; We Had to Be Expert About Babies As Well As Baby Foods." In *Great American Brands: The Success Formulas That Made Them Famous*, 112-119. New York, N.Y: Fairchild Publications, 1981.

Pottker, Jan. "Gerber Products Company: Finding Board Work Easily Digestible." In *Born to Power: Heirs to America's Leading Businesses*, 320-324. New York, N.Y.: Barron's, 1992.

GESCHKE, CHARLES

Jager, Rama Dev, and Rafael Ortiz. "John Warnock/Charles Geschke: Adobe Systems; On Partnership." In *In the Company of Giants: Candid Conversations with the Visionaries of the Digital World*, 99-113. New York, N.Y.: McGraw-Hill, 1997.

GETTY FAMILY

Getty, J. Paul. "J. Paul Getty: One Billion Dollars." In *The Very, Very Rich and How They Got That Way*, ed. Max Gunther, 106-127. Chicago, Ill.: The Playboy Press, 1972.

Klepper, Michael M., and Robert Gunther. "J. Paul Getty (1892-1976): Rockefeller Redux." In *The Wealthy 100 : From Benjamin Franklin to Bill Gates—A Ranking of the Richest Americans, Past and Present,* 231-235. Secaucus, N.J. : Carol Pub. Group, 1996.

Pottker, Jan. "P.A.J.W. Corporation: Oil Over Troubled Waters." In *Born to Power: Heirs to America's Leading Businesses,* 398-409. New York, N.Y.: Barron's, 1992.

GIANNINI, A. P.

"Bighearted Bankers: Arthur J. Morris and A.P. Giannini Sparked Revolution in Banking By Rolling Out Welcome Mat for Small Depositors and Borrowers." In *The 50 Great Pioneers of American Industry.* By the Editors of News Front and Year, 156-159. Maplewood, N.J.: C.S. Hammond, 1964.

GIANNINI, L. M.

Harrison, Mark. "L. M. Giannini." In *America's Fifty Foremost Business Leaders,* ed. B. C. Forbes, 147-158. New York, N.Y.: B.C. Forbes, 1948.

GIBBONS, FRED

Silver, A. David. "Fred Gibbons." In *Entrepreneurial Megabucks: The 100 Greatest Entrepreneurs of the Last 25 Years,* 213-215. New York, N.Y.: Wiley, 1985.

GIBSON, JOAN

Lassen, Ali. "Joan Gibson: Printing Broker, Images." In *The Secret of Their Success: Women Entrepreneurs Reveal How They Made It,* 205-212. Carlsbad, Calif.: Ali Lassen Success System, 1990.

GIBSON, VIVIAN

Harris, Wendy Beech. "Vivian Gibson, The Mill Creek Company, Inc.: The Hot Sauce Specialist." In *Against All Odds: Ten Entrepreneurs Who Followed Their Hearts and Found Success,* 47-69. New York, N.Y.:

Wiley, 2001.

GIDWITZ, RONALD J.

Pottker, Jan. "Helene Curtis Industries, Inc.: Handsome Is As Handsome Does." In *Born to Power: Heirs to America's Leading Businesses*, 4-18. New York, N.Y.: Barron's, 1992.

GIFFORD, WALTER S.

Bell, Laurence. "Walter S. Gifford." In *America's Fifty Foremost Business Leaders,* ed. B. C. Forbes, 159-168. New York, N.Y.: B.C. Forbes, 1948.

GILBRETH, FRANK

Wren, Daniel A., and Ronald G. Greenwood. "Lillian and Frank Gilbreth." In *Management Innovators: The People and Ideas That Have Shaped Modern Business*, 140-148. New York, N.Y.: Oxford University Press, 1998.

GILBRETH, LILLIAN

Wren, Daniel A., and Ronald G. Greenwood. "Lillian and Frank Gilbreth." In *Management Innovators: The People and Ideas That Have Shaped Modern Business*, 140-148. New York, N.Y.: Oxford University Press, 1998.

GILLESPIE, MARCIA ANN

Clarke, Caroline V. "Marcia Ann Gillespie: President, Liberty Media; Editor in Chief, Ms. Magazine." In *Take a Lesson: Today's Black Achievers and How They Made It and What They Learned Along the Way*, 37-46. New York, N.Y.: Wiley, 2001.

GILLETTE, KING CAMP

Cleary, David Powers. "Gillette Razors; I Was a Dreamer—I Didn't Know Enough to Quit." In *Great American Brands: The Success*

Formulas That Made Them Famous, 120-127. New York, N.Y: Fairchild Publications, 1981.

"Conquest of the Beard: King Gillette's Invention of the Safety Razor Changed the Face of the Times by Ending Male Bondage to Whiskers." In *The 50 Great Pioneers of American Industry*. By the Editors of News Front and Year, 160-162. Maplewood, N.J.: C.S. Hammond, 1964.

Davis, William. "King C. Gillette, 1855-1932: Inventor of the Safety Razor." In *The Innovators: The Essential Guide to Business Thinkers, Achievers and Entrepreneurs*, 156-160. New York, N.Y.: AMACOM, 1987.

Mariotti, Steve, and Lorraine Mooney. "King C. Gillette: Perseverance on the Cutting Edge." In *Entrepreneurs in Profile*, 78-82. London: National Foundation for Teaching Entrepreneurship, 1991.

Mariotti, Steve, and Mike Caslin. "King C. Gillette, Gillette: Perseverance on the Cutting Edge." In *The Very Very Rich: How They Got That Way and How You Can, Too!*, 47-52. Franklin Lakes, NJ: Career Press, 2000.

GIMBEL, BERNARD F.

Benson, Nathaniel A. Benson. "Bernard F. Gimbel." In *America's Fifty Foremost Business Leaders,* ed. B. C. Forbes, 169-176. New York, N.Y.: B.C. Forbes, 1948.

GINDOFF, BRYAN

Koppel, Robert. "Hard Times and Losin' It: Bryan Gindoff." In *Bulls, Bears, And Millionaires: War Stories of Trading Life*, 179-187. Chicago, Ill.: Dearborn Financial Publishers, 1997.

GIRARD, STEPHEN

Diamond, Sigmond. "Stephen Girard." In *The Reputation of the American Businessman*, 5-22. Cambridge, Mass.: Harvard University Press, 1955.

Klepper, Michael M., and Robert Gunther. "Stephen Girard (1750-1831): The Cabin Boy Who Became the Richest Man in America." In *The Wealthy 100 : From Benjamin Franklin to Bill Gates—A Ranking of the Richest Americans, Past and Present*, 26-28. Secaucus, N.J. : Carol Pub. Group, 1996.

"Stephen Girard." In *A Dozen Roads to Success: Being Graphic Sketches of Twelve of the Most Prominent Business Men of America, And Showing How They Became Millionaires*, 18-29. Philadelphia, Penn.: *Girard Pub. Co., 1894.*

GLADSTAR, ROSEMARY

Alexander, Shoshana. "Rosemary Gladstar: Sage Mountain Retreat Center, E. Barre, Vermont." In *Women's Ventures, Women's Visions: 29 Inspiring Stories From Women Who Started Their Own Businesses*, 199-205. Freedom, Calif.: The Crossing Press, 1997.

GLOVER, JACKIE

Lassen, Ali. "Jackie Glover: Branch Manager, DBA Personnel Staffing." In *The Secret of Their Success: Women Entrepreneurs Reveal How They Made It*, 117-112. Carlsbad, Calif.: Ali Lassen Success System, 1990.

GOARD, LORRAINE

Lassen, Ali. "Lorraine Goard: Partner, Progressive Development, Inc." In *The Secret of Their Success: Women Entrepreneurs Reveal How They Made It*, 105-114. Carlsbad, Calif.: Ali Lassen Success System, 1990.

GOETZE, SUSIE

Lassen, Ali. "Susie Goetze: Real Estate Agent, ERA-Best." In *The Secret of Their Success: Women Entrepreneurs Reveal How They Made It*, 91-94. Carlsbad, Calif.: Ali Lassen Success System, 1990.

GOLD, CAROL SAPIN

Gold, Carol Sapin "Why Are You Still Speaking, Your Listener Left Four Minutes Ago." In *Success Secrets: How Eighteen Everyday Women Became Fortune Builders and Famous Speakers*, 113-128. Glendora, Calif.: Royal CBS Publishing, 1978.

GOLDMAN, PHILIP M.

Hyatt, Joshua. "The Next Big Thing; Fast and Focused, Pizza Now! Is Bidding to Be the Next McDonald's." In *Anatomy of a Start-Up: Why Some New Businesses Succeed and Others Fail: 27 Real-Life Case Studies,* ed. Elizabeth K. Longsworth, 163-172. Boston, Mass.: Inc. Publishing, 1991.

GOLDWYN, SAMUEL

Foster, A. M. "Samuel Goldwyn." In *America's Fifty Foremost Business Leaders,* ed. B. C. Forbes, Samuel Goldwyn. New York, N.Y.: B.C. Forbes, 1948.

"Creating with Enthusiasm: Sam Goldwyn." In *Lessons of Leadership: 21 Executives Speak Out on Creating, Developing and Managing Success*. Presented by the editors of Nation's Business, 83-95. Garden City, N.Y.: Doubleday, 1968.

GOMPERS, SAMUEL

Fanning, Leonard M. "Samuel Gompers." In *Titans of Business,* 109-138. Philadelphia, Penn.: Lippincott, 1964. 240 p.

GOOD, MERLE

Ruth, Phil Johnson. "Merle Good and Phyllis Pellman Good: 'Sort of a Business, Sort of the Church, Sort of the Arts'." In *Entrepreneurs in the Faith Community: Profiles of Mennonites in Business,* ed. Calvin W. Redekop, and Benjamin W. Redekop, 217-239. Scottdale, Penn.: Herald Press, 1996.

GOOD, PHYLLIS PELLMAN

Ruth, Phil Johnson. "Merle Good and Phyllis Pellman Good: 'Sort of a Business, Sort of the Church, Sort of the Arts'." In *Entrepreneurs in the Faith Community: Profiles of Mennonites in Business*, ed. Calvin W. Redekop, and Benjamin W. Redekop, 217-239. Scottdale, Penn.: Herald Press, 1996.

GOODEN, C. MICHAEL

Aronoff, Craig E., and John L. Ward. "C. Michael Gooden." In *Contemporary Entrepreneurs*, 176-181. Detroit, Mich.: Omnigraphics, Inc., 1992.

Wallace, Robert L. "C. Michael Gooden: President and CEO, ISA, Inc.." In *Black Wealth: Your Road to Small Business Success*, 185-189. New York, N.Y.: Wiley, 2000.

GOODMAN, ROBERT

Kingston, Brett. "Robert Goodman of Goodtab Management Company." In *The Dynamos: Who Are They Anyway?*, 157-163. New York, N.Y.: Wiley, 1987.

GOODYEAR, CHARLES A.

"Rubber for Industry: Charles Goodyear Turned the Impractical Novelty Called 'India Rubber' into a Vital Raw Material with Hundreds of Industrial Applications." In *The 50 Great Pioneers of American Industry*. By the Editors of News Front and Year, 27-29. Maplewood, N.J.: C.S. Hammond, 1964.

GORANSON, GARY

Shook, Robert L. "Gary Goranson." In *The Entrepreneurs: Twelve Who Took Risks and Succeeded*, 93-101. New York, N.Y: Harper & Row, 1980.

GORDON, DAVID M.

Koppel, Robert. "Seeing Is Believing: David M. Gordon." In *Bulls, Bears, And Millionaires: War Stories of Trading Life*, 87-95. Chicago, Ill.: Dearborn Financial Publishers, 1997.

GORDON, ELLEN RUBIN

Pottker, Jan. "Tootsie Roll Industries, Inc.: Family Sweet." In *Born to Power: Heirs to America's Leading Businesses*, 188-194. New York, N.Y.: Barron's, 1992

GORDON, MELVIN J.

Pottker, Jan. "Tootsie Roll Industries, Inc.: Family Sweet." In *Born to Power: Heirs to America's Leading Businesses*, 188-194. New York, N.Y.: Barron's, 1992

GORDY, BERRY

Brands, H. W. "The Hero of the Hit Factory: Berry Gordy." In *Masters of Enterprise: Giants of American Business from John Jacob Astor and J.P. Morgan to Bill Gates and Oprah Winfrey*, 235-245. New York, N.Y.: Free Press, 1999.

Mariotti, Steve, and Lorraine Mooney. "Berry Gordy Jr.: Mastermind of Motown." In *Entrepreneurs in Profile*, 68-72. London: National Foundation for Teaching Entrepreneurship, 1991.

Mariotti, Steve, and Mike Caslin. "Berry Gordy, Motown: Bringing Detroit Soul to the World." In *The Very Very Rich: How They Got That Way and How You Can, Too!*, 53-58. Franklin Lakes, NJ: Career Press, 2000.

GORE, WILBERT L.

Fucini, Joseph J., and Suzy Fucini. "Wilbert L. Gore, W. L. Gore and Associates, Inc.: 'We Don't Manage People Here—They Manage Themselves'." In *Experience Inc.; Men and Women Who Founded*

Famous Companies After the Age of 40, 143-149. New York, N.Y: Free Press, 1987.

GOSNEY, MICHAEL

Murphy, Linda. "Michael Gosney: Verbum." In *Computer Entrepreneurs: People Who Built Successful Businesses Around Computers*, 93-100. San Diego, Calif.: Computer Publishing Enterprises, 1990.

GOULD, JAY

Brands, H. W. "The Speculator: Jay Gould." In *Masters of Enterprise: Giants of American Business from John Jacob Astor and J.P. Morgan to Bill Gates and Oprah Winfrey*, 37-49. New York, N.Y.: Free Press, 1999.

Klepper, Michael M., and Robert Gunther. "Jay Gould (1836-1892): Mephistopheles of Wall Street." In *The Wealthy 100 : From Benjamin Franklin to Bill Gates—A Ranking of the Richest Americans, Past and Present*, 41-45. Secaucus, N.J. : Carol Pub. Group, 1996.

Mountfield, David. "Bandits in the Palace: Gould, Fisk and the Erie." In *The Railway Barons*, 131-158. New York, N.Y.: Norton, 1979.

Wren, Daniel A., and Ronald G. Greenwood. "Jay Gould." In *Management Innovators: The People and Ideas That Have Shaped Modern Business*, 107-120. New York, N.Y.: Oxford University Press, 1998.

GRACE, EUGENE G.

Shannon, Homer H. "Eugene G. Grace." In *America's Fifty Foremost Business Leaders,* ed. B. C. Forbes, 185-194. New York, N.Y.: B.C. Forbes, 1948.

GRAHAM, BENJAMIN

Train, John. "Benjamine Graham: Quantify, Quantify." In *Money Masters of Our Time*, 108-126. New York, N.Y.: HarperBusiness, 2000.

Train, John. "Benjamin Graham: The Navigator." In *The Money Masters*, 82-113. New York, N.Y.: Harper & Row, 1980.

GRAHAM, DONALD

Coleridge, Nicholas. "All the Proprietor's Men: The Grahams and the Washington Post." In *Paper Tigers: The Latest, Greatest Newspaper Tycoons*, 74-103. New York, N.Y.: Carol Publishing Group, 1994.

Cose, Ellis. "The Underdog." In *The Press*, 27-119. New York, N.Y.: Morrow, 1989.

GRAHAM, KATHARINE

Coleridge, Nicholas. "All the Proprietor's Men: The Grahams and the Washington Post." In *Paper Tigers: The Latest, Greatest Newspaper Tycoons*, 74-103. New York, N.Y.: Carol Publishing Group, 1994.

Jeffrey, Laura S. "Katharine Graham: Publishing Powerhouse." In *Great American Businesswomen*, 46-55. Springfield, N.J.: Enslow Publishers, Inc., 1996.

GRANT, MIMI

Grant, Mimi. "In Search of a Better Way." In *Success Secrets: How Eighteen Everyday Women Became Fortune Builders and Famous Speakers*, 13-30. Glendora, Calif.: Royal CBS Publishing, 1978.

GRANVILLE, JOSEPH

King, Norman. "Joseph Granville." In *The Money Messiah$*, 49-87. New York, N.Y.: Coward-McCann, 1983.

GRAY, VALERIE

Gray, Valerie. "A Daughter's Perspective: My Mom." In *How I Became a Nurse Entrepreneur: Tales from 50 Nurses in Business*, 57-60. Petaluma, Calif.: National Nurses in Business Association, 1991.

GREEN, HETTY

Davis, William. "Hetty Green, 1834-1916: The Witch of Wall Street." In *The Innovators: The Essential Guide to Business Thinkers, Achievers and Entrepreneurs*, 164-167. New York, N.Y.: AMACOM, 1987.

Forbes, Malcolm S. "Hetty Green, 'The Witch of Wall Street'." In *Women Who Made a Difference*, 110-113. New York, N.Y.: Simon & Schuster, 1990.

Klepper, Michael M., and Robert Gunther. "Hetty Green (1834-1916): The Witch of Wall Street." In *The Wealthy 100 : From Benjamin Franklin to Bill Gates—A Ranking of the Richest Americans, Past and Present*, 139-141. Secaucus, N.J. : Carol Pub. Group, 1996.

GREEN, LOLA

Green, Lola. "Moving Towards a Fuller Life." In *Success Secrets: How Eighteen Everyday Women Became Fortune Builders and Famous Speakers*, 149-166. Glendora, Calif.: Royal CBS Publishing, 1978.

GREEN, ROBERT L.

Silver, A. David. "Robert L. Green." In *Entrepreneurial Megabucks: The 100 Greatest Entrepreneurs of the Last 25 Years*, 216-217. New York, N.Y.: Wiley, 1985.

GREEN, SYLVESTER

Clarke, Caroline V. "Sylvester Green: Executive Vice President, Chubb & Sons." In *Take a Lesson: Today's Black Achievers and How They Made It and What They Learned Along the Way*, 47-57. New York, N.Y.: Wiley, 2001.

GREENBERG, MAURICE "HANK"

Smith, Roy C. "The Great Greenberg." In *Wealth Creators: The Rise of Today's Rich and Super-Rich*, 217-220. New York, N.Y.: Truman Talley, 2001.

GREENBERG, ROBERT Y.

Aronoff, Craig E., and John L. Ward. "Robert Y. Greenberg." In *Contemporary Entrepreneurs*, 182-188. Detroit, Mich.: Omnigraphics, Inc., 1992.

GREENEWALT, CRAWFORD H.

"Sensing Who Can Command: Crawford H. Greenewalt." In *Lessons of Leadership: 21 Executives Speak Out on Creating, Developing and Managing Success*. Presented by the editors of Nation's Business, 259-271. Garden City, N.Y.: Doubleday, 1968.

GRIMES, CALVIN JR.

Wallace, Robert L. "Peter Parham and Calvin Grimes Jr.: Founders, Grime Oil, Washington, D.C. and Boston, Massachusetts." In *Black Wealth: Your Road to Small Business Success*, 129-134. New York, N.Y.: Wiley, 2000.

GRIMM, JACK

Sheehy, Sandy. "The Unsinkable Jack Grimm." In *Texas Big Rich; Exploits, Eccentricities, And Fabulous Fortunes Won and Lost*, 277-291. New York, N.Y.: Morrow, 1990.

GROGAN, BARBARA B.

Aronoff, Craig E., and John L. Ward. "Barbara B. Grogan." In *Contemporary Entrepreneurs*, 189-195. Detroit, Mich.: Omnigraphics, Inc., 1992.

GROSS, RITA BERRO

Gross, Rita Berro."What's in a No...Anyway?" In *Success Secrets: How Eighteen Everyday Women Became Fortune Builders and Famous Speakers*, 81-96. Glendora, Calif.: Royal CBS Publishing, 1978.

GROSSMAN, LOUIS

Cahill, Timothy Patrick. "The Louis Grossman Story." In *Profiles in the American Dream: The Real-Life Stories of the Struggles of American Entrepreneurs* , 7-30. Hanover, Mass.: Christopher Publishing Company, 1994.

GROSSMAN, TOM

Koppel, Robert. "Tom's Edge: Tom Grossman." In *Bulls, Bears, And Millionaires: War Stories of Trading Life*, 167-178. Chicago, Ill.: Dearborn Financial Publishers, 1997.

GROVE, ANDREW

"Andrew Grove: Chairman, CEO and Co-Founder, Intel Corporation." In *Forbes Great Minds of Business*, ed. Gretchen Morgenson, 1-34. New York, N.Y.: Wiley, 1997. 228 p.

Brands, H. W. "The Paranoia Principle: Andrew Grove." In *Masters of Enterprise: Giants of American Business from John Jacob Astor and J.P. Morgan to Bill Gates and Oprah Winfrey*, 303-314. New York, N.Y.: Free Press, 1999.

Gross, Daniel, and the Editors of Forbes Magazine. "Intel's Microcoprocessor and the Computer Revolution." In *Forbes Greatest Business Stories of All Time*, 246-265. New York, N.Y.: Wiley, 1996.

Jager, Rama Dev, and Rafael Ortiz. "Andy Grove: Intel; An Immigrant in the Trenches." In *In the Company of Giants: Candid Conversations with the Visionaries of the Digital World*, 161-174. New York, N.Y.: McGraw-Hill, 1997.

Silver, A. David. "Andrew Grove; Gordon Moore; Robert Noyce." In *Entrepreneurial Megabucks: The 100 Greatest Entrepreneurs of the Last 25 Years*, 218-221. New York, N.Y.: Wiley, 1985.

GRUENBERG, PAUL T.

Posner, Bruce G. "Class Pictures; VideOvation Is Betting That Today's TV Generation Will Want Even Their School Yearbook in Video Form." In *Anatomy of a Start-Up: Why Some New Businesses Succeed and Others Fail: 27 Real-Life Case Studies,* ed. Elizabeth K. Longsworth, 342-352. Boston, Mass.: Inc. Publishing, 1991.

GUADARRAMA, BELINDA

Alexander, Shoshana. "Belinda Guadarrama: GC Micro, Novato, California." In *Women's Ventures, Women's Visions: 29 Inspiring Stories From Women Who Started Their Own Businesses,* 49-54. Freedom, Calif.: The Crossing Press, 1997.

GUBER, PETER

Hillkirk, John, and Gary Jacobson. "Batman and Rain Man: Flip Sides of the Same Hollywood Coin." In *Grit, Guts, And Genius: True Tales of Megasuccess: Who Made Them Happen and How They Did It,* 3-19. Boston, Mass.: Houghton Mifflin, 1990.

THE GUGGENHEIM FAMILY

Simpson, Janice C. "The Guggenheims." In *American Dynasties Today,* 97-128. Homewood, Ill.: Dow Jones-Irwin, 1990.

GUMBEL, BRYANT

Clarke, Caroline V. "Bryant Gumbel: Anchor, The Early Show." In *Take a Lesson: Today's Black Achievers and How They Made It and What They Learned Along the Way,* 59-65. New York, N.Y.: Wiley, 2001.

GUY, RICHARD

Hillkirk, John, and Gary Jacobson. "GuyRex: The Sultans of Sash." In *Grit, Guts, And Genius: True Tales of Megasuccess: Who Made Them Happen and How They Did It,* 149-160. Boston, Mass.: Houghton Mifflin, 1990.

HAAS, ROBERT D.

Pottker, Jan. "Levi Strauss & Company: Fitting Ideals to Profits." In *Born to Power: Heirs to America's Leading Businesses*, 168-176. New York, N.Y.: Barron's, 1992.

HAFT, ROBERT

Pottker, Jan. "Crown Books Corp.: Discount Dynasty." In *Born to Power: Heirs to America's Leading Businesses*, 120-126. New York, N.Y.: Barron's, 1992.

HAGAN, MIKE

Ericksen, Gregory K. "Mike McNulty & Mike Hagan—VerticalNet 'We Get Qualified Eyeballs to Come to Very Focused Sites'." In *Net Entrepreneurs Only : 10 Entrepreneurs Tell the Stories of Their Success*, 21-40. New York : John Wiley, 2000.

HAGGIN, JAMES BEN ALI

Burnley, James. "James Ben Ali Haggin: The Ranch King of the West." In *Millionaires and Kings of Enterprise; The Marvellous Careers of Some Americans Who by Pluck, Foresight, And Energy Have Made Themselves Masters in the Fields of Industry and Finance*, 265-270. Philadelphia, Penn.: J. B. Lippincott, 1901.

HAIMSOHN, HENRY

Aronoff, Craig E., and John L. Ward. "Henry Haimsohn." In *Contemporary Entrepreneurs*, 196-202. Detroit, Mich.: Omnigraphics, Inc., 1992.

HAIRE, THOMAS E.

Aronoff, Craig E., and John L. Ward. "Thomas E. Haire." In *Contemporary Entrepreneurs*, 203-209. Detroit, Mich.: Omnigraphics, Inc., 1992.

HALL, DAVID

Elfstrand, Rhonda. "Dr. David Hall, M.D.: East Liberty Family Health Care Center." In *The Story Behind the Success: Learning From Pittsburgh Professionals*, 88-99. Pittsburgh, Penn.: Steel Publishing Partners, 1996.

HALL, JOSEPH B.

"Making Ideas Flow: Joseph B. Hall." In *Lessons of Leadership: 21 Executives Speak Out on Creating, Developing and Managing Success*. Presented by the editors of Nation's Business, 202-215. Garden City, N.Y.: Doubleday, 1968.

HALL, JOYCE C.

Cleary, David Powers. "Hallmark Cards; Good Taste is Good Business." In *Great American Brands: The Success Formulas That Made Them Famous*, 149-157. New York, N.Y: Fairchild Publications, 1981.

Goldwasser, Thomas. "Hallmark: Caring Enough to Send the Very Best." In *Family Pride; Profiles of Five of America's Best-Run Family Businesses*, 7-44. New York, N.Y.: Dodd, Mead and Company, 1986.

HALLIDIE, ANDREW S.

Davis, William. "Andrew S. Hallidie, 1836-1900: The Folly That Became a National Monument." In *The Innovators: The Essential Guide to Business Thinkers, Achievers and Entrepreneurs*, 167-169. New York, N.Y.: AMACOM, 1987.

HAM, AL

Levitt, Mortimer. "Al Ham: A Musician's Virtuoso Venture into Radio Programming." In *How to Start Your Own Business Without Losing Your Shirt; Secrets of Seventeen Successful Entrepreneurs*, 165-170. New York, N.Y: Atheneum, 1988.

HAMBRECHT, WILLIAM

Silver, A. David. "William Hambrecht." In *Entrepreneurial Megabucks: The 100 Greatest Entrepreneurs of the Last 25 Years*, 222-223. New York, N.Y.: Wiley, 1985.

HAMERSLAG, STEVEN J.

Ericksen, Gregory K. "Steven J. Hamerslag: MTI Technology Corp., 'Get Close to Customers'." In *What's Luck Got to Do with It; Twelve Entrepreneurs Reveal the Secrets Behind Their Success*, 181-195. New York, N.Y.: Wiley, 1997.

HAMILTON, ALEXANDER

Fanning, Leonard M. "Alexander Hamilton." In *Titans of Business*, 11-42. Philadelphia, Penn.: Lippincott, 1964. 240 p.

HAMILTON, JEAN

Pestrak, Debra. "Jean Hamilton: Chief Executive Officer, Prudential Institutional and Executive Vice-President, Prudential Insurance." In *Playing with the Big Boys: Success Stories of the Most Powerful Women in Business*, 79-94. Carlsbad, CA: SUN Publications, 2001.

HAMMER, ARMAND

Davis, William. "Armand Hammer, b. 1898: Wheeler-Dealer of East and West." In *The Innovators: The Essential Guide to Business Thinkers, Achievers and Entrepreneurs*, 169-172. New York, N.Y.: AMACOM, 1987.

HAMMOND, C. DEAN III

Pottker, Jan. "Hammond, Inc.: Mapping the Future." In *Born to Power: Heirs to America's Leading Businesses*, 50-56. New York, N.Y.: Barron's, 1992.

HAMMOND, KATHLEEN D.

Pottker, Jan. "Hammond, Inc.: Mapping the Future." In *Born to Power: Heirs to America's Leading Businesses*, 50-56. New York, N.Y.: Barron's, 1992.

HANCOCK, CAROL

Koppel, Mara. "Wild Ride—Carol Hancock." In *Women of the Pits: Shattering the Glass Ceiling in Financial Markets*, 19-28. Chicago, Ill.: Dearborn Financial Publishers, 1998.

HANCOCK, ELLEN

Pestrak, Debra. "Ellen Hancock: Chairman and Chief Executive Officer, Exodus Communications™." In *Playing with the Big Boys: Success Stories of the Most Powerful Women in Business*, 61-76. Carlsbad, CA: SUN Publications, 2001.

HANCOCK, JOHN

Klepper, Michael M., and Robert Gunther. "John Hancock (1736-1793): Poor Little Revolutionary Rich Boy." In *The Wealthy 100 : From Benjamin Franklin to Bill Gates—A Ranking of the Richest Americans, Past and Present*, 191-193. Secaucus, N.J. : Carol Pub. Group, 1996.

HANDLER, RUTH

Farnham, Alan. "Ruth Handler: Cofounder of Mattel Toys, 'I've Been Proving Myself My Whole Life; I Still Am'." In *Forbes Great Success Stories: Twelve Tales of Victory Wrested from Defeat*, 64-85. New York, N.Y.: Wiley, 2000.

Jeffrey, Laura S. "Ruth Handler: The Creator of Barbie." In *Great American Businesswomen*, 36-46. Springfield, N.J.: Enslow Publishers, Inc., 1996.

HANEY, WILLIAM M.

Haney, William M. III. "The Power of Invention." In *The Power of Boldness: Ten Master Builders of American Industry Tell Their Success Stories*, ed. Elkan Blout, 117-134. Washington, D.C.: Joseph Henry Press, 1996.

HANLEY, JOHN W.

Levinson, Harry, and Stuart Rosenthal. "John W. Hanley." In *CEO: Corporate Leadership in Action*, 137-176. New York, N.Y: Basic Books, 1984.

HANN, GEORGE R.

Trimble, William F. "George R. Hann, Pittsburgh Aviation Industries Corporation, and Pennsylvania Air Lines." In *Airline Executives and Federal Regulation: Case Studies in American Enterprise from the Airmail Era to the Dawn of the Jet Age*, ed. W. David Lewis, 47-82. Columbus, Ohio: Ohio State University Press, 2000.

HANSON, JOHN K.

Fucini, Joseph J., and Suzy Fucini. "John K. Hanson, Winnebago Industries, Inc.: 'Learning the Lessons of Small Business'." In *Experience Inc.; Men and Women Who Founded Famous Companies After the Age of 40*, 59-65. New York, N.Y: Free Press, 1987.

Silver, A. David. "John K. Hanson." In *Entrepreneurial Megabucks: The 100 Greatest Entrepreneurs of the Last 25 Years*, 224-227. New York, N.Y.: Wiley, 1985.

HARDING, RON

Tsang, Cheryl D. "Ron Harding: 'The Techie', 1986-1990." In *Microsoft First Generation: The Success Secrets of the Visionaries Who Launched a Technology Empire*, 179-194. New York, N.Y.: Wiley, 2000.

HARIG, KATHERINE

Koppel, Mara. "Burning Rubber: The S&P 500—Katherine Harig." In *Women of the Pits: Shattering the Glass Ceiling in Financial Markets*, 63-72. Chicago, Ill.: Dearborn Financial Publishers, 1998.

HARKINS, DAN

Gray, Bob, ed. "The Maverick Movie Mogul." In *How Entrepreneurs Make Business Profits: A Study of Personal Success Stories From Cordovan Business Journals*, 139-143. Houston, Tex.: Cordovan Press, 1982.

HARKNESS, EDWARD STEPHEN

Klepper, Michael M., and Robert Gunther. "Edward Stephen Harkness (1874-1940): Oil Fortune's Son." In *The Wealthy 100 : From Benjamin Franklin to Bill Gates—A Ranking of the Richest Americans, Past and Present*, 173-175. Secaucus, N.J. : Carol Pub. Group, 1996.

HARP, LORE

Zientara, Marguerite. "Lore Harp: Bored in Suburbia." In *Women, Technology & Power: Ten Stars and the History They Made*, 28-33. New York, N.Y.: AMACOM, American Management Association, 1987.

Zientara, Marguerite. "Lore Harp: Crash of a Highflyer." In *Women, Technology & Power: Ten Stars and the History They Made*, 163-172. New York, N.Y.: AMACOM, American Management Association, 1987.

Zientara, Marguerite. "Lore Harp: From Motherhood to the '8K Baby'." In *Women, Technology & Power: Ten Stars and the History They Made*, 102-106. New York, N.Y.: AMACOM, American Management Association, 1987.

HARPER, GEORGIE OLSON

Mikaelian, A. "Georgie Olson Harper." In *Women Who Mean Business: Success Stories of Women Over Forty*, 282-285. New York, N.Y.: William Morrow & Co., 1999.

HARPER, MARION

Millman, Nancy. In *Emperors of Adland; Inside the Advertising Revolution*, 37-47. New York, N.Y.: Warner Books, 1988.

HARPOLE, MURRAY J.

Fucini, Joseph J., and Suzy Fucini. "Murray J. Harpole, Pentair, Inc.: 'I Decided—I Would Give It Five Years No Matter How Tough It Got'." In *Experience Inc.; Men and Women Who Founded Famous Companies After the Age of 40*, 153-159. New York, N.Y: Free Press, 1987.

HARRIMAN, EDWARD HENRY

Hughes, Jonathan. "E. H. Harriman, The Financier and the Railroad." In *The Vital Few: The Entrepreneur and American Economic Progress*, 362-398. Expanded Edition, New York, N.Y.: Oxford University Press, 1986.

Klepper, Michael M., and Robert Gunther. "Edward Henry Harriman (1848-1909): The Wizard of Railroad Finance." In *The Wealthy 100 : From Benjamin Franklin to Bill Gates—A Ranking of the Richest Americans, Past and Present*, 91-94. Secaucus, N.J. : Carol Pub. Group, 1996.

Wren, Daniel A., and Ronald G. Greenwood. "Edward H. Harriman." In *Management Innovators: The People and Ideas That Have Shaped Modern Business*, 78-89. New York, N.Y.: Oxford University Press, 1998.

HARRIS, NINA

Harris, Nina. "Success Is an Attitude." In *Success Secrets: How Eighteen Everyday Women Became Fortune Builders and Famous Speakers*, 203-214. Glendora, Calif.: Royal CBS Publishing, 1978.

HARRISON-INGLIS, PATRICE

Alexander, Shoshana. "Patrice Harrison-Inglis: Sweetwoods Dairy, Peña Blanca, New Mexico." In *Women's Ventures, Women's Visions: 29 Inspiring Stories From Women Who Started Their Own Businesses*, 91-96. Freedom, Calif.: The Crossing Press, 1997.

HART, HARRY

Cleary, David Powers. "Hart Schaffner & Marx Suits; The Clothes a Man Wears Are to Some Extent a True Index of His Character and Taste, But They Are Also an Influence Upon His Character and Taste." In *Great American Brands: The Success Formulas That Made Them Famous*, 158-165. New York, N.Y: Fairchild Publications, 1981.

HARTMAN, ANN O'D.

Kahn, Joseph P. "The Money Game: Can Blackstone Bank Succeed by Focusing on Markets Other Lenders Ignore?" In *Anatomy of a Start-Up: Why Some New Businesses Succeed and Others Fail: 27 Real-Life Case Studies,* ed. Elizabeth K. Longsworth, 31-41. Boston, Mass.: Inc. Publishing, 1991.

HASSENFELD, ALAN G.

Pottker, Jan. "Hasbro, Inc.: Passing GO and Collecting..." In *Born to Power: Heirs to America's Leading Businesses*, 136-143. New York, N.Y.: Barron's, 1992.

HATSOPOULOS, GEORGE N.

Hatsoupolos, George N. "A Perpetual Idea Machine." In *The Power of Boldness: Ten Master Builders of American Industry Tell Their*

Success Stories, ed. Elkan Blout, 103-116. Washington, D.C.: Joseph Henry Press, 1996.

HARVEY, FRED

Beebe, Lucius. "Purveyor of the West." In *Great Stories of American Businessmen, From American Heritage, The Magazine of History,* 274-281. New York, N.Y.: American Heritage Publishing Co., 1954.

HAVEMEYER, HENRY OSBORNE

Burnley, James. "Havemeyer and Spreckels: The Sugar Kings of America." In *Millionaires and Kings of Enterprise; The Marvellous Careers of Some Americans Who by Pluck, Foresight, And Energy Have Made Themselves Masters in the Fields of Industry and Finance,* 212-223. Philadelphia, Penn.: J. B. Lippincott, 1901.

HAWKINS, TRIP

Jager, Rama Dev, and Rafael Ortiz. "Trip Hawkins: Electronic Arts/3DO; Creativity, The Ultimate Game." In *In the Company of Giants: Candid Conversations with the Visionaries of the Digital World,* 175-189. New York, N.Y.: McGraw-Hill, 1997.

HAYDEN, DAVID

Price, Christopher. "David Hayden—Critical Path 'Innovation as a Way of Life'." In *The Internet Entrepreneurs: Business Rules Are Good: Break Them,* 96-111. London, Eng.: FT.com, 2000.

HEAD, HOWARD

Landrum, Gene N. "Howard Head—Intuitive." In *Profiles of Genius: Thirteen Creative Men Who Changed the World,* 155-166. Buffalo, N.Y.: Prometheus Books, 1993.

HEARST, GEORGE

Klepper, Michael M., and Robert Gunther. "George Hearst (1820-1891): A Miner Who Founded a Media Empire." In *The Wealthy 100 : From*

Benjamin Franklin to Bill Gates—A Ranking of the Richest Americans, Past and Present, 188-190. Secaucus, N.J. : Carol Pub. Group, 1996.

HEDGEPATH, DEL

Liberman, Gail, and Alan Lavine. "Del Hedgepath: Real Estate Millionaire Ignores Financial Planner." In *Rags to Riches: Motivating Stories of How Ordinary People Achieved Extraordinary Wealth!,* 1-12. Chicago, Ill.: Dearborn, 2000.

HEFNER, CHRISTIE

Pottker, Jan. "Playboy Enterprises: Shaping Up the Figures at Playboy." In *Born to Power: Heirs to America's Leading Businesses,* 34-39. New York, N.Y.: Barron's, 1992.

HEFNER, HUGH

Davis, William. "Hugh Hefner, b. 1926: Playboy of the Western World." In *The Innovators: The Essential Guide to Business Thinkers, Achievers and Entrepreneurs,* 173-177. New York, N.Y.: AMACOM, 1987.

HEINZ FAMILY

Burnley, James. "James J. Heinz: The Condiment King." In *Millionaires and Kings of Enterprise; The Marvellous Careers of Some Americans Who by Pluck, Foresight, And Energy Have Made Themselves Masters in the Fields of Industry and Finance,* 322-328. Philadelphia, Penn.: J. B. Lippincott, 1901.

Koehn, Nancy F. "H. J. Heinz, 1844-1919." In *Brand New: How Entrepreneurs Earned Consumers' Trust from Wedgwood to Dell,* 45-90. Boston, Mass.: Harvard Business School Press, 2001.

HELBLING, ED

Elfstrand, Rhonda. "Ed Helbling: CPR Computers." In *The Story Behind the Success: Learning From Pittsburgh*

Professionals, 100-112. Pittsburgh, Penn.: Steel Publishing Partners, 1996.

HELM, POLLY

Alexander, Shoshana. "Polly Helm: Pendelton Cowgirl Company, Eugene, Oregon." In *Women's Ventures, Women's Visions: 29 Inspiring Stories From Women Who Started Their Own Businesses*, 61-68. Freedom, Calif.: The Crossing Press, 1997.

HENDERSON, LAURA

Mikaelian, A. "Laura Henderson." In *Women Who Mean Business: Success Stories of Women Over Forty*, 136-140. New York, N.Y.: William Morrow & Co., 1999.

HENDERSON, SARAHN

Alexander, Shoshana. "Sarahn Henderson: Mother's Keeper, Atlanta, Georgia." In *Women's Ventures, Women's Visions: 29 Inspiring Stories From Women Who Started Their Own Businesses*, 125-131. Freedom, Calif.: The Crossing Press, 1997.

HENDRICKS, KENNETH A.

Aronoff, Craig E., and John L. Ward. "Kenneth A. Hendricks." In *Contemporary Entrepreneurs*, 210-217. Detroit, Mich.: Omnigraphics, Inc., 1992.

HENRIKSON, LINDA J. E.

Mikaelian, A. "Linda J. E. Henrikson." In *Women Who Mean Business: Success Stories of Women Over Forty*, 11-15. New York, N.Y.: William Morrow & Co., 1999.

HENRY, JOHN B.

Aronoff, Craig E., and John L. Ward. "John B. Henry." In *Contemporary Entrepreneurs*, 218-224. Detroit, Mich.: Omnigraphics, Inc., 1992.

HENSLEY, SUSAN

Murphy, Linda. "Susan Hensley: San Diego Technical Books, Inc." In *Computer Entrepreneurs: People Who Built Successful Businesses Around Computers*, 111-117. San Diego, Calif.: Computer Publishing Enterprises, 1990.

HENTSCHEL, NOEL IRWIN

Oster, Merrill J. "It Can Be Done." In *The Entrepreneur's Creed: The Principles & Passions of 20 Successful Entrepreneurs*, 26-35. Nashville, Tenn.: Broadman & Holman Publishers, 2001.

HERRES, ROBERT T.

Wendel, Charles B. "Managing the Customer Without a Branch Network: General Robert T. Herres, Chairman & CEO, United Services Automobile Association (USAA)." In *The New Financiers*, 107-132. Chicago, Ill.: Irwin Professional Pub., 1996.

HERSHEY, MILTON S.

Cleary, David Powers. "Hershey's Milk Chocolate Bars; You Must Do Things in a Large Way." In *Great American Brands: The Success Formulas That Made Them Famous*, 166-171. New York, N.Y: Fairchild Publications, 1981.

HERZBERG, FREDERICK

Wren, Daniel A., and Ronald G. Greenwood. "Frederick Herzberg." In *Management Innovators: The People and Ideas That Have Shaped Modern Business*, 182-189. New York, N.Y.: Oxford University Press, 1998.

HEWLETT, WILLIAM R.

Jager, Rama Dev, and Rafael Ortiz. "Bill Hewlett: Hewlett-Packard; People Are Everything." In *In the Company of Giants: Candid Conversations with the Visionaries of the Digital World*, 225-232. New York, N.Y.: McGraw-Hill,

1997.

Silver, A. David. "David Packard; William R. Hewlett." In *Entrepreneurial Megabucks: The 100 Greatest Entrepreneurs of the Last 25 Years*, 344-346. New York, N.Y.: Wiley, 1985.

HICKINGBOTHAM, FRANK D.

Aronoff, Craig E., and John L. Ward. "Frank D. Hickingbotham." In *Contemporary Entrepreneurs*, 225-231. Detroit, Mich.: Omnigraphics, Inc., 1992.

Fucini, Joseph J., and Suzy Fucini. "Frank D. Hickingbotham; TCBY Enterprises, Inc.: 'The Time Was Right for a National Frozen Yogurt Chain'." In *Experience Inc.; Men and Women Who Founded Famous Companies After the Age of 40*, 9-15. New York, N.Y: Free Press, 1987.

HILFIGER, TOMMY

Agins, Teri. "Bound for Old Glory: Ralph Lauren and Tommy Hilfiger." In *The End of Fashion: The Mass Marketing of the Clothing Business*, 80-126. New York, N.Y.: William Morrow, 1999.

HILL, JAMES JEROME

Burnley, James. "James J. Hill: An American Railway Magnate." In *Millionaires and Kings of Enterprise; The Marvellous Careers of Some Americans Who by Pluck, Foresight, And Energy Have Made Themselves Masters in the Fields of Industry and Finance*, 175-187. Philadelphia, Penn.: J. B. Lippincott, 1901.

Holbrook, Stewart H. "The Legend of Jim Hill." In *Great Stories of American Businessmen*, From *American Heritage, The Magazine of History,* 302-309. New York, N.Y.: American Heritage Publishing Co., 1954.

Klepper, Michael M., and Robert Gunther. "James Jerome Hill (1838-1916): The Empire Builder of the Northwest." In *The Wealthy 100 : From Benjamin Franklin to Bill Gates—A Ranking of the Richest*

Americans, Past and Present, 142-144. Secaucus, N.J. : Carol Pub. Group, 1996.

Mountfield, David. "The Last of the Empire Builders." In *The Railway Barons,* 159-217. New York, N.Y.: Norton, 1979.

Sobel, Robert. "James J. Hill: The Business of Empire." In *The Entrepreneurs: Explorations Within the American Business Tradition,* 110-147. New York, N.Y.: Weybright and Talley, 1974.

Wren, Daniel A., and Ronald G. Greenwood. "James J. Hill." In *Management Innovators: The People and Ideas That Have Shaped Modern Business,* 72-78. New York, N.Y.: Oxford University Press, 1998.

HILL, WALTER W. JR.

Wallace, Robert L. "Walter W. Hill Jr. and Eillen E. Dorsey: Founders, ECS Technologies, Baltimore, Maryland." In *Black Wealth: Your Road to Small Business Success,* 60-66. New York, N.Y.: Wiley, 2000.

HILLARD, MOSES

Macleish, Archibald. "Portrait of a Yankee Skipper." In *Great Stories of American Businessmen,* From *American Heritage, The Magazine of History,* 59-65. New York, N.Y.: American Heritage Publishing Co., 1954.

HILLERICH, BUD

Pile, Robert B. "Bud Hillerich: The First Bat Man." In *Top Entrepreneurs and Their Businesses,* 97-109. Minneapolis, Minn.: The Oliver Press, Inc., 1993.

HILTON, CONRAD

Davis, William. "Conrad Hilton, 1887-1979: A Chain of Hotels Around the World." In *The Innovators: The Essential Guide to Business Thinkers, Achievers and Entrepreneurs,* 177-183. New York, N.Y.: AMACOM, 1987.

Gunther, Max. "Conrad Hilton: One-Hundred Million Dollars." In *The Very, Very Rich and How They Got That Way*, ed. Max Gunther, 204-213. Chicago, Ill.: The Playboy Press, 1972.

"Daring to Build on a Dream: Conrad N. Hilton." In *Lessons of Leadership: 21 Executives Speak Out on Creating, Developing and Managing Success*. Presented by the editors of Nation's Business, 3-14. Garden City, N.Y.: Doubleday, 1968.

HILTON, NANCY

Suarez, Ruth. "Nancy Hilton: Dormeuil, 'The Advantage of Being a Woman'." In *Superstar Entrepreneurs of Small and Large Businesses Reveal Their Secrets*. 181-185. Piscataway, N.J.: Research and Education Association, 1998.

HINKLE, LYNN GARDNER

Mikaelian, A. "Lynn Gardner Hinkle." In *Women Who Mean Business: Success Stories of Women Over Forty*, 113-117. New York, N.Y.: William Morrow & Co., 1999.

HINOTE, SAMUEL I.

Aronoff, Craig E., and John L. Ward. "Samuel I. Hinote." In *Contemporary Entrepreneurs*, 232-236. Detroit, Mich.: Omnigraphics, Inc., 1992.

HIRCHHORN, JOSEPH HERMAN

Hughes, Emmet John. "Joseph Hirshhorn: One-Hundred Million Dollars." In *The Very, Very Rich and How They Got That Way*, ed. Max Gunther, 57-72. Chicago, Ill.: The Playboy Press, 1972.

HIRES, CHARLES E.

"He Started Soda Sales Popping: Charles E. Hires' Root Beer Launched in 1876 Set Pattern of National Distribution." In *The 50 Great Pioneers of American Industry*. By the Editors of News Front and Year, 81-83. Maplewood, N.J.: C.S. Hammond, 1964.

HIRSCH, NEIL S.

Silver, A. David. "Neil S. Hirsch." In *Entrepreneurial Megabucks: The 100 Greatest Entrepreneurs of the Last 25 Years*, 228-230. New York, N.Y.: Wiley, 1985.

HIRSHBERG, GARY

Ericksen, Gregory K. "Gary Hirshberg: Stonyfield Farm, 'A Business Plan for the Future: Hope'." In *What's Luck Got to Do with It; Twelve Entrepreneurs Reveal the Secrets Behind Their Success*, 139-161. New York, N.Y.: Wiley, 1997.

HITCHCOCK, ROBERT

Suarez, Ruth. "Robert Hitchcock: Datavision Technologies Corporation, 'People Buying People'." In *Superstar Entrepreneurs of Small and Large Businesses Reveal Their Secrets*, 29-33. Piscataway, N.J.: Research and Education Association, 1998.

HMIELESKI, DENISE

Lassen, Ali. "Denise Hmieleski: Publisher of Fun Club Publications." In *The Secret of Their Success: Women Entrepreneurs Reveal How They Made It*, 25-34. Carlsbad, Calif.: Ali Lassen Success System, 1990.

HOCHSCHILD, ADAM

Pottker, Jan. "Mother Jones Magazine: An Incompatible Alloy, Adam Hochschild, Co-Founder—Heir to AMAX" In *Born to Power: Heirs to America's Leading Businesses*, 436-440. New York, N.Y.: Barron's, 1992.

HOFF, MARCIAN E. "TED"

Slater, Robert. "Marcian E. 'Ted' Hoff: Inventor of the 'Computer on a Chip'." In *Portraits in Silicon*, 174-181. Cambridge, Mass.: MIT Press, 1987.

HOFFACKER, THERESA MARTINEZ

Alexander, Shoshana. "Theresa Martinez Hoffacker: Constant Care DaySchool, Santa Fe, New Mexico." In *Women's Ventures, Women's Visions: 29 Inspiring Stories From Women Who Started Their Own Businesses*, 77-83. Freedom, Calif.: The Crossing Press, 1997.

HOFFMAN, PAUL G.

Westbrook, Francis Jr. "Paul G. Hoffman." In *America's Fifty Foremost Business Leaders,* ed. B. C. Forbes, 195-204. New York, N.Y.: B.C. Forbes, 1948.

HOLDER, WAYNE

Murphy, Linda. "Wayne Holder: Software Heaven/FTL Games." In *Computer Entrepreneurs: People Who Built Successful Businesses Around Computers*, 1-11. San Diego, Calif.: Computer Publishing Enterprises, 1990.

HOLDERMAN, TRICIA

Suarez, Ruth. "Tricia Holderman: T.H.E. Maintenance, 'The Grass is Always Greener...on Her Side'." In *Superstar Entrepreneurs of Small and Large Businesses Reveal Their Secrets*, 91-95. Piscataway, N.J.: Research and Education Association, 1998.

HOLLENDER, JEFFREY

Gardner, Ralph. "Jeffrey Hollender." In *Young, Gifted, and Rich: The Secrets of America's Most Successful Entrepreneurs*, 171-182. New York, N.Y.: Wallaby Books, 1984.

HOLLEY, ALEXANDER LYMAN

"A. L. Holley, Sire of Steel: Versatile Engineer Brought U.S. Bessemer Process, Laid Foundation of World's Largest Steel Industry." In *The 50 Great Pioneers of American Industry*. By the Editors of News Front and Year, 56-58. Maplewood, N.J.: C.S. Hammond, 1964.

HOLMAN, EUGENE

Spencer, Richard. "Eugene Holman." In *America's Fifty Foremost Business Leaders,* ed. B. C. Forbes, 205-214. New York, N.Y.: B.C. Forbes, 1948.

HOLT, REX

Hillkirk, John, and Gary Jacobson. "GuyRex: The Sultans of Sash." In *Grit, Guts, And Genius: True Tales of Megasuccess: Who Made Them Happen and How They Did It,* 149-160. Boston, Mass.: Houghton Mifflin, 1990.

HONAN, MARY T.

Lyons, Mary. "Mary T. Honan: Coldwell Banker Harnden Beecher, Realtor, 'It Pays to Look Like a Grandmother'." In *Maine's Achieving Women: Conversations with Entrepreneurs*, 121-127. Old Orchard Beach, ME: Lilac River Press, 1999.

HONECK, JANE

Lyons, Mary. "Jane Honeck: Honeck & O'Toole, CPA's, Founding Partner, 'No One's Ever Going to Hire a Female Accountant'." In *Maine's Achieving Women: Conversations with Entrepreneurs*, 53-63. Old Orchard Beach, ME: Lilac River Press, 1999.

HOOK, CHARLES R.

Dale, Bert. "Charles R. Hook." In *America's Fifty Foremost Business Leaders,* ed. B. C. Forbes, 215-222. New York, N.Y.: B.C. Forbes, 1948.

HOOVER, GARY E.

Buchholz, Barbara B., and Margaret Crane. "Bookstop, Austin, TX." In *Corporate Blood Lines: The Future of the Family Firm*, 145-159. New York, N.Y: Carol Publishing Group, 1989.

HOPKINS, JOHNS

"Johns Hopkins." In *A Dozen Roads to Success: Being Graphic Sketches of Twelve of the Most Prominent Business Men of America, And Showing How They Became Millionaires,* 104-116. *Philadelphia, Penn.: Girard Pub. Co., 1894.*

Klepper, Michael M., and Robert Gunther. "Johns Hopkins (1795-1873): Builder of Baltimore." In *The Wealthy 100 : From Benjamin Franklin to Bill Gates—A Ranking of the Richest Americans, Past and Present,* 239-241. Secaucus, N.J. : Carol Pub. Group, 1996.

HOPKINS, MARK

Lewis, Oscar. "Hopkins: '...The Stubbornest Man Alive'." In *The Big Four; The Story of Huntington, Stanford, Hopkins, and Crocker, And of the Building of the Central Pacific,* 124-155. New York, N.Y.: A.A. Knopf, 1938.

HORCHOW, ROGER

Shook, Robert L. "S. Roger Horchow." In *The Entrepreneurs: Twelve Who Took Risks and Succeeded,* 67-79. New York, N.Y: Harper & Row, 1980.

Silver, A. David. "Roger Horchow." In *Entrepreneurial Megabucks: The 100 Greatest Entrepreneurs of the Last 25 Years,* 234-236. New York, N.Y.: Wiley, 1985.

HOROWITZ, RUSSELL C.

Ericksen, Gregory K. "Russell C. Horowitz—Go2Net 'If You Can't Build It, Buy It'." In *Net Entrepreneurs Only : 10 Entrepreneurs Tell the Stories of Their Success,* 101-120. New York : John Wiley, 2000.

HOWARD, AGNES

Rich-McCoy, Lois. "Indian Ingenuity: Agnes Howard." In *Millionairess: Self-Made Women of America,* 189-206. New York, N.Y.: Harper & Row, 1978.

HUDIBURG, JOHN

Hillkirk, John, and Gary Jacobson. "Florida Power & Light: Providing 'Perfect' Service." In *Grit, Guts, And Genius: True Tales of Megasuccess: Who Made Them Happen and How They Did It*, 211-227. Boston, Mass.: Houghton Mifflin, 1990.

HUDSON, MARY

Shook, Robert L. "Mary Hudson." In *The Entrepreneurs: Twelve Who Took Risks and Succeeded*, 41-52. New York, N.Y: Harper & Row, 1980.

HUGG, JOYCE FLOWER

Mikaelian, A. "Joyce Flower Hugg." In *Women Who Mean Business: Success Stories of Women Over Forty*, 305-309. New York, N.Y.: William Morrow & Co., 1999.

HUGHES, GEORGE

"Household Horsepower: Earl Richardson and George Hughes, Designers of First Successful Irons and Stoves, Were Fathers of Today's $6 Billion Household Appliance Industry." In *The 50 Great Pioneers of American Industry*. By the Editors of News Front and Year, 175-177. Maplewood, N.J.: C.S. Hammond, 1964.

HUGHES, HOWARD

Davis, William. "Howard Hughes, 1905-1974: The Business Hero Turned Eccentric." In *The Innovators: The Essential Guide to Business Thinkers, Achievers and Entrepreneurs*, 192-195. New York, N.Y.: AMACOM, 1987.

Gunther, Max, "Howard Hughes: One Billion Dollars." In *The Very, Very Rich and How They Got That Way*, ed. Max Gunther, 90-104. Chicago, Ill.: The Playboy Press, 1972.

Klepper, Michael M., and Robert Gunther. "Howard Hughes (1905-1976): Hell's Angel." In *The Wealthy 100 : From Benjamin Franklin to Bill*

Gates—A Ranking of the Richest Americans, Past and Present, 276-280. Secaucus, N.J. : Carol Pub. Group, 1996.

HUGHES, PETER

Elfstrand, Rhonda. "Peter Hughes: Sport Court of Pittsburgh." In *The Story Behind the Success: Learning From Pittsburgh Professionals,* 114-126. Pittsburgh, Penn.: Steel Publishing Partners, 1996.

HUGHLEY, BARBARA

Alexander, Shoshana. "Barbara Hughley: Media Professionals, Inc., Baldwin, New York." In *Women's Ventures, Women's Visions: 29 Inspiring Stories From Women Who Started Their Own Businesses,* 20-26. Freedom, Calif.: The Crossing Press, 1997.

HUIZENGA, H. WAYNE

Aronoff, Craig E., and John L. Ward. "H. Wayne Huizenga." In *Contemporary Entrepreneurs,* 237-242. Detroit, Mich.: Omnigraphics, Inc., 1992.

HUMMEL, CARMEN

Suarez, Ruth. "Carmen Hummel: Express Personnel Services, 'From Temporary to Permanent Success'." In *Superstar Entrepreneurs of Small and Large Businesses Reveal Their Secrets.* 223-229. Piscataway, N.J.: Research and Education Association, 1998.

HUMPHREYS, KIRK

Oster, Merrill J. "Public Service." In *The Entrepreneur's Creed: The Principles & Passions of 20 Successful Entrepreneurs,* 162-171. Nashville, Tenn.: Broadman & Holman Publishers, 2001.

HUNT, H. L.

Brands, H. W. "The Gambler: H. L. Hunt." In *Masters of Enterprise: Giants of American Business from John Jacob Astor and J.P. Morgan to Bill Gates and Oprah Winfrey,* 152-167. New York, N.Y.: Free Press, 1999.

Hill, Margaret Hunt. *H. L. & Lyda: Growing Up in the H. L. Hunt and Lyda Bunker Hunt Family As Remembered by their Eldest Daughter*. Little Rock, Ark.: August House Publishers, 1994. 276 p.

Klepper, Michael M., and Robert Gunther. "H. L. Hunt (1889-1974): The Wildest of the Wildcatters." In *The Wealthy 100 : From Benjamin Franklin to Bill Gates—A Ranking of the Richest Americans, Past and Present*, 305-308. Secaucus, N.J. : Carol Pub. Group, 1996.

HUNT, J. B.

MacPhee, William. "J. B. Hunt of J. B. Hunt Transport, Inc." In *Rare Breed: The Entrepreneur, An American Culture*, 69-75. Chicago, Ill.: Probus Publishing Company, 1987.

HUNTINGTON, COLLIS P.

Lewis, Oscar. "Huntington: 'Young Man, You Can't Follow Me Through Life By the Quarters I Have Dropped'." In *The Big Four; The Story of Huntington, Stanford, Hopkins, and Crocker, And of the Building of the Central Pacific*, 211-282. New York, N.Y.: A.A. Knopf, 1938.

HUNTSMAN, JON M.

Aronoff, Craig E., and John L. Ward. "Jon M. Huntsman." In *Contemporary Entrepreneurs*, 243-249. Detroit, Mich.: Omnigraphics, Inc., 1992.

HUTCHENS, SANDRA

Murphy, Linda. "Jan Zimmerman and Sandra Hutchins." In *Computer Entrepreneurs: People Who Built Successful Businesses Around Computers*, 13-22. San Diego, Calif.: Computer Publishing Enterprises, 1990.

HUYNH, TUAN

Aronoff, Craig E., and John L. Ward. "Tuan Huynh." In *Contemporary Entrepreneurs*, 250-254. Detroit, Mich.: Omnigraphics, Inc., 1992.

HWANG, K. PHILIP

Silver, A. David. "K. Philip Hwang." In *Entrepreneurial Megabucks: The 100 Greatest Entrepreneurs of the Last 25 Years*, 237-239. New York, N.Y.: Wiley, 1985.

HYATT, JOEL ZYLBERBERG

Aronoff, Craig E., and John L. Ward. "Joel Zylberberg Hyatt." In *Contemporary Entrepreneurs*, 255-261. Detroit, Mich.: Omnigraphics, Inc., 1992.

IACOCCA, LEE

Davis, William. "Lee Iacocca, b. 1924: 'If You Can Find a Better Car, Buy It'." In *The Innovators: The Essential Guide to Business Thinkers, Achievers and Entrepreneurs*, 195-200. New York, N.Y.: AMACOM, 1987.

ICAHN, CARL

Kadlec, Daniel J. "Carl Icahn: Raider with a Pulse." In *Masters of the Universe; Winning Strategies of America's Greatest Deal Makers*, 11-38. New York, N.Y.: HarperBusiness, 1999.

Smith, Roy C. "The Loner." In *Wealth Creators: The Rise of Today's Rich and Super-Rich*, 105-110. New York, N.Y.: Truman Talley, 2001.

IDELMAN, SHERI

Mikaelian, A. "Sheri Idelman." In *Women Who Mean Business: Success Stories of Women Over Forty*, 200-204. New York, N.Y.: William Morrow & Co., 1999.

IMPERATORE, ARTHUR

Levitt, Mortimer. "Arthur Imperatore: Obsessive Drive Converts an Army Truck into a Transportation Empire." In *How to Start Your Own Business Without Losing Your Shirt; Secrets of Seventeen Successful Entrepreneurs,* 53-60. New York, N.Y: Atheneum, 1988.

INGERSOLL, RALPH

Coleridge, Nicholas. "The Emperor's New Off-The-Peg Papers: Ralph Ingersoll's $1½ Billion Shopping Spree." In *Paper Tigers: The Latest, Greatest Newspaper Tycoons*, 104-132. New York, N.Y.: Carol Publishing Group, 1994.

ISAACSON, PORTIA

Zientara, Marguerite. "Portia Isaacson: Ambitions of a Misfit." In *Women, Technology & Power: Ten Stars and the History They Made*, 38-50. New York, N.Y.: AMACOM, American Management Association, 1987.

Zientara, Marguerite. "Portia Isaacson: Champion of the Microcomputer." In *Women, Technology & Power: Ten Stars and the History They Made*, 89-102. New York, N.Y.: AMACOM, American Management Association, 1987.

Zientara, Marguerite. "Portia Isaacson: 'This Business Has Me'." In *Women, Technology & Power: Ten Stars and the History They Made*, 193-200. New York, N.Y.: AMACOM, American Management Association, 1987.

ISBELL, MARION W.

Fucini, Joseph J., and Suzy Fucini. "Marion W. Isbell, Ramada Inns: 'All of My Life I Tried to Get Ahead by Outworking the Guy Next to Me'." In *Experience Inc.; Men and Women Who Founded Famous Companies After the Age of 40*, 192-199. New York, N.Y: Free Press, 1987.

ISRAEL, STEVE

Levitt, Mortimer. "Steve Israel: Architectural Artifacts from Junk." In *How to Start Your Own Business Without Losing Your Shirt; Secrets of Seventeen Successful Entrepreneurs*, 113-119. New York, N.Y: Atheneum, 1988.

IYER, PATRICIA W

Iyer, Patricia W. "You Only Go This Way Once." In *How I Became a Nurse Entrepreneur: Tales from 50 Nurses in Business*, 191-197. Petaluma, Calif.: National Nurses in Business Association, 1991.

IZZO, JOSEPH

Gray, Bob, ed. "The Patient Data Doctor." In *How Entrepreneurs Make Business Profits: A Study of Personal Success Stories From Cordovan Business Journals*, 64-70. Houston, Tex.: Cordovan Press, 1982.

JACKSON, CHARLIE

Murphy, Linda. "Charlie Jackson: Silicon Beach Software." In *Computer Entrepreneurs: People Who Built Successful Businesses Around Computers*, 39-47. San Diego, Calif.: Computer Publishing Enterprises, 1990.

JACKSON, DAVID

Silver, A. David. "David Jackson." In *Entrepreneurial Megabucks: The 100 Greatest Entrepreneurs of the Last 25 Years*, 244-246. New York, N.Y.: Wiley, 1985.

JACKSON-HANSON, DARLENE

Mikaelian, A. "Darlene Jackson-Hanson." In *Women Who Mean Business: Success Stories of Women Over Forty*, 237-241. New York, N.Y.: William Morrow & Co., 1999.

JACOBS, ALMA

"Alma Jones." In *Women Achievers: A Series of Dialogues from the Womanagement Process*, 79-89. New York, N.Y.: American Telephone and Telegraph Co., 1997.

JACOBY, ROBERT

Millman, Nancy. In *Emperors of Adland; Inside the Advertising Revolution*, 1-17. New York, N.Y.: Warner Books, 1988.

JAKOVAC, FRANK

Elfstrand, Rhonda. "Frank Jakovac, Herman Tomer: Gateway Archives, Inc." In *The Story Behind the Success: Learning From Pittsburgh Professionals*, 128-148. Pittsburgh, Penn.: Steel Publishing Partners, 1996.

JAKUBOWSKI, CHERYL

Liberman, Gail, and Alan Lavine. "Paul and Cheryl Jakubowski: Couple Uses Software to Cut Debt and Invest Wisely." In *Rags to Riches: Motivating Stories of How Ordinary People Achieved Extraordinary Wealth!*, 77-86. Chicago, Ill.: Dearborn, 2000.

JAKUBOWSKI, PAUL

Liberman, Gail, and Alan Lavine. "Paul and Cheryl Jakubowski: Couple Uses Software to Cut Debt and Invest Wisely." In *Rags to Riches: Motivating Stories of How Ordinary People Achieved Extraordinary Wealth!*, 77-86. Chicago, Ill.: Dearborn, 2000.

JAMES, BETTY

Shook, Robert L. "The Slinky." In *Why Didn't I Think of That*, 20-36. New York, N.Y.: New American Library, 1982.

JAMES, CHARLES H. III

Dingle, Derek T. "Charles H. James III: C. H. James & Son Holding Company, Inc., 'The Strategist'." In *Black Enterprise Titans of the B.E. 100s: Black CEOs Who Redefined and Conquered American Business*, 173-192. New York, N.Y.: Wiley, 1999.

JAMES, DANIEL WILLIS

Klepper, Michael M., and Robert Gunther. "Daniel Willis James (1832-1907): Flowing in His Father's Footsteps." In *The Wealthy 100 : From Benjamin Franklin to Bill Gates—A Ranking of the Richest Americans, Past and Present,* 274-275. Secaucus, N.J. : Carol Pub. Group, 1996.

JAMISON, BOB

Elfstrand, Rhonda. "Bob Jamison: Youth Guidance, Inc." In *The Story Behind the Success: Learning From Pittsburgh Professionals,* 150-166. Pittsburgh, Penn.: Steel Publishing Partners, 1996.

JANCO, MYRA

Uris, Auren. "Myra Janco—President in a Gray Flannel Skirt." In *The Executive Breakthrough; 21 Roads to the Top,* 363-376. Garden City, N.Y.: Doubleday, 1967.

JANEWAY, ELIOT

King, Norman. "Eliot Janeway." In *The Money Messiah$,* 11-48. New York, N.Y.: Coward-McCann, 1983.

JANTZEN, CARL

Cleary, David Powers. "Jantzen Swim Suits: A Good Business." In *Great American Brands: The Success Formulas That Made Them Famous,* 182-191. New York, N.Y: Fairchild Publications, 1981.

JEANLOZ, CLAUDE

Silver, A. David. "Claude and Donna Jeanloz." In *Entrepreneurial Megabucks: The 100 Greatest Entrepreneurs of the Last 25 Years,* 247-248. New York, N.Y.: Wiley, 1985.

JEANLOZ, DONNA

Silver, A. David. "Claude and Donna Jeanloz." In *Entrepreneurial Megabucks: The 100 Greatest Entrepreneurs of the Last 25 Years*, 247-248. New York, N.Y.: Wiley, 1985.

JETT, JOAN

Gardner, Ralph. "Joan Jett." In *Young, Gifted, and Rich: The Secrets of America's Most Successful Entrepreneurs*, 183-195. New York, N.Y.: Wallaby Books, 1984.

JOBS, STEVEN P.

Aronoff, Craig E., and John L. Ward. "Steven P. Jobs." In *Contemporary Entrepreneurs*, 262-269. Detroit, Mich.: Omnigraphics, Inc., 1992.

Davis, William. "Steven Jobs, b. 1955: Genius in a Garage." In *The Innovators: The Essential Guide to Business Thinkers, Achievers and Entrepreneurs*, 204-208. New York, N.Y.: AMACOM, 1987.

Gardner, Ralph. "Steve Jobs." In *Young, Gifted, and Rich: The Secrets of America's Most Successful Entrepreneurs*, 11-23. New York, N.Y.: Wallaby Books, 1984.

Jager, Rama Dev, and Rafael Ortiz. "Steve Jobs: Apple Computer, NeXT Software, And Pixar; Only the Best—People, Product, Purpose." In *In the Company of Giants: Candid Conversations with the Visionaries of the Digital World*, 9-25. New York, N.Y.: McGraw-Hill, 1997.

Landrum, Gene N. "Steven Jobs—Autocratic." In *Profiles of Genius: Thirteen Creative Men Who Changed the World*, 73-85. Buffalo, N.Y.: Prometheus Books, 1993.

Mariotti, Steve, and Mike Caslin. "Steve Wozniak & Steve Jobs: Apple Computers." In *The Very Very Rich: How They Got That Way and How You Can, Too!*, 117-125. Franklin Lakes, NJ: Career Press, 2000.

Meyer, Michael. "The Visionary." In *The Alexander Complex: The Dreams That Drive the Great Businessmen*, 15-51. New York, N.Y.: Times Books, 1989.

Silver, A. David. "Steven P. Jobs; Steven Wozniak." In *Entrepreneurial Megabucks: The 100 Greatest Entrepreneurs of the Last 25 Years*, 250-253. New York, N.Y.: Wiley, 1985.

Slater, Robert. "Steven Jobs: Cofounder of Apple." In *Portraits in Silicon*, 308-321. Cambridge, Mass.: MIT Press, 1987.

JOCHHEIM, SUSAN

Suarez, Ruth. "Susan Jochheim: Execustaff, 'Staffing with a Vision'." In *Superstar Entrepreneurs of Small and Large Businesses Reveal Their Secrets*. 231-234. Piscataway, N.J.: Research and Education Association, 1998.

JOHN, DAYMOND

Mitchell, Niki Butler. "For Us, By Us: J. Alexander Martin, Vice President and Head Designer; Daymond John, President and CEO; Carl Brown, Co-Founder; Keith Perrin, Co-Founder, FUBU." In *The New Color of Success: Twenty Young Black Millionaires Tell You How They're Making it*, 29-42. Rocklin, Calif.: Prima Publishing, 2000.

JOHNSON, EDWARD C. "NED"

Johnson, Edward C. 3d. "Adventures of a Contrarian." In *The Power of Boldness: Ten Master Builders of American Industry Tell Their Success Stories*, ed. Elkan Blout, 189-204. Washington, D.C.: Joseph Henry Press, 1996.

Smith, Roy C. "Mr. Johnson's Company." In *Wealth Creators: The Rise of Today's Rich and Super-Rich*, 182-187. New York, N.Y.: Truman Talley, 2001.

JOHNSON FAMILY

Pottker, Jan. "Johnson Products Company: Sibling Rivalry." In *Born to Power: Heirs to America's Leading Businesses*, 360-368. New York, N.Y.: Barron's, 1992.

JOHNSON, GEORGE F.

McSherry, Ronald T. "The Valley of Fair Play." In *Nine American Self-Made Men and Their Secrets to Success*, 11-15. Denver, Colo.: U.S.A. Publishing, 1983.

JOHNSON, HOWARD DEARING

"Building from Scratch: Howard Johnson." In *Lessons of Leadership: 21 Executives Speak Out on Creating, Developing and Managing Success*. Presented by the editors of Nation's Business, 44-55. Garden City, N.Y.: Doubleday, 1968.

Cahill, Timothy Patrick. "The Howard Johnson Story." In *Profiles in the American Dream: The Real-Life Stories of the Struggles of American Entrepreneurs*, 37-72. Hanover, Mass.: Christopher Publishing Company, 1994.

JOHNSON, JOHN H.

Davis, William. "John H. Johnson, b. 1918: Black America's Publisher." In *The Innovators: The Essential Guide to Business Thinkers, Achievers and Entrepreneurs*, 209-211. New York, N.Y.: AMACOM, 1987.

Dingle, Derek T. "John H. Johnson: Johnson Publishing Company, Inc., 'The Pioneer'." In *Black Enterprise Titans of the B.E. 100s: Black CEOs Who Redefined and Conquered American Business*, 1-26. New York, N.Y.: Wiley, 1999.

Gross, Daniel, and the Editors of Forbes Magazine. "John H. Johnson: Finding the Black Consumer." In *Forbes Greatest Business Stories of All Time*, 142-156. New York, N.Y.: Wiley, 1996.

Mariotti, Steve, and Lorraine Mooney. "John H. Johnson: Prince of the Black Publishing World." In *Entrepreneurs in Profile*, 58-62. London: National Foundation for Teaching Entrepreneurship, 1991.

Mariotti, Steve, and Mike Caslin. "John Johnson, Johnson Publishing Company: Visionary Behind Ebony and Jet." In *The Very Very Rich: How They Got That Way and How You Can, Too!*, 59-64. Franklin Lakes, NJ: Career Press, 2000.

Pile, Robert B. "John Johnson: 'Don't Get Mad, Get Smart'." In *Top Entrepreneurs and Their Businesses*, 139-151. Minneapolis, Minn.: The Oliver Press, Inc., 1993.

Sobel, Robert, and David B. Sicilia. "John H. Johnson: Apostle of the Black Middle Class." In *The Entrepreneurs: An American Adventure*, 32-37. Boston, Mass.: Houghton Mifflin Company, 1986.

JOHNSON, ROBERT L.

Dingle, Derek T. "Robert L. Johnson: BET Holdings, Inc., 'The Brand Master'." In *Black Enterprise Titans of the B.E. 100s: Black CEOs Who Redefined and Conquered American Business*, New York, N.Y.: Wiley, 1999.

Mariotti, Steve, and Mike Caslin. "Robert L. Johnson, BET Holdings, Inc.: African American Television." In *The Very Very Rich: How They Got That Way and How You Can, Too!*, 65-70. Franklin Lakes, NJ: Career Press, 2000.

JOHNSON, ROBERT WOOD

Klepper, Michael M., and Robert Gunther. "Robert Wood Johnson Jr. (1893-1968): Billion-Dollar Ban-Aids." In *The Wealthy 100 : From Benjamin Franklin to Bill Gates—A Ranking of the Richest Americans, Past and Present*, 224-226. Secaucus, N.J. : Carol Pub. Group, 1996.

JOHNSON, SAMUEL CURTIS

Goldwasser, Thomas. "Johnson Wax: 100 Years and Still Shining." In *Family Pride; Profiles of Five of America's Best-Run Family*

Businesses, 163-202. New York, N.Y.: Dodd, Mead and Company, 1986.

JOHNSON, THOMAS

Mitchell, Niki Butler. "A Good Call: Thomas Johnson, President, Wireless, Inc." In *The New Color of Success: Twenty Young Black Millionaires Tell You How They're Making it*, 145-154. Rocklin, Calif.: Prima Publishing, 2000.

JOHNSON, TOM L.

Burnley, James. "Tom Loftus Johnson: The Cleveland Traction King." In *Millionaires and Kings of Enterprise; The Marvellous Careers of Some Americans Who by Pluck, Foresight, And Energy Have Made Themselves Masters in the Fields of Industry and Finance*, 454-461. Philadelphia, Penn.: J. B. Lippincott, 1901.

JOHNSTON, DEBORAH

Ericksen, Gregory K. "Deborah Johnston—Care Advantage, Inc., 'The Kind of Care Giver I Would Want for My Own Mother'." In *Women Entrepreneurs Only: Twelve Women Entrepreneurs Tell The Stories of Their Success*, 239-259. New York, N.Y.: Wiley, 1999.

JOHNSTON, DON

Millman, Nancy. In *Emperors of Adland; Inside the Advertising Revolution*, 79-90. New York, N.Y.: Warner Books, 1988.

JOHNSTON, ERIC

Bell, Laurence. "Eric Johnson." In *America's Fifty Foremost Business Leaders,* ed. B. C. Forbes, 223-232. New York, N.Y.: B.C. Forbes, 1948.

JOHNSTON, GREG

Suarez, Ruth. "Greg Johnston: Our Secret, 'Letting Entrepreneurs in on Our Secret'." In *Superstar Entrepreneurs of Small and Large Businesses*

Reveal Their Secrets. 187-191. Piscataway, N.J.: Research and Education Association, 1998.

JONES, ARTHUR

Landrum, Gene N. "Arthur Jones—Rebellious." In *Profiles of Genius: Thirteen Creative Men Who Changed the World*, 201-212. Buffalo, N.Y.: Prometheus Books, 1993.

Nayak, P. Ranganath, and John M. Ketteringham. "Nautilus: The Unfinished Breakthrough." In *Breakthroughs!*, 251-275. San Diego, Calif.: Pfeiffer & Company, 1994.

JONES, BARON

Gardner, Ralph. "Baron Jones." In *Young, Gifted, and Rich: The Secrets of America's Most Successful Entrepreneurs*, 131-142. New York, N.Y.: Wallaby Books, 1984.

JONES, CHRISTINA

Ericksen, Gregory K. "Christina Jones—pcOrder 'Such a Great Opportunity'." In *Net Entrepreneurs Only : 10 Entrepreneurs Tell the Stories of Their Success*, 41-60. New York : John Wiley, 2000.

JONES, DARLA

Lassen, Ali. "Darla Jones: Sales Director, Environment Network." In *The Secret of Their Success: Women Entrepreneurs Reveal How They Made It*, 97-102. Carlsbad, Calif.: Ali Lassen Success System, 1990.

JONES, GREGORY K.

Ericksen, Gregory K. "Gregory K. Jones—uBid, Inc. 'Where the Customer Can Set the Price'." In *Net Entrepreneurs Only : 10 Entrepreneurs Tell the Stories of Their Success*, 81-100. New York : John Wiley, 2000.

JONES, MARY

Jones, Mary. "Entrepreneurship: Passion, Belief, Perspective." In *How I Became a Nurse Entrepreneur: Tales from 50 Nurses in Business*, 113-120. Petaluma, Calif.: National Nurses in Business Association, 1991.

JONES, NEIL

Mitchell, Niki Butler. "Information Systems for the Millennium: Neil Jones, President and CEO, M-Cubed Information Systems, Inc." In *The New Color of Success: Twenty Young Black Millionaires Tell You How They're Making it*, 107-117. Rocklin, Calif.: Prima Publishing, 2000.

JONES, REGINALD H.

Levinson, Harry, and Stuart Rosenthal. "Reginald H. Jones." In *CEO: Corporate Leadership in Action*, 16-55. New York, N.Y: Basic Books, 1984.

Shook, Robert L. "Reginald H. Jones: General Electric Company." In *The Chief Executive Officers: Men Who Run Big Business in America*, 77-100. New York, N.Y.: Harper & Row, 1981.

JONES, TOM

Clarke, Caroline V. "Tom Jones: Chairman and CEO, Global Investment Management and Private Banking Group, Citigroup Inc." In *Take a Lesson: Today's Black Achievers and How They Made It and What They Learned Along the Way*, 79-91. New York, N.Y.: Wiley, 2001.

JONES, W. ALTON

Sparkes, Boydon. "W. Alton Jones." In *America's Fifty Foremost Business Leaders,* ed. B. C. Forbes, 233-242. New York, N.Y.: B.C. Forbes, 1948.

JORDAN, JAY

Kingston, Brett. "Jay Jordan of the Jordan Company." In *The Dynamos: Who Are They Anyway?*, 123-126. New York, N.Y.: William Morrow & Co., 1999.

JORDANO, ROSEMARY

Oster, Merrill J. "Kid Stuff." In *The Entrepreneur's Creed: The Principles & Passions of 20 Successful Entrepreneurs*, 88-99. Nashville, Tenn.: Broadman & Holman Publishers, 2001.

JOSEPH, ROBERT D.

Gray, Bob, ed. "The Careful Business Broker." In *How Entrepreneurs Make Business Profits: A Study of Personal Success Stories From Cordovan Business Journals*, 150- Houston, Tex.: Cordovan Press, 1982.

JOY, BILL

Kingston, Brett. "Andreas Bechtolsheim, Vinod Khosla, Bill Joy, and Scott McNealy of the SUN Microsystems Team." In *The Dynamos: Who Are They Anyway?*, 49-60. New York, N.Y.: Wiley, 1987.

JUDAH, THEODORE DEHONE

Lewis, Oscar. "Judah: 'I Have Always Had to Pit My Brains…Against Other Men's Money…'." In *The Big Four; The Story of Huntington, Stanford, Hopkins, and Crocker, And of the Building of the Central Pacific*, 3-48. New York, N.Y.: A.A. Knopf, 1938.

JURAN, JOSEPH MOSES

Wren, Daniel A., and Ronald G. Greenwood. "Joseph Moses Juran." In *Management Innovators: The People and Ideas That Have Shaped Modern Business*, 213-217. New York, N.Y.: Oxford University Press, 1998.

KAHN, PHILIPPE

Kingston, Brett. "Philippe Kahn of Borland International." In *The Dynamos: Who Are They Anyway?*, 123-127. New York, N.Y: Wiley, 1987.

KAISER, HENRY J.

Beck, Warren A., and Susanne T. Gaskins. "Henry J. Kaiser—Entrepreneur of the American West." In *Business Entrepreneurs in the West*, ed. Ted C. Hinckley, 64-72. Manhattan, Kans.: Sunflower University Press, 1986.

Bell, Laurence. "Henry J. Kaiser." In *America's Fifty Foremost Business Leaders,* ed. B. C. Forbes, 243-250. New York, N.Y.: B.C. Forbes, 1948. 483 p.

Brands, H. W. "The Faith That Launched a Thousand Ships: Henry J. Kaiser." In *Masters of Enterprise: Giants of American Business from John Jacob Astor and J.P. Morgan to Bill Gates and Oprah Winfrey*, 134-151. New York, N.Y.: Free Press, 1999.

KAPLAN, JUDITH

Aronoff, Craig E., and John L. Ward. "Judith Kaplan." In *Contemporary Entrepreneurs*, 270-276. Detroit, Mich.: Omnigraphics, Inc., 1992.

KARAN, DONNA

Agins, Teri. "Gored in a Bull Market: When Donna Karan Went to Wall Street." In *The End of Fashion: The Mass Marketing of the Clothing Business*, 200-246. New York, N.Y.: William Morrow, 1999.

KATZ, JOSEPH

Uris, Auren. "Joseph Katz—He Wraps Up Christmas." In *The Executive Breakthrough; 21 Roads to the Top*, 3-16. Garden City, N.Y.: Doubleday, 1967.

KATZENBERG, JEFFREY

Auletta, Ken. "The Human Factor; Troubles in Disneyland." In *The Highwaymen; Warriors of the Information Superhighway*, 230-247. New York, N.Y.: Random House, 1997.

KAUFFMAN FAMILY

Pottker, Jan. "Marion Merrell Dow, Inc.: You Gotta Have Heart." In *Born to Power: Heirs to America's Leading Businesses*, 314-318. New York, N.Y.: Barron's, 1992.

Silver, A. David. "Ewing Marion Kauffman." In *Entrepreneurial Megabucks: The 100 Greatest Entrepreneurs of the Last 25 Years*, 254-257. New York, N.Y.: Wiley, 1985.

KAVOVIT, BARBARA

Suarez, Ruth. "Barbara Kavovit: Anchor Construction, Inc., 'Tapping into the Boys' Club'." In *Superstar Entrepreneurs of Small and Large Businesses Reveal Their Secrets*, 71-75. Piscataway, N.J.: Research and Education Association, 1998.

KEENE, JAMES R.

Burnley, James. "James R. Keene: The King of the 'Bears'." In *Millionaires and Kings of Enterprise; The Marvellous Careers of Some Americans Who by Pluck, Foresight, And Energy Have Made Themselves Masters in the Fields of Industry and Finance*, 224-231. Philadelphia, Penn.: J. B. Lippincott, 1901.

KEENER, RICHARD N.

Case, John. "Hot Seats; Building Eurostyle Chairs for the Corporate Elite." In *Anatomy of a Start-Up: Why Some New Businesses Succeed and Others Fail: 27 Real-Life Case Studies,* ed. Elizabeth K. Longsworth, 191-200. Boston, Mass.: Inc. Publishing, 1991.

KELLER, K. T.

Finley, Bob. "K. T. Keller." In *America's Fifty Foremost Business Leaders*, ed. B. C. Forbes, 251-262. New York, N.Y.: B.C. Forbes, 1948.

KELLOGG, WILL KEITH

Folsom, Burton W. "Will Kellogg and the Cornflake Crusade." In *Empire Builders: How Michigan Entrepreneurs Helped Make America Great*, 115-138. Traverse City, Mich.: Rhodes & Easton, 1998.

KELLY, FRANCIS "FRAN" J. III

Liberman, Gail, and Alan Lavine. "Francis 'Fran' J. Kelly III: Advertising Marketer Selects Right Career." In *Rags to Riches: Motivating Stories of How Ordinary People Achieved Extraordinary Wealth!*, 41-53. Chicago, Ill.: Dearborn, 2000.

KELLY, MARJORIE

Alexander, Shoshana. "Marjorie Kelly: Business Ethics Magazine, Minneapolis, Minnesota." In *Women's Ventures, Women's Visions: 29 Inspiring Stories From Women Who Started Their Own Businesses*, 180-186. Freedom, Calif.: The Crossing Press, 1997.

"Cereal Story: W.K. Kellogg Sired Packaged Cold Cereal Flakes, Revolutionized Nation's Breakfast Habits, And Started the Trend Toward 'Convenience' Foods." In *The 50 Great Pioneers of American Industry*. By the Editors of News Front and Year, 166-168. Maplewood, N.J.: C.S. Hammond, 1964.

KELLY, THOMAS L. JR.

Silver, A. David. "Thomas L. Kelly Jr." In *Entrepreneurial Megabucks: The 100 Greatest Entrepreneurs of the Last 25 Years*, 258-260. New York, N.Y.: Wiley, 1985.

KELLY, WILLIAM RUSSELL

Uris, Auren. "William Russell Kelly—The Man with Eighty Thousand

Secretaries." In *The Executive Breakthrough; 21 Roads to the Top*, 207-219. Garden City, N.Y.: Doubleday, 1967.

KENDALL, B. J.

Lassen, Ali. "B. J. Kendall: Consultant, Image Enhancement, Partner, Clean Connecions, And Property Management." In *The Secret of Their Success: Women Entrepreneurs Reveal How They Made It*, 51-54. Carlsbad, Calif.: Ali Lassen Success System, 1990.

KENDALL, DONALD M.

Uris, Auren. "Donald M. Kendall—Hard Cash in a Soft Drink." In *The Executive Breakthrough; 21 Roads to the Top*, 45-53. Garden City, N.Y.: Doubleday, 1967.

KENNEDY, JIM COX

Coleridge, Nicholas. "Little Empire on the Prairie: Jim Cox Kennedy's Atlanta Constitution." In *Paper Tigers: The Latest, Greatest Newspaper Tycoons*, 179-199. New York, N.Y.: Carol Publishing Group, 1994.

KENNEDY, JOE II

Gardner, Ralph. "Joe Kennedy II." In *Young, Gifted, and Rich: The Secrets of America's Most Successful Entrepreneurs*, 65-78. New York, N.Y.: Wallaby Books, 1984.

KESSLER, HOWARD

Posner Bruce G. "Good Vibrations; A New Recording Studio Stakes Its Pitch on Service, But Will Its Customers Care?" In *Anatomy of a Start-Up: Why Some New Businesses Succeed and Others Fail: 27 Real-Life Case Studies,* ed. Elizabeth K. Longsworth, 46-55. Boston, Mass.: Inc. Publishing, 1991.

KESSLER, RICHARD C.

Silver, A. David. "Cecil B. Day; Richard C. Kessler." In *Entrepreneurial Megabucks: The 100 Greatest Entrepreneurs of the Last 25 Years*, 178-180. New York, N.Y.: Wiley, 1985.

KESSMAN, ALAN

Aronoff, Craig E., and John L. Ward. "Alan Kessman." In *Contemporary Entrepreneurs*, 277-283. Detroit, Mich.: Omnigraphics, Inc., 1992.

KHOSLA, VINOD

Kingston, Brett. "Andreas Bechtolsheim, Vinod Khosla, Bill Joy, and Scott McNealy of the SUN Microsystems Team." In *The Dynamos: Who Are They Anyway?*, 49-60. New York, N.Y.: Wiley, 1987.

KHOURY, AMIN J.

Silver, A. David. "Amin J. Khoury." In *Entrepreneurial Megabucks: The 100 Greatest Entrepreneurs of the Last 25 Years*, 261-263. New York, N.Y.: Wiley, 1985.

KIELBASA, MAUREEN GREICHEN

Mikaelian, A. "Maureen Greichen Kielbasa." In *Women Who Mean Business: Success Stories of Women Over Forty*, 272-276. New York, N.Y.: William Morrow & Co., 1999.

KIGHT, PETE

Suarez, Ruth. "Pete Kight: Checkfree, 'Automatic Withdrawal of the Competition'." In *Superstar Entrepreneurs of Small and Large Businesses Reveal Their Secrets*, 35-41. Piscataway, N.J.: Research and Education Association, 1998.

KILBY, JACK

Slater, Robert. "Jack Kilby: Co-Inventor of the Integrated Circuit." In *Portraits in Silicon*, 162-173. Cambridge, Mass.: MIT

Press, 1987.

KILDALL, GARY

Slater, Robert. "Gary Kildall: Making It Easier to Use a Computer—With CP/M." In *Portraits in Silicon*, 250-261. Cambridge, Mass.: MIT Press, 1987.

KIMBRELL, W. DAVID

Aronoff, Craig E., and John L. Ward. "W. David Kimbrell." In *Contemporary Entrepreneurs*, 284-290. Detroit, Mich.: Omnigraphics, Inc., 1992.

KING, DON

Farnham, Alan. "Don King: Founder of Don King Productions, 'I Totally Eradicated the Word Failure from My Vocabulary'." In *Forbes Great Success Stories: Twelve Tales of Victory Wrested from Defeat*, 148-167. New York, N.Y.: Wiley, 2000.

KING, MICHAEL

Pottker, Jan. "King World Productions, Inc.: Will the Wheel of Fortune Turn?" In *Born to Power: Heirs to America's Leading Businesses*, 20-27. New York, N.Y.: Barron's, 1992.

KING, ROGER

Pottker, Jan. "King World Productions, Inc.: Will the Wheel of Fortune Turn?" In *Born to Power: Heirs to America's Leading Businesses*, 20-27. New York, N.Y.: Barron's, 1992.

KING, SHARON

Koppel, Mara. "Lion Trade—Sharon King." In *Women of the Pits: Shattering the Glass Ceiling in Financial Markets*, 91-106. Chicago, Ill.: Dearborn Financial Publishers, 1998.

KIPLINGER, KNIGHT A.

Pottker, Jan. "The Kiplinger Washington Editors, Inc.: Financing the Future." In *Born to Power: Heirs to America's Leading Businesses*, 178-186. New York, N.Y.: Barron's, 1992.

KIPLINGER, TODD

Pottker, Jan. "The Kiplinger Washington Editors, Inc.: Financing the Future." In *Born to Power: Heirs to America's Leading Businesses*, 178-186. New York, N.Y.: Barron's, 1992.

KIRSCH, STEVE

Kingston, Brett. "Steve Kirsch of Mouse Systems Corporation." In *The Dynamos: Who Are They Anyway?*, 77-83. New York, N.Y.: Wiley, 1987.

Price, Christopher. "Steve Kirsch—Infoseek 'Altruism Born of Technology Talent'." In *The Internet Entrepreneurs: Business Rules Are Good: Break Them*, 112-125. London, Eng.: FT.com, 2000.

KITTLE, PAUL A.

Finegan, Jay. "Down in the Dump; We're Quickly Running Out of Room for Our Solid Waste, And Innovative Companies Like Rusmar, Inc. Stand to Get Rich. But Can This Start-Up First Navigate Through a Maze of Government Regulations?" In *Anatomy of a Start-Up: Why Some New Businesses Succeed and Others Fail: 27 Real-Life Case Studies,* ed. Elizabeth K. Longsworth, 291-299. Boston, Mass.: Inc. Publishing, 1991.

KLEIMAN, HARLAN

Richman, Tom. "Hollywood Shuffle; Filmstar Inc. Is Out to Free Hollywood Procedures from the Studios' Stranglehold. But Will Producers Take the Risk?" In *Anatomy of a Start-Up: Why Some New Businesses Succeed and Others Fail: 27 Real-Life Case Studies,* ed. Elizabeth K. Longsworth, 73-83. Boston, Mass.: Inc. Publishing, 1991.

KLEIN, RAPHAEL

Silver, A. David. "Raphael Klein." In *Entrepreneurial Megabucks: The 100 Greatest Entrepreneurs of the Last 25 Years*, 264-266. New York, N.Y.: Wiley, 1985.

KLINGER, KATHRYN

Pottker, Jan. "Georgette Klinger Salons, Inc.: Monday's Child." In *Born to Power: Heirs to America's Leading Businesses*, 244-253. New York, N.Y.: Barron's, 1992.

KLIPSCH, PAUL

MacPhee, William. "Paul Klipsch of Klipsch Loudspeaker Systems." In *Rare Breed: The Entrepreneur, An American Culture*, 79-88. Chicago, Ill.: Probus Publishing Company, 1987.

KLUGE, JOHN WERNER

Klepper, Michael M., and Robert Gunther. "John Werner Kluge (1914-): High-Tech High Roller." In *The Wealthy 100 : From Benjamin Franklin to Bill Gates—A Ranking of the Richest Americans, Past and Present*, 242-245. Secaucus, N.J. : Carol Pub. Group, 1996.

KNERR, RICHARD "RICH"

Shook, Robert L. "The Hula Hoop Toy, The Frisbee Disc, And the Super Ball Toy." In *Why Didn't I Think of That*, 50-65. New York, N.Y.: New American Library, 1982.

KNIGHT, CHARLES L.

Cose, Ellis. "The Chains: Gannett and Knight-Ridder." In *The Press*, 281-356. New York, N.Y.: Morrow, 1989.

KNIGHT, PHILIP H.

Brands, H. W. "Just Do It: Phil Knight." In *Masters of Enterprise: Giants of American Business from John Jacob Astor and J.P. Morgan to Bill Gates and Oprah Winfrey*, 256-266. New York, N.Y.: Free Press, 1999.

Nayak, P. Ranganath, and John M. Ketteringham. "Nike: The Competitive Response." In *Breakthroughs!*, 227-250. San Diego, Calif.: Pfeiffer & Company, 1994.

Silver, A. David. "Philip H. Knight." In *Entrepreneurial Megabucks: The 100 Greatest Entrepreneurs of the Last 25 Years*, 267-269. New York, N.Y.: Wiley, 1985.

KNOX, ROSE

Forbes, Malcolm S. "Rose Knox, 'America's Foremost Women Industrialist'." In *Women Who Made a Difference*, 153-155. New York, N.Y.: Simon & Schuster, 1990.

KOCH FAMILY

Pottker, Jan. "Koch Industries, Inc.: Blood, Oil, and Money." In *Born to Power: Heirs to America's Leading Businesses*, 376-382. New York, N.Y.: Barron's, 1992.

KOCH, JIM

Aronoff, Craig E., and John L. Ward. "James Koch." In *Contemporary Entrepreneurs*, 291-296. Detroit, Mich.: Omnigraphics, Inc., 1992.

Ericksen, Gregory K. "Jim Koch: The Boston Beer Company, 'I Wanted to Make a Great Beer'." In *What's Luck Got to Do with It; Twelve Entrepreneurs Reveal the Secrets Behind Their Success*, 43-60. New York, N.Y.: Wiley, 1997.

KOHLBERG, JEROME JR

Smith, Roy C. "The Buyout Kings." In *Wealth Creators: The Rise of Today's Rich and Super-Rich*, 113-122. New York, N.Y.: Truman

Talley, 2001.

KOHLER, JOSEPH

Levitt, Mortimer. "Joseph Kohler: A 'Burma Shave' Advertising Twist Worth $2.5 Million." In *How to Start Your Own Business Without Losing Your Shirt; Secrets of Seventeen Successful Entrepreneurs*, 61-68. New York, N.Y: Atheneum, 1988.

KOMANSKY, DAVID H.

Wendel, Charles B. "Inheriting the Mantle: David H. Komansky, President and CEO, Merrill Lynch & Co., Inc.." In *The New Financiers*, 133-151. Chicago, Ill.: Irwin Professional Pub., 1996.

KOPPEL, ROBERT

Koppel, Robert. "A Personal Tale." In *Bulls, Bears, And Millionaires: War Stories of Trading Life*, 1-7. Chicago, Ill.: Dearborn Financial Publishers, 1997.

KOSOWSKY, DAVID I.

Silver, A. David. "David I. Kosowsky." In *Entrepreneurial Megabucks: The 100 Greatest Entrepreneurs of the Last 25 Years*, 270-272. New York, N.Y.: Wiley, 1985.

KOSS FAMILY

Buchholz, Barbara B., and Margaret Crane. "Koss Corporation, Milwaukee, WI." In *Corporate Blood Lines: The Future of the Family Firm*, 175-192. New York, N.Y: Carol Publishing Group, 1989.

KOVACEVICH, RICHARD M.

Wendel, Charles B. "Creating a Nonbank Mentality—Within a Bank: Richard M. Kovacevich, Chairman & CEO, Norwest Corporation." In *The New Financiers*, 153-169. Chicago, Ill.: Irwin Professional Pub., 1996.

KRAUS, JOE

Price, Christopher. "Joe Kraus—Excite 'Passion and Commitment to a Business Ideal'." In *The Internet Entrepreneurs: Business Rules Are Good: Break Them*, 142-159. London, Eng.: FT.com, 2000.

KRAVIS, HENRY

Gross, Daniel, and the Editors of Forbes Magazine. "Kohlberg Kravis Roberts & Co. and the Leveraged Buyout." In *Forbes Greatest Business Stories of All Time*, 314-333. New York, N.Y.: Wiley, 1996.

KRAY, MARGRETTA

Kray, Margretta, and Valerie Nielsen. "Let's Get Down to Business: The Story of N.P.A." In *How I Became a Nurse Entrepreneur: Tales from 50 Nurses in Business*, 215-219. Petaluma, Calif.: National Nurses in Business Association, 1991.

KRIEBLE, VERNON K.

Fucini, Joseph J., and Suzy Fucini. "Vernon K. Krieble, Loctite Corporation: 'Work is Too Much Fun to Give Up'." In *Experience Inc.; Men and Women Who Founded Famous Companies After the Age of 40*, 200-206. New York, N.Y: Free Press, 1987.

KROC, RAY

Brands, H. W. "Sweating Burgers: Ray Kroc." In *Masters of Enterprise: Giants of American Business from John Jacob Astor and J.P. Morgan to Bill Gates and Oprah Winfrey*, 2111-222. New York, N.Y.: Free Press, 1999.

Davis, William. "Ray Kroc, b. 1902-1984: Popularizer of Franchising." In *The Innovators: The Essential Guide to Business Thinkers, Achievers and Entrepreneurs*, 215-221. New York, N.Y.: AMACOM, 1987.

Gross, Daniel, and the Editors of Forbes Magazine. "Ray Kroc, McDonald's, And the Fast-Food Industry." In *Forbes Greatest*

Business Stories of All Time, 176-192. New York, N.Y.: Wiley, 1996.

Hinckley. Ted C., and Roderick C. Johnson. "Ray Kroc, Embodiment of Mid-Twentieth Century America." In *Business Entrepreneurs in the West*, ed. Ted C. Hinckley, 94-102. Manhattan, Kans.: Sunflower University Press, 1986.

Lukas, J. Anthony. "Ray Kroc: One-Hundred Million Dollars." In *The Very, Very Rich and How They Got That Way*, ed. Max Gunther, 256-275. Chicago, Ill.: The Playboy Press, 1972.

Mariotti, Steve, and Lorraine Mooney. "Ray Kroc: McDonald's Magnate." In *Entrepreneurs in Profile*, 106-108. London: National Foundation for Teaching Entrepreneurship, 1991.

Mariotti, Steve, and Mike Caslin. "Ray Kroc: McDonald's." In *The Very Very Rich: How They Got That Way and How You Can, Too!*, 71-74. Franklin Lakes, NJ: Career Press, 2000.

Shook, Carrie, and Robert L. Shook. "McDonald's Corporation: The Franchisor That Has Influenced the Culture of the World." In *Franchising: The Business Strategy That Changed the World*, 139-166. Englewood Cliffs, NJ: Prentice Hall, 1993.

Silver, A. David. "Raymond A. Kroc." In *Entrepreneurial Megabucks: The 100 Greatest Entrepreneurs of the Last 25 Years*, 273-275. New York, N.Y.: Wiley, 1985.

KROFTA, MILOS

Gilder, George. "The Man Who Wanted to Clean the Water." In *The Spirit of Enterprise*, 71-92. New York, N.Y: Simon and Schuster, 1984.

KROLL, BARBARA NELSON

Kroll, Barbara Nelson. "Openness and Flexibility: A Nurse Entrepreneur." In *How I Became a Nurse Entrepreneur: Tales from 50 Nurses in Business*, 295-298. Petaluma, Calif.: National Nurses in Business Association, 1991.

KROLL, STANLEY

Train, John. "Stanley Kroll: 'We Who Are About to Die...'." In *The Money Masters*, 114-138. New York, N.Y.: Harper & Row, 1980.

KUGLEN, FRANCESCA

Suarez, Ruth. "Francesca Kuglen—Jontee, 'Guerilla Warfare with Green Barrettes'." In *Superstar Entrepreneurs of Small and Large Businesses Reveal Their Secrets*. 193-202. Piscataway, N.J.: Research and Education Association, 1998.

KUPERSTEIN, MICHAEL

Welles, Edward O. "Decisions, Decisions; Unschooled in the Ways of Commerce, Scientist Michael Kuperstein Finds Himself the Owner of a Technology with Unlimited Applications. Now All He Needs to Do Is Choose the Right Niche." In *Anatomy of a Start-Up: Why Some New Businesses Succeed and Others Fail: 27 Real-Life Case Studies,* ed. Elizabeth K. Longsworth, 278-287. Boston, Mass.: Inc. Publishing, 1991.

KUPRIONIS, M. DENISE

Mikaelian, A. "M. Denise Kuprionis, Esq." In *Women Who Mean Business: Success Stories of Women Over Forty*, 247-251. New York, N.Y.: William Morrow & Co., 1999.

KURTZIG, SANDRA L.

Jager, Rama Dev, and Rafael Ortiz. "Sandy Kurtzig, ASK: Go for It!" In *In the Company of Giants: Candid Conversations with the Visionaries of the Digital World*, 87-98. New York, N.Y.: McGraw-Hill, 1997.

Silver, A. David. "Sandra L. Kurtzig." In *Entrepreneurial Megabucks: The 100 Greatest Entrepreneurs of the Last 25 Years*, 276-278. New York, N.Y.: Wiley, 1985.

KURZWEIL, RAYMOND C.

Aronoff, Craig E., and John L. Ward. "Raymond C. Kurzweil." In *Contemporary Entrepreneurs*, 297-303. Detroit, Mich.: Omnigraphics, Inc., 1992.

LA MAGNA, DAL

Liberman, Gail, and Alan Lavine. "Dal La Magna: Failing Entrepreneur Succeeds with Tweezer Business." In *Rags to Riches: Motivating Stories of How Ordinary People Achieved Extraordinary Wealth!*, 100-116. Chicago, Ill.: Dearborn, 2000.

LABRECQUE, FRANCIS

Silver, A. David. "Francis Labrecque." In *Entrepreneurial Megabucks: The 100 Greatest Entrepreneurs of the Last 25 Years*, 279-281. New York, N.Y.: Wiley, 1985.

LAFORGE, MARGARET GETCHELL

Forbes, Malcolm S. "Margaret Getchell LaForge, 'She Ran Macy's Department Store'." In *Women Who Made a Difference*, 160-162. New York, N.Y.: Simon & Schuster, 1990.

LAKER, FREDDIE

Davis, William. "Freddie Laker, b.1922: Revolutionary of the Aviation Industry." In *The Innovators: The Essential Guide to Business Thinkers, Achievers and Entrepreneurs*, 221-224. New York, N.Y.: AMACOM, 1987.

LAMB, DICK

Buchholz, Barbara B., and Margaret Crane. "Blake-Lamb Funeral Homes, Oak Park, IL." In *Corporate Blood Lines: The Future of the Family Firm*, 212-228. New York, N.Y: Carol Publishing Group, 1989.

LAMB, MATT III

Buchholz, Barbara B., and Margaret Crane. "Blake-Lamb Funeral Homes, Oak Park, IL." In *Corporate Blood Lines: The Future of the Family Firm*, 212-228. New York, N.Y: Carol Publishing Group, 1989.

LAMONT, BARBARA

Fraser, Jill Andresky. "Broadcast News; Can Positioning Yourself As the Low-Cost Producer Work in Television Broadcasting?" In *Anatomy of a Start-Up: Why Some New Businesses Succeed and Others Fail: 27 Real-Life Case Studies,* ed. Elizabeth K. Longsworth, 316-324. Boston, Mass.: Inc. Publishing, 1991.

LAND, EDWIN H.

Bello, Francis. "Edwin H. Land: Five-Hundred Million Dollars." In *The Very, Very Rich and How They Got That Way*, ed. Max Gunther, 162-175. Chicago, Ill.: The Playboy Press, 1972.

Davis, William. "Edwin Land, b. 1909: Inventor of the Instant Camera." In *The Innovators: The Essential Guide to Business Thinkers, Achievers and Entrepreneurs*, 225-227. New York, N.Y.: AMACOM, 1987.

Livesay, Harold C. "The Philosopher Scientist: Edwin Land." In *American Made: Men Who Shaped the American Economy*, 268-288. Boston, Mass.: Little, Brown, 1979.

LANDAU, RALPH

Landau, Ralph. "Entrepreneurs, Managers, and the Importance of Finance." In *The Power of Boldness: Ten Master Builders of American Industry Tell Their Success Stories*, ed. Elkan Blout, 41-60. Washington, D.C.: Joseph Henry Press, 1996.

LANE, EDWARD HUDSON

Cleary, David Powers. "Lane Cedar Chests; Make a Good Product, And Sell with an Idea." In *Great American Brands: The Success Formulas That*

Made Them Famous, 202-210. New York, N.Y: Fairchild Publications, 1981.

LANE, JENAI

Alexander, Shoshana. "Jenai Lane: Respect, San Francisco, California." In *Women's Ventures, Women's Visions: 29 Inspiring Stories From Women Who Started Their Own Businesses*, 153-160. Freedom, Calif.: The Crossing Press, 1997.

LANG, DALE W.

Shook, Robert L. "Dale W. Lang." In *The Entrepreneurs: Twelve Who Took Risks and Succeeded*, 53-65. New York, N.Y: Harper & Row, 1980.

LANE, KENNETH JAY

Levitt, Mortimer. "Kenneth Jay Lane: An Eye for Fashion Trends Finds a Gold Mine in Rhinestones." In *How to Start Your Own Business Without Losing Your Shirt; Secrets of Seventeen Successful Entrepreneurs*, 77-84. New York, N.Y: Atheneum, 1988.

LANSBURGH, DAVID

Koppel, Robert. "West of Eden: David Lansburgh." In *Bulls, Bears, And Millionaires: War Stories of Trading Life*, 157-166. Chicago, Ill.: Dearborn Financial Publishers, 1997.

LARDON, DENNIS L.

Liberman, Gail, and Alan Lavine. "Dennis L. Lardon: Ramp Agent Grows with Southwest Airlines." In *Rags to Riches: Motivating Stories of How Ordinary People Achieved Extraordinary Wealth!*, 175-183. Chicago, Ill.: Dearborn, 2000.

LARSEN, TERRENCE A.

Wendel, Charles B. "Adhering to Core Values and Business Strategies: Terrence A. Larsen, Chairman & CEO, CoreStates Financial

Corporation." In *The New Financiers*, 171-194. Chicago, Ill.: Irwin Professional Pub., 1996.

LAU, JOANNA

Ericksen, Gregory K. "Joanna Lau: LAU Technologies, 'You Need to Be in a State of Readiness'." In *What's Luck Got to Do with It; Twelve Entrepreneurs Reveal the Secrets Behind Their Success*, 61-80. New York, N.Y.: Wiley, 1997.

LAUDER, ESTÉE

Koehn, Nancy F. "Estée Lauder." In *Brand New: How Entrepreneurs Earned Consumers' Trust from Wedgwood to Dell*, 137-199. Boston, Mass.: Harvard Business School Press, 2001.

Landrum, Gene N. "Estée Lauder—Impatient Overachiever." In *Profiles of Female Genius: Thirteen Creative Women Who Changed the World*, 244-259. Amherst, N.Y.: Prometheus Books, 1994.

Taylor, Russel R. "Estée Lauder; High Priestess of Cosmetics." In *Exceptional Entrepreneurial Women*, 111-119. New York, N.Y: Quorum Books, 1988.

LAUDER, WILLIAM

Pottker, Jan. "Estee Lauder, Inc.: Will Green Turn to Gold?" In *Born to Power: Heirs to America's Leading Businesses*, 260-269. New York, N.Y.: Barron's, 1992.

LAUREN, RALPH

Agins, Teri. "Bound for Glory: Ralph Lauren and Tommy Hilfiger." In *The End of Fashion: The Mass Marketing of the Clothing Business*, 80-126. New York, N.Y.: William Morrow, 1999.

LAUTENBERG, FRANK

Silver, A. David. "Henry Taub; Frank Lautenberg; Joseph Taub." In *Entrepreneurial Megabucks: The 100 Greatest Entrepreneurs of the Last 25 Years*, 423-425. New York, N.Y.: Wiley, 1985.

LAZARUS, CHARLES

Silver, A. David. "Charles Lazarus." In *Entrepreneurial Megabucks: The 100 Greatest Entrepreneurs of the Last 25 Years*, 282-284. New York, N.Y.: Wiley, 1985.

LAZARUS, FRED R. JR.

"Expanding with Confidence: Fred R. Lazarus Jr." In *Lessons of Leadership: 21 Executives Speak Out on Creating, Developing and Managing Success*. Presented by the editors of Nation's Business, 15-31. Garden City, N.Y.: Doubleday, 1968.

LAZARUS, RALPH

Shook, Robert L. "Ralph Lazarus: Federated Department Stores." In *The Chief Executive Officers: Men Who Run Big Business in America*, 101-122. New York, N.Y.: Harper & Row, 1981.

LAZZARA FAMILY

Buchholz, Barbara B., and Margaret Crane. "Lazzara Optical, Villa Park, IL." In *Corporate Blood Lines: The Future of the Family Firm*, 29-42. New York, N.Y: Carol Publishing Group, 1989.

LEACH, SHERYL

Ericksen, Gregory K. "Sheryl Leach—Barney, 'Business Is Common Sense'." In *Women Entrepreneurs Only: Twelve Women Entrepreneurs Tell The Stories of Their Success*, 1-21. New York, N.Y.: Wiley, 1999.

LEAR, WILLIAM

Davis, William. "William Lear, 1902-1978: The Classic Inventor-Entrepreneur." In *The Innovators: The Essential Guide to Business Thinkers, Achievers and Entrepreneurs*, 227-229. New York, N.Y.: AMACOM, 1987.

Gilmore, C. P. "William Lear: Two-Hundred Million Dollars." In *The Very, Very Rich and How They Got That Way*, ed. Max Gunther, 146-160. Chicago, Ill.: The Playboy Press, 1972.

Landrum, Gene N. "William Lear—Passionette." In *Profiles of Genius: Thirteen Creative Men Who Changed the World*, 167-179. Buffalo, N.Y.: Prometheus Books, 1993.

LECKIE, JIM

Elfstrand, Rhonda. "Jim Leckie: Family Ministries, Inc." In *The Story Behind the Success: Learning From Pittsburgh Professionals*, 168-183. Pittsburgh, Penn.: Steel Publishing Partners, 1996.

LECLAIR, CORA

LeClair, Cora. "Maybe I Can..." In *How I Became a Nurse Entrepreneur: Tales from 50 Nurses in Business*, 129-133. Petaluma, Calif.: National Nurses in Business Association, 1991.

LEE, DEBRA L.

Clarke, Caroline V. "Debra L. Lee: President and Chief Operating Officer, BET Holdings Inc.." In *Take a Lesson: Today's Black Achievers and How They Made It and What They Learned Along the Way*, 93-103. New York, N.Y.: Wiley, 2001.

LEE, IVY LEDBETTER

"Image Maker for PR: Ivy Lee Persuaded U.S. Industry That Good Public Relations Is Good Business, Raised PR Man's Status in Eyes of Public." In *The 50 Great Pioneers of American Industry*. By the Editors of

News Front and Year, 163-165. Maplewood, N.J.: C.S. Hammond, 1964.

LEE, SPIKE

Clarke, Caroline V. "Spike Lee: CEO, Forty Acres and a Mule." In *Take a Lesson: Today's Black Achievers and How They Made It and What They Learned Along the Way*, 105-112. New York, N.Y.: Wiley, 2001.

Mariotti, Steve, and Mike Caslin. "Spike Lee, 40 Acres and a Mule: The Artist As Entrepreneur." In *The Very Very Rich: How They Got That Way and How You Can, Too!*, 75-80. Franklin Lakes, NJ: Career Press, 2000.

LEEBOW, STEVEN B.

Aronoff, Craig E., and John L. Ward. "Steven B. Leebow." In *Contemporary Entrepreneurs*, 305-311. Detroit, Mich.: Omnigraphics, Inc., 1992.

LEHMAN, JAY

Lehman, Celia. "Jay Lehman: Successful Alternatives." In *Entrepreneurs in the Faith Community: Profiles of Mennonites in Business*, ed. Calvin W. Redekop, and Benjamin W. Redekop, 181-195. Scottdale, Penn.: Herald Press, 1996.

LEIGHTON, CHARLIE

Kao, John J. "Managing Entrepreneurship at the CML Group." In *The Entrepreneur*, 155-163. Englewood Cliffs, New Jersey: Prentice Hall, 1991.

LEITER, LEVI Z.

Burnley, James. "Levi Z. Leiter: An American Nabob." In *Millionaires and Kings of Enterprise; The Marvellous Careers of Some Americans Who by Pluck, Foresight, And Energy Have Made Themselves Masters in the Fields of Industry and Finance*, 110-121. Philadelphia, Penn.: J. B. Lippincott, 1901.

LENYOUN, ESTEAN H. III

Oster, Merrill J. "Diamonds in the Rough." In *The Entrepreneur's Creed: The Principles & Passions of 20 Successful Entrepreneurs*, 152-161. Nashville, Tenn.: Broadman & Holman Publishers, 2001.

LEONARD, STEW

Levitt, Mortimer. "Stew Leonard: Selling Milk and Groceries in a 'Magic Kingdom' Setting." In *How to Start Your Own Business Without Losing Your Shirt; Secrets of Seventeen Successful Entrepreneurs*, 85-95. New York, N.Y: Atheneum, 1988.

LEONSIS, TED

Kingston, Brett. "Ted Leonsis of Redgate Communications Corporation." In *The Dynamos: Who Are They Anyway?*, 217-223. New York, N.Y.: Wiley, 1987.

LETTERMAN, JERRY

Koppel, Robert. "The Comeback Kid: Jerry Letterman." In *Bulls, Bears, And Millionaires: War Stories of Trading Life*, 149-156. Chicago, Ill.: Dearborn Financial Publishers, 1997.

LEVINE, BILL

Fucini, Joseph J., and Suzy Fucini. "Bill Levine, Postal Instant Press: 'I Saw a Good Opportunity and I Jumped in'." In *Experience Inc.; Men and Women Who Founded Famous Companies After the Age of 40*, 16-22. New York, N.Y: Free Press, 1987.

LEVINE, MARJORIE R.

"Marjorie R. Levine." In *Women Achievers: A Series of Dialogues from the Womanagement Process*, 9-25. New York, N.Y.: American Telephone and Telegraph Co., 1997.

LEVINGSTON, JOYCE

Levingston, Joyce Lee. "Confessions of a 'Shady' Lady." In *Success Secrets: How Eighteen Everyday Women Became Fortune Builders and Famous Speakers*, 215-234. Glendora, Calif.: Royal CBS Publishing, 1978.

LEVINSON, SARA

White, Jane. "Sara Levinson of MTV: Just Don't Ask Her to Type." In *A Few Good Women: Breaking the Barriers to Top Management*, 143-150. Englewood Cliffs, N.J.: Prentice Hall, 1992.

LEVITT FAMILY

Gunther, Max. "The Levitts: One-Hundred Million Dollars." In *The Very, Very Rich and How They Got That Way*, ed. Max Gunther, 215-220. Chicago, Ill.: The Playboy Press, 1972.

"Revolutionizing an Industry: William J. Levitt." In *Lessons of Leadership: 21 Executives Speak Out on Creating, Developing and Managing Success*. Presented by the editors of Nation's Business, 56-69. Garden City, N.Y.: Doubleday, 1968.

LEVITT, MORTIMER

Levitt, Mortimer. "The Custom Shop's Preposterous Beginnings." In *How to Start Your Own Business Without Losing Your Shirt; Secrets of Seventeen Successful Entrepreneurs*, 15-26. New York, N.Y: Atheneum, 1988.

LEVY, LAWRENCE F.

Silver, A. David. "Lawrence F. Levy." In *Entrepreneurial Megabucks: The 100 Greatest Entrepreneurs of the Last 25 Years*, 285-287. New York, N.Y.: Wiley, 1985.

LEVY, SUSAN

Alexander, Shoshana. "Susan Levy: Femi-9 Contracting Corporation, Lindenhurst, New York." In *Women's Ventures, Women's Visions: 29 Inspiring Stories From Women Who Started Their Own Businesses*, 112-118. Freedom, Calif.: The Crossing Press, 1997.

LEWIS, BYRON E.

Dingle, Derek T. "Byron E. Lewis: UniWorld Group, Inc., 'Mr. Madison Avenue'." In *Black Enterprise Titans of the B.E. 100s: Black CEOs Who Redefined and Conquered American Business*, 93-114. New York, N.Y.: Wiley, 1999.

LEWIS, CURTIS, J.

Mitchell, Niki Butler. "Mojo Highway Is a Rough Road to Success: Lee M. Chapman III, Chairman and CEO; Curtis J. Lewis II, President and COO, Mojo Highway Brewing Company, LLC." In *The New Color of Success: Twenty Young Black Millionaires Tell You How They're Making it*, 183-198. Rocklin, Calif.: Prima Publishing, 2000.

LEWIS, GEORGE R.

Clarke, Caroline V. "George R. Lewis: President and CEO, Philip Morris Capital Corporation." In *Take a Lesson: Today's Black Achievers and How They Made It and What They Learned Along the Way*, 113-120. New York, N.Y.: Wiley, 2001.

LEWIS, JOHN L.

Fanning, Leonard M. "John L. Lewis." In *Titans of Business*, 175-204. Philadelphia, Penn.: Lippincott, 1964. 240 p.

LEWIS, SYDNEY

Silver, A. David. "Sydney Lewis." In *Entrepreneurial Megabucks: The 100 Greatest Entrepreneurs of the Last 25 Years*, 288-290. New York, N.Y.: Wiley, 1985.

LEWIS, WILLIAM M. JR.

Clarke, Caroline V. "William M. Lewis, Jr.: Managing Director, Morgan Stanley Dean Witter & Co." In *Take a Lesson: Today's Black Achievers and How They Made It and What They Learned Along the Way*, 121-131. New York, N.Y.: Wiley, 2001.

LEYSHON, WALLACE

Richman, Tom. "Made in the U.S.A.; Can Appliance-Control maker ACT Inc. Become Both the Low-Cost Producer and the High-Quality Provider?" In *Anatomy of a Start-Up: Why Some New Businesses Succeed and Others Fail: 27 Real-Life Case Studies*, ed. Elizabeth K. Longsworth, 241-249. Boston, Mass.: Inc. Publishing, 1991.

LIENHARD, JANET

Murphy, Linda. "Janet Lienhard: Lienhard Consulting Group." In *Computer Entrepreneurs: People Who Built Successful Businesses Around Computers*, 81-89. San Diego, Calif.: Computer Publishing Enterprises, 1990.

LIGGETT, LANNIE

"Diversification and Determination: A Magic Formula." In *How I Became a Nurse Entrepreneur: Tales from 50 Nurses in Business*, 125-128. Petaluma, Calif.: National Nurses in Business Association, 1991.

LINCOLN, JAMES F.

Bell, Laurence. "James F. Lincoln." In *America's Fifty Foremost Business Leaders*, ed. B. C. Forbes, 263-270. New York, N.Y.: B.C. Forbes, 1948. 483 p.

LINCOLN, LEROY A.

Shannon, Homer H. "Leroy A. Lincoln." In *America's Fifty Foremost Business Leaders*, ed. B. C. Forbes, 271-278. New York, N.Y.: B.C. Forbes, 1948.

LINCOLN, LILLIAN

Suarez, Ruth. "Lillian Lincoln: Centennial, 'The Heights of Great Confidence'." In *Superstar Entrepreneurs of Small and Large Businesses Reveal Their Secrets*, 97-101. Piscataway, N.J.: Research and Education Association, 1998.

LINDBERG, LOUISE

Gray, Bob, ed. "Keeping Control of Growth." In *How Entrepreneurs Make Business Profits: A Study of Personal Success Stories From Cordovan Business Journals*, 7-10. Houston, Tex.: Cordovan Press, 1982.

LINDERMANN, GEORGE

Levitt, Mortimer. "George Lindermann: Filling an Old Prescription in a Lucrative New Way." In *How to Start Your Own Business Without Losing Your Shirt; Secrets of Seventeen Successful Entrepreneurs*, 177-185. New York, N.Y: Atheneum, 1988.

LINDT, MARTHA

Alexander, Shoshana. "Carol Rivendell & Martha Lindt: Wild Women Adventures, Sebastopol, California." In *Women's Ventures, Women's Visions: 29 Inspiring Stories From Women Who Started Their Own Businesses*, 186-192. Freedom, Calif.: The Crossing Press, 1997.

LING, JAMES JOSEPH

Davis, William. "James Joseph Ling, b. 1922: King of the Conglomerateurs." In *The Innovators: The Essential Guide to Business Thinkers, Achievers and Entrepreneurs*, 230-234. New York, N.Y.: AMACOM, 1987.

Gunther, Max. "James J. Ling: One-Hundred Million Dollars." In *The Very, Very Rich and How They Got That Way*, ed. Max Gunther, 192-201. Chicago, Ill.: The Playboy Press, 1972.

Sobel, Robert. "James Ling and the Conglomerate Era." In *Dangerous Dreamers: The Financial Innovators from Charles Merrill to Michael Milken*, 37-51. New York, N.Y.: Wiley, 1993.

Sobel, Robert. "James Ling: The Magician." In *The Rise and Fall of the Conglomerate Kings*, 77-100. New York, N.Y.: Stein and Day, 1984.

LIONE, GAIL ANN

Mikaelian, A. "Gail Ann Lione, Esq." In *Women Who Mean Business: Success Stories of Women Over Forty*, 325-329. New York, N.Y.: William Morrow & Co., 1999.

LITTLE, ROYAL

Silver, A. David. "Royal Little." In *Entrepreneurial Megabucks: The 100 Greatest Entrepreneurs of the Last 25 Years*, 291-293. New York, N.Y.: Wiley, 1985.

Sobel, Robert. "Royal Little: The Pioneer." In *The Rise and Fall of the Conglomerate Kings*, 23-45. New York, N.Y.: Stein and Day, 1984.

Sobel, Robert. "Royal Little: The Spider and His Webs." In *The Entrepreneurs: Explorations Within the American Business Tradition*, 341-383. New York, N.Y.: Weybright and Talley, 1974.

LIVERMORE, ANN

Pestrak, Debra. "Ann Livermore: President, Business Customer Organization at Hewlett-Packard and Member of the Hewlett-Packard Executive Council." In *Playing with the Big Boys: Success Stories of the Most Powerful Women in Business*, 49-59. Carlsbad, CA: SUN Publications, 2001.

LLOYD, DAVID

Woodard, Michael D. "Bay City Marina—David Lloyd." In *Black Entrepreneurs in America: Stories of Struggle and Success*, 184-199. New Brunswick, N.J.: Rutgers University Press, 1997.

LOBEL, SHARON

Ericksen, Gregory K. "Sharon Lobel—Seal It, Inc., 'I'm Always Thinking About Different Ideas to Try'." In *Women Entrepreneurs Only: Twelve Women Entrepreneurs Tell The Stories of Their Success*, 173-195. New York, N.Y.: Wiley, 1999.

LOBSENZ, AMELIA

Uris, Auren. "Amelia Lobsenz—From Writer's Study to Executive Suite." In *The Executive Breakthrough; 21 Roads to the Top*, 153-165. Garden City, N.Y.: Doubleday, 1967.

LOCKHART, H. EUGENE

Wendel, Charles B. "Redefining the Credit Card: H. Eugene Lockhart, Chairman & CEO, MasterCard International." In *The New Financiers*, 195-214. Chicago, Ill.: Irwin Professional Pub., 1996.

LOCKLEAR, SUZANNE

Mikaelian, A. "Suzanne Locklear." In *Women Who Mean Business: Success Stories of Women Over Forty*, 83-87. New York, N.Y.: William Morrow & Co., 1999.

LOEW, MARCUS

"The Men Who Made the Movies: Furrier Loew, Scrap Dealer Mayer, Made Movies Mass Medium, Hollywood World Film Capital." In *The 50 Great Pioneers of American Industry*. By the Editors of News Front and Year, 178-181. Maplewood, N.J.: C.S. Hammond, 1964.

Sobel, Robert. "Marcus Loew: An Artist in Spite of Himself." In *The Entrepreneurs: Explorations Within the American Business Tradition*, 247-288. New York, N.Y.: Weybright and Talley, 1974.

LONGWORTH, NICHOLAS

Klepper, Michael M., and Robert Gunther. "Nicholas Longworth (1782-1863): The Man Who Owned Cincinnati." In *The Wealthy 100 : From*

Benjamin Franklin to Bill Gates—A Ranking of the Richest Americans, Past and Present, 120-122. Secaucus, N.J. : Carol Pub. Group, 1996.

LOVE, GEORGE H.

"Uniting for Strength: George H. Love." In *Lessons of Leadership: 21 Executives Speak Out on Creating, Developing and Managing Success*. Presented by the editors of Nation's Business, 155-168. Garden City, N.Y.: Doubleday, 1968.

LOVING, JUDY R.

Mikaelian, A. "Judy R. Loving." In *Women Who Mean Business: Success Stories of Women Over Forty*, 26-30. New York, N.Y.: William Morrow & Co., 1999.

LOWDER, MICHELLE

"Nurse-Publisher Finds Her Niche." In *How I Became a Nurse Entrepreneur: Tales from 50 Nurses in Business*, 87-90. Petaluma, Calif.: National Nurses in Business Association, 1991.

LOWELL, FRANCIS CABOT

Sobel, Robert. "Francis Cabot Lowell: The Patrician as Factory Master." In *The Entrepreneurs: Explorations Within the American Business Tradition*, 1-40. New York, N.Y.: Weybright and Talley, 1974.

LUCAS, GEORGE

Silver, A. David. "George Lucas." In *Entrepreneurial Megabucks: The 100 Greatest Entrepreneurs of the Last 25 Years*, 294-296. New York, N.Y.: Wiley, 1985.

LUCE, HENRY R.

Bell, Laurence. "Henry R. Luce." In *America's Fifty Foremost Business Leaders,* ed. B. C. Forbes, 279-288. New York, N.Y.: B.C. Forbes, 1948.

Davis, William. "Henry Luce, 1898-1967: Founder of Picture Magazine." In *The Innovators: The Essential Guide to Business Thinkers, Achievers and Entrepreneurs*, 238-242. New York, N.Y.: AMACOM, 1987.

LUCKMAN, CHARLES

Benson, Nathaniel A. "Charles Luckman." In *America's Fifty Foremost Business Leaders,* ed. B. C. Forbes, 289-298. New York, N.Y.: B.C. Forbes, 1948.

LUDWIG, DANIEL

Gunther, Max. "Daniel Ludwig: One Billion Dollars." In *The Very, Very Rich and How They Got That Way*, ed. Max Gunther, 183-189. Chicago, Ill.: The Playboy Press, 1972.

Meyer, Michael. "Obsession." In *The Alexander Complex: The Dreams That Drive the Great Businessmen*, 235-250. New York, N.Y.: Times Books, 1989.

LUICK, NANCY

Gray, Bob, ed. "Growing Big in Graphic Arts." In *How Entrepreneurs Make Business Profits: A Study of Personal Success Stories From Cordovan Business Journals*, 22-26. Houston, Tex.: Cordovan Press, 1982.

LUKINS, SHEILA

Levitt, Mortimer. "Julee Rosso and Sheila Lukins: Gourmet Takeout, Palatable at Any Price." In *How to Start Your Own Business Without Losing Your Shirt; Secrets of Seventeen Successful Entrepreneurs*, 188-194. New York, N.Y: Atheneum, 1988.

LYNCH, PETER

Hillkirk, John, and Gary Jacobson. "Peter Lynch and the Magellan Fund: Zen and the Art of Investing." In *Grit, Guts, And Genius: True Tales of Megasuccess: Who Made Them*

Happen and How They Did It, 64-69. Boston, Mass.: Houghton Mifflin, 1990.

"Peter Lynch: Former Manager of Fidelity, Magellan Fund." In *Forbes Great Minds of Business*, ed. Gretchen Morgenson, 73-120. New York, N.Y.: Wiley, 1997. 228 p.

Train, John. "Peter Lynch: Relentless Pursuit." In *Money Masters of Our Time*, 274-298. New York, N.Y.: HarperBusiness, 2000.

Train, John. "Peter Lynch: Relentless Pursuit." In *The New Money Masters : Winning Investment Strategies of Soros, Lynch, Steinhardt, Rogers, Neff, Wanger, Michaelis, Carret*, 192-226. New York, N.Y.: Harper & Row, 1989.

LYNN, ANNETTE

Gray, Bob, ed. "The Thorough Matchmaker." In *How Entrepreneurs Make Business Profits: A Study of Personal Success Stories From Cordovan Business Journals*, 116-121. Houston, Tex.: Cordovan Press, 1982.

MA, SUE LAN

Mikaelian, A. "Sue Lan Ma." In *Women Who Mean Business: Success Stories of Women Over Forty*, 242-246. New York, N.Y.: William Morrow & Co., 1999.

MACADAMS, DOREEN

"A Spa Retreat." In *How I Became a Nurse Entrepreneur: Tales from 50 Nurses in Business*, 61-64. Petaluma, Calif.: National Nurses in Business Association, 1991.

MCADAMS, LISA DANIEL

Mikaelian, A. "Lisa Daniel McAdams." In *Women Who Mean Business: Success Stories of Women Over Forty*, 170-174. New York, N.Y.: William Morrow & Co., 1999.

MCAFEE, JERRY

Shook, Robert L. "Jerry McAfee: Gulf Oil Corporation." In *The Chief Executive Officers: Men Who Run Big Business in America*, 123-142. New York, N.Y.: Harper & Row, 1981.

MACARTHUR, JOHN D.

Darby, Edwin. "MacArthur." In *The Fortune Builders*, 117-135. Garden City, N.Y.: Doubleday and Company, Inc., 1986.

MACASKILL, BRIDGET

Herera, Sue. "Bridget Macaskill: President and CEO, Oppenheimer Funds." In *Women of the Street: Making It on Wall Street—The World's Toughest Business*, 15-34. New York, N.Y.: Wiley, 1997.

MCAULIFFE, TIMOTHY

Koppel, Robert. "Fly on the Rhino's Back: Timothy McAuliffe." In *Bulls, Bears, And Millionaires: War Stories of Trading Life*, 47-55. Chicago, Ill.: Dearborn Financial Publishers, 1997.

MCAVITY, IAN

King, Norman. "Ian McAvity." In *The Money Messiah$*, 188-189. New York, N.Y.: Coward-McCann, 1983.

MCBRIDE, CORNELL

Gray, Bob, ed. "Hair Care From Grass Roots." In *How Entrepreneurs Make Business Profits: A Study of Personal Success Stories From Cordovan Business Journals*, 107-109. Houston, Tex.: Cordovan Press, 1982.

MCBRIDE, TERESA

Suarez, Ruth. "Teresa McBride: McBride and Associates, 'Success and the Single Parent'." In *Superstar Entrepreneurs of Small and Large*

Businesses Reveal Their Secrets, 43-50. Piscataway, N.J.: Research and Education Association, 1998.

MCCABE, THOMAS B.

"Enriching Life by Broad Experience: Thomas B. McCabe." In *Lessons of Leadership: 21 Executives Speak Out on Creating, Developing and Managing Success*. Presented by the editors of Nation's Business, 248-258. Garden City, N.Y.: Doubleday, 1968.

MCCALL, ALVIN A. JR.

Aronoff, Craig E., and John L. Ward. "Alvin A. McCall Jr." In *Contemporary Entrepreneurs*, 325-330. Detroit, Mich.: Omnigraphics, Inc., 1992.

MCCAMPBELL, CHARLES

Woodard, Michael D. "Heritage Paper Company—Charles McCampbell." In *Black Entrepreneurs in America: Stories of Struggle and Success*, New Brunswick, N.J.: Rutgers University Press, 1977.

MCCANN, JIM

Ericksen, Gregory K. "Jim McCann: 1-800-FLOWERS, 'I'm a Builder'." In *What's Luck Got to Do with It; Twelve Entrepreneurs Reveal the Secrets Behind Their Success*, 19-41. New York, N.Y.: Wiley, 1997.

MCCARTHY, LAURA J.

"Consulting Services Through PHA." In *How I Became a Nurse Entrepreneur: Tales from 50 Nurses in Business*, 143-150. Petaluma, Calif.: National Nurses in Business Association, 1991.

MCCAW, CRAIG O.

Pottker, Jan. "McCaw Cellular Communications, Inc.: Goodbye, Ma Bell; Hello, Craig McCaw." In *Born to Power: Heirs to America's Leading Businesses*, 68-75. New York, N.Y.: Barron's, 1992.

MCCLURE, SAMUEL SIDNEY

"How Magazines Went National: Cyrus H. K. Curtis Led the Turn-Of-The Century Publishing Revolution That Created the Mass Circulation Magazine; S. S. McClure Dramatized Its Power As a National Opinion-Maker." In *The 50 Great Pioneers of American Industry*. By the Editors of News Front and Year, 148-151. Maplewood, N.J.: C.S. Hammond, 1964.

"How Magazines Went National Part 2: McClure and the 'Muckrakers'... Curtis and the Saturday Evening Post... National Magazines and National Advertisers..." In *The 50 Great Pioneers of American Industry*. By the Editors of News Front and Year, 152-155. Maplewood, N.J.: C.S. Hammond, 1964.

MCCOLL, HUGH

Kadlec, Daniel J. "Hugh McColl: Southern Dynamite." In *Masters of the Universe; Winning Strategies of America's Greatest Deal Makers*, 39-70. New York, N.Y.: HarperBusiness, 1999.

MCCOLLUM, L. F.

"Spurring Growth with Imagination: L.F. McCollum." In *Lessons of Leadership: 21 Executives Speak Out on Creating, Developing and Managing Success*. Presented by the editors of Nation's Business, 123-131. Garden City, N.Y.: Doubleday, 1968.

MCCONNELL, MARY P.

Mikaelian, A. "Mary P. McConnell, Esq." In *Women Who Mean Business: Success Stories of Women Over Forty*, 161-164. New York, N.Y.: William Morrow & Co., 1999.

MCCORMACK, MARK H.

Davis, William. "Mark H. McCormack, b. 1930: The Man Who Marketed Sportsman." In *The Innovators: The Essential Guide to Business Thinkers, Achievers and Entrepreneurs*, 243-246. New York, N.Y.: AMACOM, 1987.

MCCORMICK, BERNADETTE S.

Mikaelian, A. "Bernadette S. McCormick." In *Women Who Mean Business: Success Stories of Women Over Forty*, 165-169. New York, N.Y.: William Morrow & Co., 1999.

THE MCCORMICK FAMILY

Benson, Nathaniel A. "Fowler McCormick." In *America's Fifty Foremost Business Leaders,* ed. B. C. Forbes, 339-350. New York, N.Y.: B.C. Forbes, 1948.

Brands, H. W. "Golden Grains: Cyrus McCormick." In *Masters of Enterprise: Giants of American Business from John Jacob Astor and J.P. Morgan to Bill Gates and Oprah Winfrey*, 26-36. New York, N.Y.: Free Press, 1999.

Burnley, James. "The McCormicks of Chicago: The Harvesting Machine Magnates." In *Millionaires and Kings of Enterprise; The Marvellous Careers of Some Americans Who by Pluck, Foresight, And Energy Have Made Themselves Masters in the Fields of Industry and Finance*, 251-264. Philadelphia, Penn.: J. B. Lippincott, 1901.

Darby, Edwin. "McCormick." In *The Fortune Builders*, 203-267. Garden City, N.Y.: Doubleday and Company, Inc., 1986.

Fishwick, Marshall. "Sheaves of Golden Grain." In *Great Stories of American Businessmen*, From *American Heritage, The Magazine of History,* 74-80. New York, N.Y.: American Heritage Publishing Co., 1954.

Forbes, Malcolm S. "Katherine McCormick, 'Financial Backer of the Pill'." In *Women Who Made a Difference*, New York, N.Y.: Simon & Schuster, 1990.

Gross, Daniel, and the Editors of Forbes Magazine. "Cyrus McCormick's Reaper and the Industrialization of Farming." In *Forbes Greatest Business Stories of All Time*, 22-38. New York, N.Y.: Wiley, 1996.

"Harvester of the Prairies." In *The 50 Great Pioneers of American Industry*. By the Editors of News Front and Year, 14-18. Maplewood, N.J.: C.S. Hammond, 1964.

Klepper, Michael M., and Robert Gunther. "Cyrus H. McCormick (1809-1884): Reaping a Fortune." In *The Wealthy 100 : From Benjamin Franklin to Bill Gates—A Ranking of the Richest Americans, Past and Present*, 259-261. Secaucus, N.J. : Carol Pub. Group, 1996.

Ingrassia, Paul. "The McCormicks." In *American Dynasties Today*, 129-164. Homewood, Ill.: Dow Jones-Irwin, 1990.

Livesay, Harold C. "The Grim Reaper: Cyrus Hall McCormick." In *American Made: Men Who Shaped the American Economy*, 53-84. Boston, Mass.: Little, Brown, 1979.

Sobel, Robert. "Cyrus Hall McCormick: From Farm Boy to Tycoon." In *The Entrepreneurs: Explorations Within the American Business Tradition*, 42-72. New York, N.Y.: Weybright and Talley, 1974.

Wren, Daniel A., and Ronald G. Greenwood. "Cyrus H. McCormick." In *Management Innovators: The People and Ideas That Have Shaped Modern Business*, 25-33. New York, N.Y.: Oxford University Press, 1998.

MCCORMICK, MIKE

Elfstrand, Rhonda. "Mike McCormick: Class, Inc./Candidate for Congress, 20th District." In *The Story Behind the Success: Learning From Pittsburgh Professionals*, 184-200. Pittsburgh, Penn.: Steel Publishing Partners, 1996.

MCCOY, JAMES M.

Aronoff, Craig E., and John L. Ward. "James M. McCoy." In *Contemporary Entrepreneurs*, 331-336. Detroit, Mich.: Omnigraphics, Inc., 1992.

MCCOY, JOHN B.

Wendel, Charles B. "Leveraging the Uncommon Partnership: John B. McCoy, Chairman & CEO, Banc One Corporation." In *The New Financiers*, 215-238. Chicago, Ill.: Irwin Professional Pub., 1996.

MCCOY, JOSEPH G.

Wickman, John E. "A Visionary on the Prairie: Joseph G. McCoy." In *Business Entrepreneurs in the West*, ed. Ted C. Hinckley, 22-27. Manhattan, Kans.: Sunflower University Press, 1986.

MCCRACKEN, ED

Jager, Rama Dev, and Rafael Ortiz. "Ed McCracken: Silicon Graphics; Meditative Management." In *In the Company of Giants: Candid Conversations with the Visionaries of the Digital World*, 191-207. New York, N.Y.: McGraw-Hill, 1997.

MCCRACKEN, JARRELL

Sheehy, Sandy. "Jarrell McCracken; Show Biz and Salvation." In *Texas Big Rich; Exploits, Eccentricities, And Fabulous Fortunes Won and Lost*, 197-205. New York, N.Y.: Morrow, 1990.

MACDIARMID, MARY

Koppel, Mara. "Oh No—Mary MacDiarmid." In *Women of the Pits: Shattering the Glass Ceiling in Financial Markets*, 49-62. Chicago, Ill.: Dearborn Financial Publishers, 1998.

MCDONALD, MARSHALL

Hillkirk, John, and Gary Jacobson. "Florida Power & Light: Providing "Perfect" Service." In *Grit, Guts, And Genius: True Tales of Megasuccess: Who Made Them Happen and How They Did It*, 211-227. Boston, Mass.: Houghton Mifflin, 1990.

MCDONOGH, JOHN

Klepper, Michael M., and Robert Gunther. "John McDonogh (1779-1850): The King of the Merchant's Mardi Gras." In *The Wealthy 100 : From Benjamin Franklin to Bill Gates—A Ranking of the Richest Americans, Past and Present,* 284-287. Secaucus, N.J. : Carol Pub. Group, 1996.

MCENROE, GAYLE

Alexander, Shoshana. "Gayle McEnroe: Metal Service Inc., St. Paul, Minnesota." In *Women's Ventures, Women's Visions: 29 Inspiring Stories From Women Who Started Their Own Businesses,* 139-145. Freedom, Calif.: The Crossing Press, 1997.

MCGOVERN, PATRICK J.

Silver, A. David. "Patrick J. McGovern." In *Entrepreneurial Megabucks: The 100 Greatest Entrepreneurs of the Last 25 Years,* 300-303. New York, N.Y.: Wiley, 1985.

MCGOWAN, WILLIAM G.

Gross, Daniel, and the Editors of Forbes Magazine. "William McGowan and MCI: A New World of Telecommunications." In *Forbes Greatest Business Stories of All Time,* 284-297. New York, N.Y.: Wiley, 1996.

Shook, Robert L. "William G. McGowen." In *The Entrepreneurs: Twelve Who Took Risks and Succeeded,* 139-156. New York, N.Y: Harper & Row, 1980.

Silver, A. David. "William G. McGowan." In *Entrepreneurial Megabucks: The 100 Greatest Entrepreneurs of the Last 25 Years,* 304-306. New York, N.Y.: Wiley, 1985.

MCGREGOR, DOUGLAS M.

Wren, Daniel A., and Ronald G. Greenwood. "Douglas M. McGregor." In *Management Innovators: The People and Ideas That Have Shaped*

Modern Business, 198-203. New York, N.Y.: Oxford University Press, 1998.

MCGREGOR, IAN K.

Levinson, Harry, and Stuart Rosenthal. "Ian K. MacGregor." In *CEO: Corporate Leadership in Action*, 96-136. New York, N.Y: Basic Books, 1984.

MACHIAVELLI, NICOLÒ

Wren, Daniel A., and Ronald G. Greenwood. "Nicolò Machiavelli." In *Management Innovators: The People and Ideas That Have Shaped Modern Business*, 191-194. New York, N.Y.: Oxford University Press, 1998.

MACKAY, ELIZABETH

Herera, Sue. "Elizabeth Mackay: Chief Investment Strategist and Managing Director, Bear Stearns." In *Women of the Street: Making It on Wall Street—The World's Toughest Business*, 71-82. New York, N.Y.: Wiley, 1997.

MACKAY, JOHN W.

Burnley, James. "The 'Bonanza' Kings: John W. Mackay and His Partners." In *Millionaires and Kings of Enterprise; The Marvellous Careers of Some Americans Who by Pluck, Foresight, And Energy Have Made Themselves Masters in the Fields of Industry and Finance*, 376-384. Philadelphia, Penn.: J. B. Lippincott, 1901.

MCKEEVER, JEFF

Oster, Merrill J. "Virtual Reality." In *The Entrepreneur's Creed: The Principles & Passions of 20 Successful Entrepreneurs*, 110-119. Nashville, Tenn.: Broadman & Holman Publishers, 2001.

MCLEAN, MALCOM P.

Silver, A. David. "Malcom P. McLean." In *Entrepreneurial Megabucks: The 100 Greatest Entrepreneurs of the Last 25 Years*, 307-310. New York, N.Y.: Wiley, 1985.

MCMANUS, JAMES

Levitt, Mortimer. "James McManus: A Money-Making Smorgasbord of Marketing, Advertising, And Management Innovations." In *How to Start Your Own Business Without Losing Your Shirt; Secrets of Seventeen Successful Entrepreneurs*, 143-156. New York, N.Y: Atheneum, 1988.

MCNAMARA, FRANK

Davis, William. "Frank McNamara: Inventor of the Charge Card." In *The Innovators: The Essential Guide to Business Thinkers, Achievers and Entrepreneurs*, 247-250. New York, N.Y.: AMACOM, 1987.

MCNEALY, SCOTT

Aronoff, Craig E., and John L. Ward. "Scott McNealy." In *Contemporary Entrepreneurs*, 337-342. Detroit, Mich.: Omnigraphics, Inc., 1992.

Kingston, Brett. "Andreas Bechtolsheim, Vinod Khosla, Bill Joy, and Scott McNealy of the SUN Microsystems Team." In *The Dynamos: Who Are They Anyway?*, 49-60. New York, N.Y.: Wiley, 1987.

MCNULTY, MIKE

Ericksen, Gregory K. "Mike McNulty & Mike Hagan—VerticalNet 'We Get Qualified Eyeballs to Come to Very Focused Sites'." In *Net Entrepreneurs Only : 10 Entrepreneurs Tell the Stories of Their Success*, 21-40. New York : John Wiley, 2000.

MACY, ROWLAND HUSSEY

"Selling Was Never the Same: R.H. Macy Combined Old Ideas into New, Under-One-Roof Formula, Created Modern Department Store." In *The*

50 Great Pioneers of American Industry. By the Editors of News Front and Year, 42-44. Maplewood, N.J.: C.S. Hammond, 1964.

MAHER, FRANCESCA M.

Mikaelian, A. "Francesca M. Maher, Esq." In *Women Who Mean Business: Success Stories of Women Over Forty*, 88-92. New York, N.Y.: William Morrow & Co., 1999.

MALEC, JOHN

Hillkirk, John, and Gary Jacobson. "Information Resources: A Revolution in Marketing." In *Grit, Guts, And Genius: True Tales of Megasuccess: Who Made Them Happen and How They Did It*, 186-196. Boston, Mass.: Houghton Mifflin, 1990.

MALLERY, SUZY

Mallery, Suzy. "Talk to Yourself." In *Success Secrets: How Eighteen Everyday Women Became Fortune Builders and Famous Speakers*, 167-174. Glendora, Calif.: Royal CBS Publishing, 1978.

MALONE, JOHN

Auletta, Ken. "The Cowboy: John Malone's Cable Kingdom." In *The Highwaymen; Warriors of the Information Superhighway*, 25-55. New York, N.Y.: Random House, 1997.

MANGANO, JOY

Ericksen, Gregory K. "Joy Mangano—Ingenious Designs, Inc., 'The Product is Always King'." In *Women Entrepreneurs Only: Twelve Women Entrepreneurs Tell The Stories of Their Success*, 67-85. New York, N.Y.: Wiley, 1999.

MANGO, NABILA

Alexander, Shoshana. "Nabila Mango: Mango Trading Services, San Francisco, California." In *Women's Ventures, Women's Visions: 29*

Inspiring Stories From Women Who Started Their Own Businesses, 161-166. Freedom, Calif.: The Crossing Press, 1997.

MANNING, THOMAS J.

Fisher, Anne B. "House Calls; Can Buddy Systems Inc. Persuade Doctors, Insurers, And Patients to Accept Its New Home Monitoring Device." In *Anatomy of a Start-Up: Why Some New Businesses Succeed and Others Fail: 27 Real-Life Case Studies,* ed. Elizabeth K. Longsworth, 266-274. Boston, Mass.: Inc. Publishing, 1991.

MANOOGIAN, ALEX

Silver, A. David. "Alex Manoogian." In *Entrepreneurial Megabucks: The 100 Greatest Entrepreneurs of the Last 25 Years*, 297-299. New York, N.Y.: Wiley, 1985.

MANSON, MICHAEL

Oster, Merrill J. "In Search of Truth." In *The Entrepreneur's Creed: The Principles & Passions of 20 Successful Entrepreneurs*, 142-151. Nashville, Tenn.: Broadman & Holman Publishers, 2001.

MARCUS, BERNARD

Aronoff, Craig E., and John L. Ward. "Bernard Marcus." In *Contemporary Entrepreneurs*, 312-318. Detroit, Mich.: Omnigraphics, Inc., 1992.

MARKS, CAROLYNA

Alexander, Shoshana. "Carolyna Marks: Blue Rider School of Art; The World Wall for Peace, Berkeley, California." In *Women's Ventures, Women's Visions: 29 Inspiring Stories From Women Who Started Their Own Businesses*, 97-103. Freedom, Calif.: The Crossing Press, 1997.

MARKS, SIMON

Davis, William. "Simon Marks, 1888-1964: 'Don't Ask the Price, It's a Penny'." In *The Innovators: The Essential Guide to Business*

Thinkers, Achievers and Entrepreneurs, 251-256. New York, N.Y.: AMACOM, 1987.

MARRIOTT FAMILY

Goldwasser, Thomas. "Marriott: A Hamburger Stand Becomes a Food and Lodging Empire." In *Family Pride; Profiles of Five of America's Best-Run Family Businesses*, 85-124. New York, N.Y.: Dodd, Mead and Company, 1986.

Pottker, Jan. "Marriott Corporation: Starting at the Bottom." In *Born to Power: Heirs to America's Leading Businesses*, 230-235. New York, N.Y.: Barron's, 1992.

MARSH, STANLEY

Sheehy, Sandy. "Stanley Marsh 3: Cristo of the Cap Rock." In *Texas Big Rich; Exploits, Eccentricities, And Fabulous Fortunes Won and Lost*, 294-306. New York, N.Y.: Morrow, 1990.

MARTIN, GLENN L.

Bell, Laurence. "Glenn L. Martin." In *America's Fifty Foremost Business Leaders,* ed. B. C. Forbes, 299-308. New York, N.Y.: B.C. Forbes, 1948.

MARTIN, HAROLD

Woodard, Michael D. "Economic Rights." In *Black Entrepreneurs in America: Stories of Struggle and Success*, 3-8. New Brunswick, N.J.: Rutgers University Press, 1997.

MARTIN, J. ALEXANDER

Mitchell, Niki Butler. "For Us, By Us: J. Alexander Martin, Vice President and Head Designer; Daymond John, President and CEO; Carl Brown, Co-Founder; Keith Perrin, Co-Founder, FUBU." In *The New Color of Success: Twenty Young Black Millionaires Tell You How They're Making it*, 29-42. Rocklin, Calif.: Prima Publishing, 2000.

MARTIN, THOMAS W.

Shannon, Homer H. "Thomas W. Martin." In *America's Fifty Foremost Business Leaders,* ed. B. C. Forbes, 309-318. New York, N.Y.: B.C. Forbes, 1948.

MARTZ, CARRIE ABRAHAM

Mikaelian, A. "Carrie Abraham Martz." In *Women Who Mean Business: Success Stories of Women Over Forty,* 16-20. New York, N.Y.: William Morrow & Co., 1999.

MARX, MARCUS

Cleary, David Powers. "Hart Schaffner & Marx Suits; The Clothes a Man Wears Are to Some Extent a True Index of His Character and Taste, But They Are Also an Influence Upon His Character and Taste." In *Great American Brands: The Success Formulas That Made Them Famous,* 158-165. New York, N.Y: Fairchild Publications, 1981.

MASCUCH, J. J.

Uris, Auren. "J. J. Mascuch—Spark-Plug Tamer Extraordinary." In *The Executive Breakthrough; 21 Roads to the Top,* 255-270. Garden City, N.Y.: Doubleday, 1967.

MASLAK, SAMUEL H.

Aronoff, Craig E., and John L. Ward. "Samuel H. Maslak." In *Contemporary Entrepreneurs,* 319-324. Detroit, Mich.: Omnigraphics, Inc., 1992.

MASLOW, ABRAHAM H.

Wren, Daniel A., and Ronald G. Greenwood. "Abraham H. Maslow." In *Management Innovators: The People and Ideas That Have Shaped Modern Business,* 177-182. New York, N.Y.: Oxford University Press, 1998.

MASON, STEVENS T.

Folsom, Burton W. "Governor Stevens T. Mason and Michigan's First Railroad." In *Empire Builders: How Michigan Entrepreneurs Helped Make America Great*, 31-54. Traverse City, Mich.: Rhodes & Easton, 1998.

MASTERS, JOHN

Gilder, George. "The Explorer." In *The Spirit of Enterprise*, 57-70. New York, N.Y.: Simon & Schuster, 1984. 338 p.

MATHEWS, JOHN

Morrison, Joseph L. "The Soda Fountain." In *Great Stories of American Businessmen*, From *American Heritage, The Magazine of History*, 136-145. New York, N.Y.: American Heritage Publishing Co., 1954.

MATHIS, SHARON A.

Mathis, Sharon A. "Udderitis: A Nursing Challenge." In *How I Became a Nurse Entrepreneur: Tales from 50 Nurses in Business*, 281-284. Petaluma, Calif.: National Nurses in Business Association, 1991.

MATLOCK, KENT

Mitchell, Niki Butler. "Changing the Way the World Thinks: Kent Matlock, Chairman and CEO, Matlock and Associates, Inc." In *The New Color of Success: Twenty Young Black Millionaires Tell You How They're Making it*, 95-106. Rocklin, Calif.: Prima Publishing, 2000.

MATTHIAS, REBECCA

Mikaelian, A. "Rebecca Matthias." In *Women Who Mean Business: Success Stories of Women Over Forty*, 267-271. New York, N.Y.: William Morrow & Co., 1999.

MAUCHLY, JOHN W.

"Computers Come of Age: Electronic Data Processing, Miracle of Modern Technology, Was Spawned in Basement of University of Pennsylvania's Moore School of Engineering." In *The 50 Great Pioneers of American Industry*. By the Editors of News Front and Year, 200-203. Maplewood, N.J.: C.S. Hammond, 1964.

MAXFIELD, ROBERT R.

Silver, A. David. "M. Kenneth Oshman; Robert R. Maxfield." In *Entrepreneurial Megabucks: The 100 Greatest Entrepreneurs of the Last 25 Years*, 342-343. New York, N.Y.: Wiley, 1985.

MAXIM, HIRAM

Burnley, James. "Sir Hiram Maxim: The Man Behind the Gun." In *Millionaires and Kings of Enterprise; The Marvellous Careers of Some Americans Who by Pluck, Foresight, And Energy Have Made Themselves Masters in the Fields of Industry and Finance*, 93-109. Philadelphia, Penn.: J. B. Lippincott, 1901.

MAXWELL, KEVIN

Farnham, Alan. "Kevin Maxwell: Founder of Telemonde and Former CEO of Maxwell Communications, 'One Could Have—Should Have— Abandoned Ship'." In *Forbes Great Success Stories: Twelve Tales of Victory Wrested from Defeat*, 226-254. New York, N.Y.: Wiley, 2000.

MAYER, LOUIS B.

Davis, William. "Louis B. Mayer, 1885-1957: 'More Stars Than There Are in Heaven'." In *The Innovators: The Essential Guide to Business Thinkers, Achievers and Entrepreneurs*, 261-264. New York, N.Y.: AMACOM, 1987.

"The Men Who Made the Movies: Furrier Loew, Scrap Dealer Mayer, Made Movies Mass Medium, Hollywood World Film Capital." In *The 50 Great Pioneers of American Industry*. By the Editors of News Front and Year, 178-181. Maplewood, N.J.: C.S. Hammond, 1964.

MAYO, ELTON

Wren, Daniel A., and Ronald G. Greenwood. "Elton Mayo." In *Management Innovators: The People and Ideas That Have Shaped Modern Business*, 171-176. New York, N.Y.: Oxford University Press, 1998.

MAYS, BILL

Woodard, Michael D. "Mays Chemical Company—Bill Mays." In *Black Entrepreneurs in America: Stories of Struggle and Success*, 102-127. New Brunswick, N.J.: Rutgers University Press, 1997.

MECCA, LORRAINE

Zientara, Marguerite. "Lorraine Mecca: Hitting an Industry Nerve." In *Women, Technology & Power: Ten Stars and the History They Made*, 120-127. New York, N.Y.: AMACOM, American Management Association, 1987.

Zientara, Marguerite. "Lorraine Mecca: Seizing Control." In *Women, Technology & Power: Ten Stars and the History They Made*, 25-28. New York, N.Y.: AMACOM, American Management Association, 1987.

Zientara, Marguerite. "Lorraine Mecca: Take the Money and Run." In *Women, Technology & Power: Ten Stars and the History They Made*, 187-193. New York, N.Y.: AMACOM, American Management Association, 1987.

MEDINA, SHERRI

Suarez, Ruth. "Sherri Medina: Southcoast Rehabilitation, 'Staying Above the Competition'." In *Superstar Entrepreneurs of Small and Large Businesses Reveal Their Secrets*. 235-241. Piscataway, N.J.: Research and Education Association, 1998.

MEEHAN, SHARON

Mikaelian, A. "Sharon Meehan." In *Women Who Mean Business: Success Stories of Women Over Forty*, 291-295. New York, N.Y.: William Morrow & Co., 1999.

MELIN, ARTHUR "SPUD"

Shook, Robert L. "The Hula Hoop Toy, The Frisbee Disc, And the Super Ball Toy." In *Why Didn't I Think of That*, 50-65. New York, N.Y.: New American Library, 1982.

MELLINGER FAMILY

Pottker, Jan. "Frederick's of Hollywood: Naughty to Nice." In *Born to Power: Heirs to America's Leading Businesses*, 332-336. New York, N.Y.: Barron's, 1992.

THE MELLON FAMILY

Klepper, Michael M., and Robert Gunther. "Andrew W. Mellon (1855-1937), Richard B. Mellon (1858-1933): Banking Brothers." In *The Wealthy 100 : From Benjamin Franklin to Bill Gates—A Ranking of the Richest Americans, Past and Present*, 60-64. Secaucus, N.J. : Carol Pub. Group, 1996.

Seas, Douglas R. "The Mellons." In *American Dynasties Today,* 199-232. Homewood, Ill.: Dow Jones-Irwin, 1990.

Shannon, Homer H. "Richard K. Mellon." In *America's Fifty Foremost Business Leaders,* ed. B. C. Forbes, 319-328. New York, N.Y.: B.C. Forbes, 1948.

MELNICK, NORMAN

Aronoff, Craig E., and John L. Ward. "Norman Melnick." In *Contemporary Entrepreneurs*, 343-347. Detroit, Mich.: Omnigraphics, Inc., 1992.

MENDEL, PERRY

Fucini, Joseph J., and Suzy Fucini. "Perry Mendel, Kinder-Care Learning Centers, Inc.: 'An Idea Will Remain Just an Idea Until Someone Moves on It'." In *Experience Inc.; Men and Women Who Founded Famous Companies After the Age of 40*, 75-81. New York, N.Y: Free Press, 1987.

MERCADO-VALDES, FRANK

Harris, Wendy Beech. "Frank Mercado-Valdes, African Heritage Network: He's Mad About Movies." In *Against All Odds: Ten Entrepreneurs Who Followed Their Hearts and Found Success*, 113-142. New York, N.Y.: Wiley, 2001.

MERGENTHALER, OTTMAR

"He Unplugged Printing's Bottleneck: Mergenthaler's Linotype Transformed Typesetting." In *The 50 Great Pioneers of American Industry*. By the Editors of News Front and Year, 102-105. Maplewood, N.J.: C.S. Hammond, 1964.

MERNS, SY SYMS

Silver, A. David. "Sy Syms Merns." In *Entrepreneurial Megabucks: The 100 Greatest Entrepreneurs of the Last 25 Years*, 311-312. New York, N.Y.: Wiley, 1985.

MERRILL, CHARLES

Gross, Daniel, and the Editors of Forbes Magazine. "Charles Merril and the Democratization of Stock Ownership." In *Forbes Greatest Business Stories of All Time*, 90-105. New York, N.Y.: Wiley, 1996.

Shannon, Homer H. "Charles E. Merrill." In *America's Fifty Foremost Business Leaders,* ed. B. C. Forbes, 329-338. New York, N.Y.: B.C. Forbes, 1948.

Sobel, Robert. "Charles Merrill and the Rebirth of Wall Street." In *Dangerous Dreamers: The Financial Innovators from Charles Merrill to Michael Milken*, 23-36. New York, N.Y.: Wiley, 1993.

MESCH, ROBIN

Koppel, Mara. "Financial Fishing—Robin Mesch." In *Women of the Pits: Shattering the Glass Ceiling in Financial Markets*, 107-116. Chicago, Ill.: Dearborn Financial Publishers, 1998.

Koppel, Robert. "Trades to the Beat of Her Own Drummond: Robin Mesch." In *Bulls, Bears, And Millionaires: War Stories of Trading Life*, 106-115. Chicago, Ill.: Dearborn Financial Publishers, 1997.

METCALF, ROBERT

Aronoff, Craig E., and John L. Ward. "Robert Metcalf." In *Contemporary Entrepreneurs*, 348-353. Detroit, Mich.: Omnigraphics, Inc., 1992.

MEYER, DEBORAH

Suarez, Ruth. "Deborah Meyer: Deborah Meyer Associates, 'Color Schemes'." In *Superstar Entrepreneurs of Small and Large Businesses Reveal Their Secrets*, 123-128. Piscataway, N.J.: Research and Education Association, 1998.

MEYER, PAUL J.

Gunther, Max, "The Tenth-Multiple Man." In *The Very, Very Rich and How They Got That Way*, ed. Max Gunther, 50-53. Chicago, Ill.: The Playboy Press, 1972.

MICHAELIS, GEORGE

Train, John. "George Michaelis: Apostle of Return on Equities." In *The New Money Masters : Winning Investment Strategies of Soros, Lynch, Steinhardt, Rogers, Neff, Wanger, Michaelis, Carret*, 122-137. New York, N.Y.: Harper & Row, 1989.

MILKIN, MICHAEL

Davis, William. "Michael Milkin, b. 1946: 'The Premier Financier of His Generation'." In *The Innovators: The Essential Guide to Business Thinkers, Achievers and Entrepreneurs*, 264-266. New York, N.Y.: AMACOM, 1987.

Smith, Roy C. "The Midas Touch." In *Wealth Creators: The Rise of Today's Rich and Super-Rich*, 122-131. New York, N.Y.: Truman Talley, 2001.

Sobel, Robert. "Michael Milken—The Outsider." In *Dangerous Dreamers: The Financial Innovators from Charles Merrill to Michael Milken*, 55-80. New York, N.Y.: Wiley, 1993.

MILLARD, WILLIAM H.

Fucini, Joseph J., and Suzy Fucini. "William H. Millard, ComputerLand Corporation: 'Anybody Had the Opportunity to Observe This Phenomenon'." In *Experience Inc.; Men and Women Who Founded Famous Companies After the Age of 40*, 82-88. New York, N.Y: Free Press, 1987.

Silver, A. David. "William H. Millard." In *Entrepreneurial Megabucks: The 100 Greatest Entrepreneurs of the Last 25 Years*, 313-316. New York, N.Y.: Wiley, 1985.

Slater, Robert. "William Millard: The Man Who Built ComputerLand." In *Portraits in Silicon*, 330-340. Cambridge, Mass.: MIT Press, 1987.

MILLER, DANE ALAN

Aronoff, Craig E., and John L. Ward. "Dane Alan Miller." In *Contemporary Entrepreneurs*, 354-359. Detroit, Mich.: Omnigraphics, Inc., 1992.

MILLER, JANATHIN

Murphy, Linda. "Janathin Miller Lindsey Ware: Access Research Corporation." In *Computer Entrepreneurs: People Who Built*

Successful Businesses Around Computers, 71-79. San Diego, Calif.: Computer Publishing Enterprises, 1990.

MILLER, JUDITH C.

Miller, Judith C. "Watching the Lights Go On." In *How I Became a Nurse Entrepreneur: Tales from 50 Nurses in Business*, 159-164. Petaluma, Calif.: National Nurses in Business Association, 1991.

MILLER, LOUISE

Lassen, Ali. "Louise Miller: Office Furniture Salesperson and Representative, Amway." In *The Secret of Their Success: Women Entrepreneurs Reveal How They Made It*, 183-188. Carlsbad, Calif.: Ali Lassen Success System, 1990.

MILLER, NORMAN

Oster, Merrill J. "Recharged." In *The Entrepreneur's Creed: The Principles & Passions of 20 Successful Entrepreneurs*, 66-75. Nashville, Tenn.: Broadman & Holman Publishers, 2001.

MILLIKEN FAMILY

Pottker, Jan. "Milliken & Co., Inc.: Unraveling the Family Shares." In *Born to Power: Heirs to America's Leading Businesses*, 384-389. New York, N.Y.: Barron's, 1992.

MILLS, GLENNA B.

Mills, Glenna B., and Katherine T. Pollin. "Getting Started..." In *How I Became a Nurse Entrepreneur: Tales from 50 Nurses in Business*, 261-265. Petaluma, Calif.: National Nurses in Business Association, 1991.

MINCHAK, BOB

Suarez, Ruth. "Joan and Bob Minchak: JB Dollar Stretcher Magazine, 'Married to Work'." In *Superstar Entrepreneurs of Small and Large*

Businesses Reveal Their Secrets, 9-13. Piscataway, N.J.: Research and Education Association, 1998.

MINCHAK, JOAN

Suarez, Ruth. "Joan and Bob Minchak: JB Dollar Stretcher Magazine, 'Married to Work'." In *Superstar Entrepreneurs of Small and Large Businesses Reveal Their Secrets*, 9-13. Piscataway, N.J.: Research and Education Association, 1998.

MINNITI, MARTHA JEAN

Minniti, Martha Jean. "The Evolving Dream." In *How I Became a Nurse Entrepreneur: Tales from 50 Nurses in Business*, 255-260. Petaluma, Calif.: National Nurses in Business Association, 1991.

MINTZ, DAVID

Fucini, Joseph J., and Suzy Fucini. "David Mintz, Tofutti Brands, Inc.: 'A Little Voice Kept Whispering, Keep Going'." In *Experience Inc.; Men and Women Who Founded Famous Companies After the Age of 40*, 66-71. New York, N.Y: Free Press, 1987.

MINYARD, LIZ

Enkelis, Liane, and Karen Olsen. "Liz Minyard & Gretchen Minyard Williams: Co-Chairmen of the Board, Minyard Foods Stores, Inc." In *On Our Own Terms: Portraits of Women Business Leaders*, 102-111. San Francisco, Calif.: Berrett-Koehler, 1995.

MISCHER, WALTER

Sheehy, Sandy. "Walter Mischer: The Kingmaker." In *Texas Big Rich; Exploits, Eccentricities, And Fabulous Fortunes Won and Lost*, 76-83. New York, N.Y.: Morrow, 1990.

MITCHELL, DAVID W.

Shook, Robert L. "David W. Mitchell: Avon Products, Inc." In *The Chief Executive Officers: Men Who Run Big Business in America*, 143-160. New York, N.Y.: Harper & Row, 1981.

MITCHELL, ED

Levitt, Mortimer. "Ed. Mitchell: A Retail Clothier Brings In the Crowds with a Warm Family Touch." In *How to Start Your Own Business Without Losing Your Shirt; Secrets of Seventeen Successful Entrepreneurs*, 171-176. New York, N.Y: Atheneum, 1988.

MITCHELL, FRANK

Brokaw, Leslie. "Play by Play; When Is a Great Product Not a Great Business? Maybe, Just Maybe, In the Case of SportsBand Network." In *Anatomy of a Start-Up: Why Some New Businesses Succeed and Others Fail: 27 Real-Life Case Studies,* ed. Elizabeth K. Longsworth, 328-338. Boston, Mass.: Inc. Publishing, 1991.

MITCHELL, GILLIAN

Rich-McCoy, Lois. "Synergy and Swimsuits: Gillian Mitchell and Jacqueline Baird." In *Millionairess: Self-Made Women of America*, 23-48. New York, N.Y.: Harper & Row, 1978.

MOFFATT, D. H.

Burnley, James. "D. H. Moffatt: The Banker King of Denver." In *Millionaires and Kings of Enterprise; The Marvellous Careers of Some Americans Who by Pluck, Foresight, And Energy Have Made Themselves Masters in the Fields of Industry and Finance*, 407-413. Philadelphia, Penn.: J. B. Lippincott, 1901.

MOFFITT, PHILIP

Silver, A. David. "Philip Moffitt; Christopher Whittle." In *Entrepreneurial Megabucks: The 100 Greatest Entrepreneurs of the Last 25 Years*, 317-319. New York, N.Y.: Wiley, 1985.

MONAGHAN, TOM

Farnham, Alan. "Tom Monaghan, Founder of Domino's Pizza: 'I Feel That All These Setbacks Were Tools for Me to Learn From.'" In *Forbes Great Success Stories: Twelve Tales of Victory Wrested from Defeat*, 24-43. New York, N.Y.: Wiley, 2000.

Landrum, Gene N. "Tom Monaghan—Competitive." In *Profiles of Genius: Thirteen Creative Men Who Changed the World*, 96-105. Buffalo, N.Y.: Prometheus Books, 1993.

MONDAVI, ROBERT

MacPhee, William. "Robert Mondavi of Robert Mondavi Winery." In *Rare Breed: The Entrepreneur, An American Culture*, 91-101. Chicago, Ill.: Probus Publishing Company, 1987.

MONIZ, JOSEPH A.

Clarke, Caroline V. "Joseph A. Moniz: Partner, Day, Berry & Howard." In *Take a Lesson: Today's Black Achievers and How They Made It and What They Learned Along the Way*, 133-140. New York, N.Y.: Wiley, 2001.

MONTGOMERY, PARKER G.

Silver, A. David. "Parker G. Montgomery." In *Entrepreneurial Megabucks: The 100 Greatest Entrepreneurs of the Last 25 Years*, 320-322. New York, N.Y.: Wiley, 1985.

MOORE, GORDON E.

Gross, Daniel, and the Editors of Forbes Magazine. "Intel's Microcoprocessor and the Computer Revolution." In *Forbes Greatest Business Stories of All Time*, 246-265. New York, N.Y.: Wiley, 1996.

Moore, Gordon E. "Intel—Memories and the Microprocessor." In *The Power of Boldness: Ten Master Builders of American Industry Tell Their Success Stories*, ed. Elkan Blout, 77-102. Washington, D.C.: Joseph Henry Press, 1996.

Silver, A. David. "Andrew Grove; Gordon Moore; Robert Noyce." In *Entrepreneurial Megabucks: The 100 Greatest Entrepreneurs of the Last 25 Years*, 218-221. New York, N.Y.: Wiley, 1985.

MOORE, SHERYL

Lassen, Ali. "Sheryl Moore: Owner, Moore and Associates." In *The Secret of Their Success: Women Entrepreneurs Reveal How They Made It*, 125-130. Carlsbad, Calif.: Ali Lassen Success System, 1990.

MOORE, VERA

Harris, Wendy Beech. "Vera Moore, Vera Moore Cosmetics: Madam Makeover." In *Against All Odds: Ten Entrepreneurs Who Followed Their Hearts and Found Success*, 163-180. New York, N.Y.: Wiley, 2001.

MORALES, RAMON

Kingston, Brett. "Raphael Collado and Ramon Morales of Protocom Devices." In *The Dynamos: Who Are They Anyway?*, 35-44. New York, N.Y.: Wiley, 1987.

MORBY, JACQUELINE

Zientara, Marguerite. "Jacqueline Morby: Discovering Her Own Worth." In *Women, Technology & Power: Ten Stars and the History They Made*, 33-38. New York, N.Y.: AMACOM, American Management Association, 1987.

Zientara, Marguerite. "Jacqueline Morby: First on the Scene." In *Women, Technology & Power: Ten Stars and the History They Made*, 127-134. New York, N.Y.: AMACOM, American Management Association, 1987.

MORGAN, J. PIERPONT

Brands, H. W. "By Jupiter: J. Pierpont Morgan." In *Masters of Enterprise: Giants of American Business from John Jacob Astor and J.P.*

Morgan to Bill Gates and Oprah Winfrey, 64-79. New York, N.Y.: Free Press, 1999.

Burnley, James. "J. Pierpont Morgan: King of the Trusts." In *Millionaires and Kings of Enterprise; The Marvellous Careers of Some Americans Who by Pluck, Foresight, And Energy Have Made Themselves Masters in the Fields of Industry and Finance*, 79-92. Philadelphia, Penn.: J. B. Lippincott, 1901.

Diamond, Sigmond. "J. P. Morgan." In *The Reputation of the American Businessman*, 79-106. Cambridge, Mass.: Harvard University Press, 1955.

Fanning, Leonard M. "J. Pierpont Morgan." In *Titans of Business*, 45-72. Philadelphia, Penn.: Lippincott, 1964. 240 p.

Garraty, John A. "A Lion in the Street: How J. P. Morgan, like a 'One-Man Federal Reserve,' Calmed the Bankers and Helped Ease the Panic of 1907." In *Great Stories of American Businessmen, From American Heritage, The Magazine of History*, 317-325. New York, N.Y.: American Heritage Publishing Co., 1954.

Gross, Daniel, and the Editors of Forbes Magazine. "J. P. Morgan Saves the Country." In *Forbes Greatest Business Stories of All Time*, 58-73. New York, N.Y.: Wiley, 1996.

Hughes, Jonathan. "J. Pierpornt Morgan, The Investment Banker as Statesman." In *The Vital Few: The Entrepreneur and American Economic Progress*, 399-454. Expanded Edition, New York, N.Y.: Oxford University Press, 1986.

Klepper, Michael M., and Robert Gunther. "John Pierpont Morgan (1837-1913): The Most Powerful Banker in American History." In *The Wealthy 100 : From Benjamin Franklin to Bill Gates—A Ranking of the Richest Americans, Past and Present*, 98-103. Secaucus, N.J. : Carol Pub. Group, 1996.

Means, Howard B. "J. Pierpont Morgan: The American Colossus." In *Money & Power: The History of Business*, 125-143. New York, N.Y.: Wiley, 2001.

Wren, Daniel A., and Ronald G. Greenwood. "J. Pierpont Morgan." In *Management Innovators: The People and Ideas That Have Shaped Modern Business*, 120-129. New York, N.Y.: Oxford University Press, 1998.

MORITZ, JEFF

Kingston, Brett. "Jeff Moritz of SATCORP." In *The Dynamos: Who Are They Anyway?*, 23-30. New York, N.Y.: Wiley, 1987.

MORRIS, ARTHUR J.

"Bighearted Bankers: Arthur J. Morris and A. P. Giannini Sparked Revolution in Banking By Rolling Out Welcome Mat for Small Depositors and Borrowers." In *The 50 Great Pioneers of American Industry*. By the Editors of News Front and Year, 156-159. Maplewood, N.J.: C.S. Hammond, 1964.

MORRIS, JOHN L.

MacPhee, William. "John L. Morris of Bass Pro Shops." In *Rare Breed: The Entrepreneur, An American Culture*, 105-114. Chicago, Ill.: Probus Publishing Company, 1987.

MORRIS, ROBERT

Dos Passos, John. "Robert Morris and the 'Art Magick'." In *Great Stories of American Businessmen*, From *American Heritage, The Magazine of History*, 19-25. New York, N.Y.: American Heritage Publishing Co., 1954.

Gross, Daniel, and the Editors of Forbes Magazine. "Robert Morris: America's First Financier." In *Forbes Greatest Business Stories of All Time*, 4-21. New York, N.Y.: Wiley, 1996.

MORRIS, SAMUEL

Roberts, Edward B. "Samuel Morris and Transducer Devices, Inc." In *Entrepreneurs in High Technology: Lessons from MIT and Beyond*, 16-21. New York: Oxford University Press, 1991.

MORSE, SAMUEL FINLEY BREESE

Wren, Daniel A., and Ronald G. Greenwood. "Samuel Finley Breese Morse." In *Management Innovators: The People and Ideas That Have Shaped Modern Business*, 91-94. New York, N.Y.: Oxford University Press, 1998.

MORTON, LEVI PARSONS

Stoddard, William Osborn. "Levi Parsons Morton—Development." In *Men of Business*, 94-110. New York, N.Y.: Scribner's Sons, 1893. 317 p.

MOTTA, GLENDA

"Reimbursement: A Consultant's Focus." In *How I Became a Nurse Entrepreneur: Tales from 50 Nurses in Business*, 165-168. Petaluma, Calif.: National Nurses in Business Association, 1991.

MULLANY, DAVID

Fucini, Joseph J., and Suzy Fucini. "David Mullany, Wiffle Ball, Inc.: 'I Wanted to Control My Own Company'." In *Experience Inc.; Men and Women Who Founded Famous Companies After the Age of 40*, 23-29. New York, N.Y: Free Press, 1987.

MULLET, EMANUEL E.

Sommer, Willis J. "Emanuel E. Mullet: In Partnership with People and the Land." In *Entrepreneurs in the Faith Community: Profiles of Mennonites in Business*, ed. Calvin W. Redekop, and Benjamin W. Redekop, 98-122. Scottdale, Penn.: Herald Press, 1996.

MUNN, IRA Y.

Magrath, C. Peter. "Munn v. Illinois: A foot in the Door." In *Great Stories of American Businessmen*, From *American Heritage, The Magazine of*

History, 230-239. New York, N.Y.: American Heritage Publishing Co., 1954.

MURPHY, OWEN K.

Uris, Auren. "Owen K. Murphy—There's Money in Circulation." In *The Executive Breakthrough; 21 Roads to the Top*, 21-37. Garden City, N.Y.: Doubleday, 1967.

MURPHY, PATRICIA

Uris, Auren. "Patricia Murphy—Success by Candlelight." In *The Executive Breakthrough; 21 Roads to the Top*, 275-292. Garden City, N.Y.: Doubleday, 1967.

MURPHY, TERRY

Gray, Bob, ed. "Cashing in on Information." In *How Entrepreneurs Make Business Profits: A Study of Personal Success Stories From Cordovan Business Journals*, 159-162. Houston, Tex.: Cordovan Press, 1982.

MURPHY, THOMAS A.

Shook, Robert L. "Thomas A. Murphy: General Motors Corporation." In *The Chief Executive Officers: Men Who Run Big Business in America*, 161-182. New York, N.Y.: Harper & Row, 1981.

MURPHY, THOMAS S.

Silver, A. David. "Thomas S. Murphy." In *Entrepreneurial Megabucks: The 100 Greatest Entrepreneurs of the Last 25 Years*, 323-325. New York, N.Y.: Wiley, 1985.

MURRAY, ALBERT

Harris, Wendy Beech. "Albert and Odetta Murray, Hillside Inn: Mr. and Mrs. Hospitality." In *Against All Odds: Ten Entrepreneurs Who Followed Their Hearts and Found Success*, 203-227. New York, N.Y.: Wiley, 2001.

MURRAY, ODETTA

Harris, Wendy Beech. "Albert and Odetta Murray, Hillside Inn: Mr. and Mrs. Hospitality." In *Against All Odds: Ten Entrepreneurs Who Followed Their Hearts and Found Success*, 203-227. New York, N.Y.: Wiley, 2001.

MUTH, CATHERINE COLAN

Mikaelian, A. "Catherine Colan Muth." In *Women Who Mean Business: Success Stories of Women Over Forty*, 330-334. New York, N.Y.: William Morrow & Co., 1999.

MYERS, C. VERNE

King, Norman. "C. Verne Myers." In *The Money Messiah$*, 193-195. New York, N.Y.: Coward-McCann, 1983.

MYERS, SHERRIE

Ericksen, Gregory K. "Sherrie Myers—Lansing Lugnuts, 'We've Made Service Our Priority'." In *Women Entrepreneurs Only: Twelve Women Entrepreneurs Tell The Stories of Their Success*, 217-237. New York, N.Y.: Wiley, 1999.

MYERS, THERESE

Zientara, Marguerite. "Therese Myers: Adversity Builds Strength." In *Women, Technology & Power: Ten Stars and the History They Made*, 148-155. New York, N.Y.: AMACOM, American Management Association, 1987.

Zientara, Marguerite. "Therese Myers: The Need to Achieve." In *Women, Technology & Power: Ten Stars and the History They Made*, 62-69. New York, N.Y.: AMACOM, American Management Association, 1987.

Zientara, Marguerite. "Therese Myers: The Underdog Bites Back." In *Women, Technology & Power: Ten Stars and the History They Made*,

209-214. New York, N.Y.: AMACOM, American Management Association, 1987.

NASH, VON

Nash, Von. "A Knock on the Broken Screen Door!" In *Success Secrets: How Eighteen Everyday Women Became Fortune Builders and Famous Speakers*, 175-188. Glendora, Calif.: Royal CBS Publishing, 1978.

NATORI, JOSIE CRUZ

Aronoff, Craig E., and John L. Ward. "Josie Cruz Natori." In *Contemporary Entrepreneurs*, 360-366. Detroit, Mich.: Omnigraphics, Inc., 1992.

Enkelis, Liane, and Karen Olsen. "Josie Natori: President, The Natori Company." In *On Our Own Terms: Portraits of Women Business Leaders*, 8-17. San Francisco, Calif.: Berrett-Koehler, 1995.

Suarez, Ruth. "Josie Natori: Natori Co., 'Entrepreneurial Melody'." In *Superstar Entrepreneurs of Small and Large Businesses Reveal Their Secrets*. 203-207. Piscataway, N.J.: Research and Education Association, 1998.

Taylor, Russel R. "Josie Natori; She Made a Blouse into a Nightshirt." In *Exceptional Entrepreneurial Women*, 47-51. New York, N.Y: Quorum Books, 1988.

NEFF, JOHN

Train, John. "John Neff: Discipline, Patience…and Income." In *The New Money Masters : Winning Investment Strategies of Soros, Lynch, Steinhardt, Rogers, Neff, Wanger, Michaelis, Carret*, 138-151. New York, N.Y.: Harper & Row, 1989.

Train, John. "John Neff: Systematic Bargain Hunter." In *Money Masters of Our Time*, 144-155. New York, N.Y.: HarperBusiness, 2000.

NEIR, DAVE

Tsang, Cheryl D. "Dave Neir: 'The CPA', 1983-1993." In *Microsoft First Generation: The Success Secrets of the Visionaries Who Launched a Technology Empire*, 113-130. New York, N.Y.: Wiley, 2000.

NELSON, ORVIS M.

Launius, Roger D. "Right Man, Right Place, Right Time? Orvis M. Nelson and the Politics of Supplemental Air Carriers." In *Airline Executives and Federal Regulation: Case Studies in American Enterprise from the Airmail Era to the Dawn of the Jet Age*, ed. W. David Lewis, 322-355. Columbus, Ohio: Ohio State University Press, 2000.

NELSON, RAYMOND L.

Aronoff, Craig E., and John L. Ward. "Raymond L. Nelson Jr." In *Contemporary Entrepreneurs*, 367-371. Detroit, Mich.: Omnigraphics, Inc., 1992.

NEMETH, LANE

Aronoff, Craig E., and John L. Ward. "Lane Nemeth." In *Contemporary Entrepreneurs*, 372-377. Detroit, Mich.: Omnigraphics, Inc., 1992.

Silver, A. David. "Lane Nemeth." In *Entrepreneurial Megabucks: The 100 Greatest Entrepreneurs of the Last 25 Years*, 326-327. New York, N.Y.: Wiley, 1985.

Suarez, Ruth. "Lane Nemeth: Discovery Toys, 'Quality Time for Working Parents'." In *Superstar Entrepreneurs of Small and Large Businesses Reveal Their Secrets*. 209-213. Piscataway, N.J.: Research and Education Association, 1998.

Taylor, Russel R. "Lane Nemeth: 'Learning Should Be Fun'." In *Exceptional Entrepreneurial Women*, 79-85. New York, N.Y: Quorum Books, 1988.

NEUHARTH, ALLEN

Cose, Ellis. "The Chains: Gannett and Knight-Ridder." In *The Press*, 281-356. New York, N.Y.: Morrow, 1989.

NEUMANN, VERA

Rich-McCoy, Lois. "Earth Mother: Vera Neumann." In *Millionairess: Self-Made Women of America*, 1-22. New York, N.Y.: Harper & Row, 1978.

NEWHOUSE, SAMUEL I.

Klepper, Michael M., and Robert Gunther. "Samuel I. Newhouse (1895-1979): Paper Tiger." In *The Wealthy 100 : From Benjamin Franklin to Bill Gates—A Ranking of the Richest Americans, Past and Present*, 329-332. Secaucus, N.J. : Carol Pub. Group, 1996.

NEWTON FAMILY

Buchholz, Barbara B., and Margaret Crane. "Fox Photo, Inc., San Antonio, TX." In *Corporate Blood Lines: The Future of the Family Firm*, 160-174. New York, N.Y: Carol Publishing Group, 1989.

NG, ASSUNTA

Alexander, Shoshana. "Assunta NG: Seattle Chinese Post, Northwest Asian Weekly, Seattle, Washington." In *Women's Ventures, Women's Visions: 29 Inspiring Stories From Women Who Started Their Own Businesses*, 69-76. Freedom, Calif.: The Crossing Press, 1997.

NICHOLS, J. C.

Rose, Mark H. " 'There is Less Smoke in the District': J. C. Nichols, Urban Change, and Technological Systems." In *Business Entrepreneurs in the West*, ed. Ted C. Hinckley, 44-54. Manhattan, Kans.: Sunflower University Press, 1986.

NIELSEN, VALARIE

Kray, Margretta, and Valerie Nielsen. "Let's Get Down to Business: The Story of N.P.A." In *How I Became a Nurse Entrepreneur: Tales from 50 Nurses in Business*, 215-219. Petaluma, Calif.: National Nurses in Business Association, 1991.

NOE, DOROTHY COLE

Aronoff, Craig E., and John L. Ward. "Dorothy Cole Noe." In *Contemporary Entrepreneurs*, 378-382. Detroit, Mich.: Omnigraphics, Inc., 1992.

NOLAN, CHRISTOPHER P.

Hyatt, Joshua. "Cheap Counsel; Does Every Citizen Need a Lawyer on Private Retainer? The Founder of Landmark Legal Plans Inc. Thinks So." In *Anatomy of a Start-Up: Why Some New Businesses Succeed and Others Fail: 27 Real-Life Case Studies,* ed. Elizabeth K. Longsworth, 59-69. Boston, Mass.: Inc. Publishing, 1991.

NORMAN, DAVID A.

Fucini, Joseph J., and Suzy Fucini. "David A. Norman, Businessland, Inc.: 'There Was an Opportunity to Build a Very Large Company Very Quickly in a Whole New Industry'." In *Experience Inc.; Men and Women Who Founded Famous Companies After the Age of 40*, 105-111. New York, N.Y: Free Press, 1987.

NORMAN, MERLE N.

Fucini, Joseph J., and Suzy Fucini. "Merle N. Norman, Merle Norman Cosmetics: 'If They Like the Results They'll Buy the Product'." In *Experience Inc.; Men and Women Who Founded Famous Companies After the Age of 40*, 160-166. New York, N.Y: Free Press, 1987.

NORRIS, ERNEST E.

Farrar, Larston D. "Ernest E. Norris." In *America's Fifty Foremost Business Leaders,* ed. B. C. Forbes, 351-360. New York, N.Y.: B.C. Forbes, 1948.

NORRIS, WILLIAM C.

Fucini, Joseph J., and Suzy Fucini. "William C. Norris, Control Data Corporation: 'Address Society's Unmet Needs As Profitable Business Opportunities'." In *Experience Inc.; Men and Women Who Founded Famous Companies After the Age of 40*, 112-118. New York, N.Y: Free Press, 1987.

Pine, Carol, and Susan Mundale. "William Norris; There Ain't No Backin' Up." In *Self-Made: The Stories of 12 Minnesota Entrepreneurs*, 101-124. Minneapolis, Minn.: Dorn Books, 1982.

Silver, A. David. "William C. Norris." In *Entrepreneurial Megabucks: The 100 Greatest Entrepreneurs of the Last 25 Years*, 328-335. New York, N.Y.: Wiley, 1985.

Slater, Robert. "William Norris: Founder of Control Data Corporation." In *Portraits in Silicon*, 112-125. Cambridge, Mass.: MIT Press, 1987.

NORTON, CAROL "MICKEY"

Koppel, Mara. "Number One—Carol 'Mickey' Norton." In *Women of the Pits: Shattering the Glass Ceiling in Financial Markets*, 11-18. Chicago, Ill.: Dearborn Financial Publishers, 1998.

NOYCE, ROBERT

Gross, Daniel, and the Editors of Forbes Magazine. "Intel's Microcoprocessor and the Computer Revolution." In *Forbes Greatest Business Stories of All Time*, 246-265. New York, N.Y.: Wiley, 1996.

Silver, A. David. "Andrew Grove; Gordon Moore; Robert Noyce." In *Entrepreneurial Megabucks: The 100 Greatest Entrepreneurs of the Last 25 Years*, 218-221. New York, N.Y.: Wiley, 1985.

Slater, Robert. "Robert Noyce: The Mayor of Silicon Valley." In *Portraits in Silicon*, 152-161. Cambridge, Mass.: MIT Press, 1987.

NYE, AMY

Suarez, Ruth. "Amy Nye: AltiTunes, 'Business Junkie'." In *Superstar Entrepreneurs of Small and Large Businesses Reveal Their Secrets*, 129-132. Piscataway, N.J.: Research and Education Association, 1998.

NYE, TIM

Suarez, Ruth. "Tim Nye: Sunshine Interactive Network, 'A Web of Talent and Creativity'." In *Superstar Entrepreneurs of Small and Large Businesses Reveal Their Secrets*, 133-136. Piscataway, N.J.: Research and Education Association, 1998.

NYROP, DONALD W.

Corbett, Donna M. "Donald W. Nyrop: Airline Regulator, Airline Executive." In *Airline Executives and Federal Regulation: Case Studies in American Enterprise from the Airmail Era to the Dawn of the Jet Age*, ed. W. David Lewis, 125-168. Columbus, Ohio: Ohio State University Press, 2000.

OCHOA, ESTEBAN

Meier, Matt S. "Esteban Ochoa, Enterpriser." In *Business Entrepreneurs in the West*, ed. Ted C. Hinckley, 15-21. Manhattan, Kans.: Sunflower University Press, 1986.

O'CONNELL, PETER

Cahill, Timothy Patrick. "The Peter O'Connell Story." In *Profiles in the American Dream: The Real-Life Stories of the Struggles of American Entrepreneurs* , 111-132. Hanover, Mass.: Christopher Publishing Company, 1994.

O'DOWD, RON

Elfstrand, Rhonda. "Ron O'Dowd, Rick Tidball: Oakwood Financial Group, Inc." In *The Story Behind the Success: Learning From Pittsburgh Professionals*, 202-216. Pittsburgh, Penn.: Steel Publishing Partners, 1996.

OGILVY, DAVID

Gross, Daniel, and the Editors of Forbes Magazine. "David Ogilvy and the Creation of Modern Advertising." In *Forbes Greatest Business Stories of All Time*, 158-175. New York, N.Y.: Wiley, 1996.

O'KEEFE, MARY A.

Mikaelian, A. "Mary A. O'Keefe." In *Women Who Mean Business: Success Stories of Women Over Forty*, 108-112. New York, N.Y.: William Morrow & Co., 1999.

OKI, SCOTT

Liberman, Gail, and Alan Lavine. "Scott D. Oki: Microsoft Millionaire." In *Rags to Riches: Motivating Stories of How Ordinary People Achieved Extraordinary Wealth!*, 163-174. Chicago, Ill.: Dearborn, 2000.

Tsang, Cheryl D. "Scott Oki: 'The Force' 1982-1992." In *Microsoft First Generation: The Success Secrets of the Visionaries Who Launched a Technology Empire*, 23-46. New York, N.Y.: Wiley, 2000.

OLDFIELD, JULIA COOPER

Oldfield, Julia Cooper. "The Visionary Enterprise of Kind Hearts, Caring Hands." In *How I Became a Nurse Entrepreneur: Tales from 50 Nurses in Business*, 211-214. Petaluma, Calif.: National Nurses in Business Association, 1991.

OLSON, EARL

Pine, Carol, and Susan Mundale. "Earl Olson; Betting on the Bird." In *Self-Made: The Stories of 12 Minnesota Entrepreneurs*, 175-190. Minneapolis, Minn.: Dorn Books, 1982.

OLSON, KENNETH H.

Davis, William. "Ken Olson, b. 1926: The Ultimate Team Leader." In *The Innovators: The Essential Guide to Business Thinkers, Achievers and Entrepreneurs*, 274-276. New York, N.Y.: AMACOM, 1987.

Jager, Rama Dev, and Rafael Ortiz. "Ken Olsen: Digital Equipment Corporation; Reflections on the Revolution." In *In the Company of Giants: Candid Conversations with the Visionaries of the Digital World*, 209-224. New York, N.Y.: McGraw-Hill, 1997.

Roberts, Edward B. "Kenneth Olsen and Digital Equipment Corporation." In *Entrepreneurs in High Technology: Lessons From MIT and Beyond*, 5-12. New York: Oxford University Press, 1991.

Silver, A. David. "Kenneth H. Olsen." In *Entrepreneurial Megabucks: The 100 Greatest Entrepreneurs of the Last 25 Years*, 336-338. New York, N.Y.: Wiley, 1985.

OMIDYAR, PIERRE

Ericksen, Gregory K. "Pierre Omidyar—eBay 'Bring Power to the Individual'." In *Net Entrepreneurs Only : 10 Entrepreneurs Tell the Stories of Their Success*, 161-183. New York : John Wiley, 2000.

Price, Christopher. "Pierre Omidyar—eBay 'Bidding to Distance the Competition'." In *The Internet Entrepreneurs: Business Rules Are Good: Break Them*, 176-190. London, Eng.: FT.com, 2000.

O'REAR, BOB

Tsang, Cheryl D. "Bob O'Rear: 'The Mathematician', 1977-1993." In *Microsoft First Generation: The Success Secrets of the Visionaries*

Who Launched a Technology Empire, 1-22. New York, N.Y.: Wiley, 2000.

ORTENBERG, ELISABETH CLAIBORNE

Silver, A. David. "Elisabeth Claiborne Ortenberg." In *Entrepreneurial Megabucks: The 100 Greatest Entrepreneurs of the Last 25 Years*, 339-341. New York, N.Y.: Wiley, 1985.

O'RYAN, THOMAS MICHAEL

Uris, Auren. "Thomas O'Ryan—Advertising on Wheels." In *The Executive Breakthrough; 21 Roads to the Top*, 59-69. Garden City, N.Y.: Doubleday, 1967.

OSBORNE, ADAM

Slater, Robert. "Adam Osborne: He made the Computer Portable." In *Portraits in Silicon*, 322-329. Cambridge, Mass.: MIT Press, 1987.

OSHMAN, M. KENNETH

Silver, A. David. "M. Kenneth Oshman; Robert R. Maxfield." In *Entrepreneurial Megabucks: The 100 Greatest Entrepreneurs of the Last 25 Years*, 342-343. New York, N.Y.: Wiley, 1985.

OTIS, ELISHA GRAVES

"Going Up: Elisha Graves Otis' Invention of Safety Elevator in 1853 Started the Rise of Modern Cities by Making Multi-Story Buildings Practicable. Elevator Industry Sales Volume Today Is Over $500 Million a Year." In *The 50 Great Pioneers of American Industry*. By the Editors of News Front and Year, 48-52. Maplewood, N.J.: C.S. Hammond, 1964.

OWADES, RUTH M.

Enkelis, Liane, and Karen Olsen. "Ruth M. Owades: President, Calyx & Corolla." In *On Our Own Terms: Portraits of Women Business Leaders* , 50-59. San Francisco, Calif.: Berrett-Koehler, 1995.

OWEN, DIAN GRAVE

Enkelis, Liane, and Karen Olsen. "Dian Owen: Chairman of the Board, Owen Healthcare." In *On Our Own Terms: Portraits of Women Business Leaders* , 124-133. San Francisco, Calif.: Berrett-Koehler, 1995.

OWENS, MICHAEL J.

"Glass Giant: Untutored Mike Owens Replaced Blowpipe with Machine, Founded $2-Billion-A-Year Glass Industry." In *The 50 Great Pioneers of American Industry*. By the Editors of News Front and Year, 141-143. Maplewood, N.J.: C.S. Hammond, 1964.

PABST, FREDERICK

Burnley, James. "Captain Frederick Pabst: The King of Lager Beer." In *Millionaires and Kings of Enterprise; The Marvellous Careers of Some Americans Who by Pluck, Foresight, And Energy Have Made Themselves Masters in the Fields of Industry and Finance*, 463-475. Philadelphia, Penn.: J. B. Lippincott, 1901.

PACKARD, DAVID

Klepper, Michael M., and Robert Gunther. "David Packard (1912-1996): The H-P Way." In *The Wealthy 100 : From Benjamin Franklin to Bill Gates—A Ranking of the Richest Americans, Past and Present,* 336-339. Secaucus, N.J. : Carol Pub. Group, 1996.

Silver, A. David. "David Packard; William R. Hewlett." In *Entrepreneurial Megabucks: The 100 Greatest Entrepreneurs of the Last 25 Years*, 344-346. New York, N.Y.: Wiley, 1985.

PALMER, POTTER

Burnley, James. "Potter Palmer: A Successful Pioneer." In *Millionaires and Kings of Enterprise; The Marvellous Careers of Some Americans Who by Pluck, Foresight, And Energy Have Made Themselves Masters in the Fields of Industry and Finance*, 414-421. Philadelphia, Penn.: J. B. Lippincott, 1901.

PAPPALARADO, NEIL

Roberts, Edward B. "Neil Pappalarado and Medical Information Technology, Inc." In *Entrepreneurs in High Technology: Lessons from MIT and Beyond*, 21-26. New York: Oxford University Press, 1991.

PARHAM, PETER

Wallace, Robert L. "Peter Parham and Calvin Grimes Jr.: Founders, Grime Oil, Washington, D.C. and Boston, Massachusetts." In *Black Wealth: Your Road to Small Business Success*, 129-134. New York, N.Y.: Wiley, 2000.

PARK, ROY HAMPTON

Silver, A. David. "Roy Hampton Park." In *Entrepreneurial Megabucks: The 100 Greatest Entrepreneurs of the Last 25 Years*, 347-351. New York, N.Y.: Wiley, 1985.

PARKER, GEORGE S.

Cleary, David Powers. "Parker Pens; 'Our Pens Can Write in Any Language'." In *Great American Brands: The Success Formulas That Made Them Famous*, 223-231. New York, N.Y: Fairchild Publications, 1981.

PARKINSON, JOSEPH C.

Silver, A. David. "Joseph C. Parkinson; Ward Parkinson." In *Entrepreneurial Megabucks: The 100 Greatest Entrepreneurs of the Last 25 Years*, 352-354. New York, N.Y.: Wiley, 1985.

PARKINSON, WARD

Aronoff, Craig E., and John L. Ward. "Ward D. Parkinson." In *Contemporary Entrepreneurs*, 383-388. Detroit, Mich.: Omnigraphics, Inc., 1992.

Gilder, George. "The Rise of Micron." In *The Spirit of Enterprise*, 218-244. New York, N.Y: Simon and Schuster, 1984.

Silver, A. David. "Joseph C. Parkinson; Ward Parkinson." In *Entrepreneurial Megabucks: The 100 Greatest Entrepreneurs of the Last 25 Years*, 352-354. New York, N.Y.: Wiley, 1985.

PARROT-FONSECA, JOAN

Clarke, Caroline V. "Joan Parrot-Fonseca: President, JPF & Associates." In *Take a Lesson: Today's Black Achievers and How They Made It and What They Learned Along the Way*, 141-150. New York, N.Y.: Wiley, 2001.

PARSONS, RICHARD D.

Clarke, Caroline V. "Richard D. Parsons: President, Time Warner, Inc." In *Take a Lesson: Today's Black Achievers and How They Made It and What They Learned Along the Way*, 151-160. New York, N.Y.: Wiley, 2001.

PASTERNAK, KEN

Ericksen, Gregory K. "Ken Pasternak—Knight Trading Group 'Figure Things Out and Build a Business'." In *Net Entrepreneurs Only : 10 Entrepreneurs Tell the Stories of Their Success*, 121-140. New York : John Wiley, 2000.

PATTERSON, JOHN HENRY

Carson, Gerald. "The Machine That Kept Them Honest." In *Great Stories of American Businessmen*, From *American Heritage, The Magazine of History,* 335-347. New York, N.Y.: American Heritage Publishing Co., 1954.

"Making Sales Register: NCR's John Patterson Blazed Salesmanship's Sawdust Trail, Pioneered 'Education' of Customer." In *The 50 Great Pioneers of American Industry*. By the Editors of News Front and Year, 114-118. Maplewood, N.J.: C.S. Hammond, 1964.

PAUL, REBECCA GRAHAM

Mikaelian, A. "Rebecca Graham Paul." In *Women Who Mean Business: Success Stories of Women Over Forty*, 64-68. New York, N.Y.: William Morrow & Co., 1999.

PAULSON, ALLEN E.

Silver, A. David. "Allen E. Paulson." In *Entrepreneurial Megabucks: The 100 Greatest Entrepreneurs of the Last 25 Years*, 355-357. New York, N.Y.: Wiley, 1985.

PAULUCCI, JENO FRANCO

Davis, William. "Jeno Paulucci, b. 1918: Maverick of the Grocery Trade." In *The Innovators: The Essential Guide to Business Thinkers, Achievers and Entrepreneurs*, 280-283. New York, N.Y.: AMACOM, 1987.

Gunther, Max. "Jeno Paulucci: One-Hundred Million Dollars." In *The Very, Very Rich and How They Got That Way*, ed. Max Gunther, 244-254. Chicago, Ill.: The Playboy Press, 1972.

Pine, Carol, and Susan Mundale. "Jeno Paulucci: The Kid with the Argentine Bananas." In *Self-Made: The Stories of 12 Minnesota Entrepreneurs*, 19-37. Minneapolis, Minn.: Dorn Books, 1982.

Silver, A. David. "Luigino Franco Paulucci." In *Entrepreneurial Megabucks: The 100 Greatest Entrepreneurs of the Last 25 Years*, 358-361. New York, N.Y.: Wiley, 1985.

Uris, Auren. "Jeno Paulucci—He Brings Exotic Foods to America's Tables." In *The Executive Breakthrough; 21 Roads to the Top*, 299-312. Garden City, N.Y.: Doubleday, 1967.

PAYNE, OLIVER HAZARD

Klepper, Michael M., and Robert Gunther. "Col. Oliver H. Payne (1839-1917): Colonel Cash." In *The Wealthy 100 : From Benjamin Franklin to Bill Gates—A Ranking of the Richest Americans, Past and Present*, 104-105. Secaucus, N.J. : Carol Pub. Group, 1996.

PAXSON, LOWELL W.

Fucini, Joseph J., and Suzy Fucini. "Lowell W. Paxson, Roy M. Speer, Home Shopping Network, Inc.: 'We Knew We Were on a Rocket'." In *Experience Inc.; Men and Women Who Founded Famous Companies After the Age of 40*, 89-95. New York, N.Y: Free Press, 1987.

PEABODY, GEORGE

Hellman, Geoffrey T. "The First Great Cheerful Giver." In *Great Stories of American Businessmen, From American Heritage, The Magazine of History*, 119-125. New York, N.Y.: American Heritage Publishing Co., 1954.

Klepper, Michael M., and Robert Gunther. "George Peabody (1795-1869): Spanning the Atlantic." In *The Wealthy 100 : From Benjamin Franklin to Bill Gates—A Ranking of the Richest Americans, Past and Present*, 156-158. Secaucus, N.J. : Carol Pub. Group, 1996.

PEACH, ROBERT E.

Leary, William M. "Robert E. Peach and Mohawk Airlines: A Study in Entrepreneurship." In *Airline Executives and Federal Regulation: Case Studies in American Enterprise from the Airmail Era to the Dawn of the Jet Age*, ed. W. David Lewis, 293-321. Columbus, Ohio: Ohio State University Press, 2000.

PEARSONS, D. K.

Burnley, James. "Dr. D. K. Pearsons: The Millionaire Philosopher." In *Millionaires and Kings of Enterprise; The Marvellous Careers of Some Americans Who by Pluck, Foresight, And Energy Have Made Themselves Masters in the Fields of Industry and Finance*, 422-429. Philadelphia, Penn.: J. B. Lippincott, 1901.

PECKHAM, JOHN M. III

"John M. Peckham III, The Peckham Boston Company." In *Profiles in Success: How Six Entrepreneurs Have Prospered in a Tough*

Business Environment, 46-53. By the editors of *Managing*. New York, N.Y.: HBJ Newsletters, 1981.

PEMBERTON, JOHN S.

Cleary, David Powers. "Coca-Cola; There Is No Limit to What a Man Can Do or Where He Can Go." In *Great American Brands: The Success Formulas That Made Them Famous*, 60-74. New York, N.Y: Fairchild Publications, 1981.

Davis, William. "John S. Pemberton, 1841-1886: Coke Is It." In *The Innovators: The Essential Guide to Business Thinkers, Achievers and Entrepreneurs*, 284-288. New York, N.Y.: AMACOM, 1987.

PENNEY, J. C.

Davis, William. "James Cash Penney, 1875-1971: The Man with a Thousand Partners." In *The Innovators: The Essential Guide to Business Thinkers, Achievers and Entrepreneurs*, 288-292. New York, N.Y.: AMACOM, 1987.

PERDUE, FRANK

Sobel, Robert, and David B. Sicilia. "Frank Perdue: The Man of 270 Million Chickens." In *The Entrepreneurs: An American Adventure*, 77-81. Boston, Mass.: Houghton Mifflin Company, 1986.

PERELMAN, RONALD OWEN

Klepper, Michael M., and Robert Gunther. "Ronald Owen Perelman (1943-): Super Investor." In *The Wealthy 100 : From Benjamin Franklin to Bill Gates—A Ranking of the Richest Americans, Past and Present*, 319-321. Secaucus, N.J. : Carol Pub. Group, 1996.

Smith, Roy C. "The Beauty Queen." In *Wealth Creators: The Rise of Today's Rich and Super-Rich*, 95-99. New York, N.Y.: Truman Talley, 2001.

PERKINS, THOMAS HANDASYD

Klepper, Michael M., and Robert Gunther. "Thomas Handasyd Perkins (1764-1854): Bigger Than the U.S. Navy." In *The Wealthy 100 : From Benjamin Franklin to Bill Gates—A Ranking of the Richest Americans, Past and Present*, 266-269. Secaucus, N.J. : Carol Pub. Group, 1996.

PEROT, H. ROSS

Davis, William. "H. Ross Perot, b. 1930: The Texan Who Managed Japanese-Style." In *The Innovators: The Essential Guide to Business Thinkers, Achievers and Entrepreneurs*, 292-296. New York, N.Y.: AMACOM, 1987.

Meyer, Michael. "The Patriarch." In *The Alexander Complex; The Dreams That Drive the Great Businessmen*, 63-103. New York, N.Y.: Times Books, 1989.

Sheehy, Sandy. "H. Ross Perot: Beyond Cowboy Capitalism." In *Texas Big Rich; Exploits, Eccentricities, And Fabulous Fortunes Won and Lost*, 387-405. New York, N.Y.: Morrow, 1990.

Silver, A. David. "H. Ross Perot." In *Entrepreneurial Megabucks: The 100 Greatest Entrepreneurs of the Last 25 Years*, 362-363. New York, N.Y.: Wiley, 1985.

Slater, Robert. "H. Ross Perot." In *Portraits in Silicon*, 126-137. Cambridge, Mass.: MIT Press, 1987.

PERRIN, KEITH

Mitchell, Niki Butler. "For Us, By Us: J. Alexander Martin, Vice President and Head Designer; Daymond John, President and CEO; Carl Brown, Co-Founder; Keith Perrin, Co-Founder, FUBU." In *The New Color of Success: Twenty Young Black Millionaires Tell You How They're Making it*, 29-42. Rocklin, Calif.: Prima Publishing, 2000.

PETERS, JON

Hillkirk, John, and Gary Jacobson. "Batman and Rain Man: Flip Sides of the Same Hollywood Coin." In *Grit, Guts, And Genius: True Tales of Megasuccess: Who Made Them Happen and How They Did It*, 3-19. Boston, Mass.: Houghton Mifflin, 1990.

PETERS, LOIS

Wallace, Robert L. "Lois Peters: President and Founder, Aathome Pediatrics Nursing Team, Clarksville, Maryland." In *Black Wealth: Your Road to Small Business Success*, 67-72. New York, N.Y.: Wiley, 2000.

PETERSEN, DONALD

Hillkirk, John, and Gary Jacobson. "Ford's Donald Petersen: CEO of the Decade." In *Grit, Guts, And Genius: True Tales of Megasuccess: Who Made Them Happen and How They Did It*, 73-83. Boston, Mass.: Houghton Mifflin, 1990.

PETERSON, MYRA

Mitchell, Niki Butler. "From the Universe to Omniverse: Myra Peterson, President and CEO, Omniverse Digital Solutions, LLC." In *The New Color of Success: Twenty Young Black Millionaires Tell You How They're Making it*, 55-67. Rocklin, Calif.: Prima Publishing, 2000.

PETGRAVE, ROBIN

Mitchell, Niki Butler. "Fly Guy: Robin Petgrave, President, Bravo Helicopter and Wing." In *The New Color of Success: Twenty Young Black Millionaires Tell You How They're Making it*, 43-54. Rocklin, Calif.: Prima Publishing, 2000.

PETRIE, MILTON S.

Silver, A. David. "Milton S. Petrie." In *Entrepreneurial Megabucks: The 100 Greatest Entrepreneurs of the Last 25 Years*, 364-365. New York, N.Y.: Wiley, 1985.

PHILLIPS, COLETTE

Suarez, Ruth. "Colette Phillips: Colette Phillips Communications, Inc., 'Innovation in Communication'." In *Superstar Entrepreneurs of Small and Large Businesses Reveal Their Secrets*. 243-247. Piscataway, N.J.: Research and Education Association, 1998.

PHILLIPS, LAWRENCE S.

Pottker, Jan. "Phillips-Van Heusen Corporation: No Heart on His Sleeve." In *Born to Power: Heirs to America's Leading Businesses*, 298-305. New York, N.Y.: Barron's, 1992.

PHILLIPS, PERIAN HASLAM

Lyons, Mary. "Perian Haslam Phillips: FrontierVision, Regional Marketing Manager, 'I Worked a Million Hours a Week'." In *Maine's Achieving Women: Conversations with Entrepreneurs*, 141-151. Old Orchard Beach, ME: Lilac River Press, 1999.

PHIPPS, HENRY

Klepper, Michael M., and Robert Gunther. "Henry Phipps (1839-1930): The Flywheel of Carnegie's Steel Company." In *The Wealthy 100 : From Benjamin Franklin to Bill Gates—A Ranking of the Richest Americans, Past and Present,* 313-315. Secaucus, N.J. : Carol Pub. Group, 1996.

PICKENS, T. BOONE

Sheehy, Sandy. "T. Boone Pickens: The 'Attila of Amarilla'." In *Texas Big Rich; Exploits, Eccentricities, And Fabulous Fortunes Won and Lost,* 307-319. New York, N.Y.: Morrow, 1990.

Sobel, Robert. "T. Boone Pickens and the New Corporate Raiders." In *Dangerous Dreamers: The Financial Innovators from Charles Merrill to Michael Milken,* 136-153. New York, N.Y.: Wiley, 1993.

PIESTRUP, ANN

Zientara, Marguerite. "Ann Piestrup: 'I Wanted to Make the World Better'." In *Women, Technology & Power: Ten Stars and the History They Made*, 50-56. New York, N.Y.: AMACOM, American Management Association, 1987.

Zientara, Marguerite. "Ann Piestrup: Making the Abstract Concrete." In *Women, Technology & Power: Ten Stars and the History They Made*, 107-119. New York, N.Y.: AMACOM, American Management Association, 1987.

Zientara, Marguerite. "Ann Piestrup: Uprooted." In *Women, Technology & Power: Ten Stars and the History They Made*, 178-183. New York, N.Y.: AMACOM, American Management Association, 1987.

PILAND, LARRY

Murphy, Linda. "Larry Piland: & Bill Blue: Datel Systems, Inc." In *Computer Entrepreneurs: People Who Built Successful Businesses Around Computers*, 57-64. San Diego, Calif.: Computer Publishing Enterprises, 1990.

PILLSBURY FAMILY

Burnley, James. "The Pillsbury's: The Flour Kings of America." In *Millionaires and Kings of Enterprise; The Marvellous Careers of Some Americans Who by Pluck, Foresight, And Energy Have Made Themselves Masters in the Fields of Industry and Finance*, 476-489. Philadelphia, Penn.: J. B. Lippincott, 1901.

Pottker, Jan. "The Funding Exchange: He's Pillsbury—He's Got to Do Good, George Pillsbury, Co-Founder." In *Born to Power: Heirs to America's Leading Businesses*, 428-433. New York, N.Y.: Barron's, 1992.

PINKERTON, ALLAN

Davis, William. "Allan Pinkerton, 1819-1884: Pioneer of Private Security." In *The Innovators: The Essential Guide to*

Business Thinkers, Achievers and Entrepreneurs, 301-304. New York, N.Y.: AMACOM, 1987.

PIPER, WILLIAM T.

Cleary, David Powers. "Piper Aircraft—Because Air Is Everywhere." In *Great American Brands: The Success Formulas That Made Them Famous*, 232-238. New York, N.Y: Fairchild Publications, 1981.

PLACETTE, GREIG

Gray, Bob, ed. "Customer Service Is the Key." In *How Entrepreneurs Make Business Profits: A Study of Personal Success Stories From Cordovan Business Journals*, 96-101. Houston, Tex.: Cordovan Press, 1982.

PLUMLY, GEORGE W.

Fucini, Joseph J., and Suzy Fucini. "George W. Plumly, Plumly Industries: 'People Will Always Say It Can't Be Done, Until Someone Comes Along and Does It'." In *Experience Inc.; Men and Women Who Founded Famous Companies After the Age of 40*, 207-214. New York, N.Y: Free Press, 1987.

PODUSKA, JOHN WILLIAM SR.

Aronoff, Craig E., and John L. Ward. "John William Poduska Sr." In *Contemporary Entrepreneurs*, 389-395. Detroit, Mich.: Omnigraphics, Inc., 1992.

Silver, A. David. "John William Poduska." In *Entrepreneurial Megabucks: The 100 Greatest Entrepreneurs of the Last 25 Years*, 366-369. New York, N.Y.: Wiley, 1985.

POE, KRISTEN N.

Harris, Wendy Beech. "Renée E. Warren and Kristen N. Poe, Noelle-Elaine Media Consultants: PR's Dynamic Duo." In *Against All Odds: Ten Entrepreneurs Who Followed Their Hearts and Found Success*, 181-201. New York, N.Y.: Wiley, 2001.

POE, SHERI

Aronoff, Craig E., and John L. Ward. "Sheri Poe." In *Contemporary Entrepreneurs*, 396-401. Detroit, Mich.: Omnigraphics, Inc., 1992.

POLLIN, KATHERINE T.

Mills, Glenna B., and Katherine T. Pollin. "Getting Started..." In *How I Became a Nurse Entrepreneur: Tales from 50 Nurses in Business*, 261-265. Petaluma, Calif.: National Nurses in Business Association, 1991.

POLLOCK, ELSIE FRANKFURT

Rich-McCoy, Lois. "A Pregnant Pattern: Edna Ravkind and Elsie Frankfurt Pollock." In *Millionairess: Self-Made Women of America*, 96-126. New York, N.Y.: Harper & Row, 1978.

POOR, HENRY VARNUM

"He Opened Industry's Books: Henry Varnum Poor, Pioneer of Financial Research, Defended the Investor's Right to Know About His Company in an Era When the Annual Report Was Unknown." In *The 50 Great Pioneers of American Industry*. By the Editors of News Front and Year, 53-55. Maplewood, N.J.: C.S. Hammond, 1964.

POPCORN, FAITH

Taylor, Russel R. "Faith Popcorn; She Discerns the Future." In *Exceptional Entrepreneurial Women*, 25-31. New York, N.Y: Quorum Books, 1988.

POPE, ALBERT A.

Cleary, David Powers. "Columbia Bicycles; Could It Have Become 'The First General Motors'?" In *Great American Brands: The Success Formulas That Made Them Famous*, 75-79. New York, N.Y: Fairchild Publications, 1981.

POPEIL, RON

Farnham, Alan. "Ron Popeil: Founder of Ronco, 'You Might as Well Go for It'." In *Forbes Great Success Stories: Twelve Tales of Victory Wrested from Defeat*, 86-105. New York, N.Y.: Wiley, 2000.

PORTER, WILLIAM

Ericksen, Gregory K. "William Porter & Christos Cotsakos—E*TRADE 'Go For It'." In *Net Entrepreneurs Only : 10 Entrepreneurs Tell the Stories of Their Success*, 61-80. New York : John Wiley, 2000.

POST, CHARLES WILLIAM

Klepper, Michael M., and Robert Gunther. "Charles W. Post (1854-1914): Cereal Czar." In *The Wealthy 100 : From Benjamin Franklin to Bill Gates—A Ranking of the Richest Americans, Past and Present*, 325-328`. Secaucus, N.J. : Carol Pub. Group, 1996.

POWELL, ELIOT

Wallace, Robert L. "Jerome Sanders, Eliot Powell, Robert (Bob) Wallace: Founders, The SDGG Holding Company, Inc., Summit, New Jersey." In *Black Wealth: Your Road to Small Business Success*, 175-184. New York, N.Y.: Wiley, 2000.

PRATT, ENOCH

"Enoch Pratt." In *A Dozen Roads to Success: Being Graphic Sketches of Twelve of the Most Prominent Business Men of America, And Showing How They Became Millionaires*, 60-71. Philadelphia, Penn.: Girard Pub. Co., 1894.

PRECHTER, ROBERT

King, Norman. "Robert Prechter." In *The Money Messiah$*, 199-201. New York, N.Y.: Coward-McCann, 1983.

PRESSMAN, GENE

Pottker, Jan. "Barneys New York: Innovation by Generation." In *Born to Power: Heirs to America's Leading Businesses*, 40-49. New York, N.Y.: Barron's, 1992.

PRESSMAN, ROBERT L.

Pottker, Jan. "Barneys New York: Innovation by Generation." In *Born to Power: Heirs to America's Leading Businesses*, 40-49. New York, N.Y.: Barron's, 1992.

PRICE, PETER O.

Welles, Edward O. "A Whole New Game; At Birth, It's Already Bigger and Richer Than Most Businesses Ever Get. But Like Many Start-Ups, America's First All-Sports Daily Newspaper Is Gambling on a Hunch." In *Anatomy of a Start-Up: Why Some New Businesses Succeed and Others Fail: 27 Real-Life Case Studies,* ed. Elizabeth K. Longsworth, 303-312. Boston, Mass.: Inc. Publishing, 1991.

PRICE, SOLOMON

Landrum, Gene N. "Solomon Price—Impatient." In *Profiles of Genius: Thirteen Creative Men Who Changed the World*, 144-154. Buffalo, N.Y.: Prometheus Books, 1993.

Silver, A. David. "Sol Price." In *Entrepreneurial Megabucks: The 100 Greatest Entrepreneurs of the Last 25 Years*, 370-371. New York, N.Y.: Wiley, 1985.

PRICE, T. ROWE

Train, John. "T. Rowe Price: Fertile Field for Growth." In *The Money Masters*, 139-157. New York, N.Y.: Harper & Row, 1980.

Train, John. "T. Rowe Price: Mr. Growth Stock." In *Money Masters of Our Time*, 1-13. New York, N.Y.: HarperBusiness, 2000.

PRITZKER, JAY ARTHUR

Darby, Edwin. "Pritzker." In *The Fortune Builders*, 95-116. Garden City, N.Y.: Doubleday and Company, Inc., 1986.

PROCTER FAMILY

Cleary, David Powers. "Ivory Soap; 99 44/100% Pure—It Floats." In *Great American Brands: The Success Formulas That Made Them Famous*, 172-181. New York, N.Y: Fairchild Publications, 1981.

Pottker, Jan. "University of Massachusetts: Brewing Controversy at P&G, James Gamble, Researcher." In *Born to Power: Heirs to America's Leading Businesses*, 420-425. New York, N.Y.: Barron's, 1992.

"Soap's First Big Splash: When Harley Procter in 1878, Used Direct-to-Consumer, Large-Scale Advertising and Merchandising to Launch Ivory Soap, He Charted a New Course for the Entire Soap Industry. Today the Combined Advertising Expenditures of the Three Leading Soap Firms Have Passed a New High of Over $300 Million." In *The 50 Great Pioneers of American Industry*. By the Editors of News Front and Year, 72-75. Maplewood, N.J.: C.S. Hammond, 1964.

PROCTOR, BARBARA GARDNER

Rich-McCoy, Lois. "Right Smart: Barbara Gardner Proctor." In *Millionairess: Self-Made Women of America*, 207-227. New York, N.Y.: Harper & Row, 1978.

PRUTCH, SHIRLEY

White, Jane. "Shirley Prutch of Martin Marietta: A Pioneer Who Did It Her Way." In *A Few Good Women: Breaking the Barriers to Top Management*, 53-75. Englewood Cliffs, N.J.: Prentice Hall, 1992.

PSAROUTHAKIS, JOHN

Fucini, Joseph J., and Suzy Fucini. "John Psarouthakis: 'Define a Problem Before Trying to Solve It'." In *Experience Inc.; Men and Women Who*

Founded Famous Companies After the Age of 40, 167-172. New York, N.Y: Free Press, 1987.

PULITZER, JOSEPH

Klepper, Michael M., and Robert Gunther. "Joseph Pulitzer (1847-1911): The Pauper Who Became a Publishing Prince." In *The Wealthy 100 : From Benjamin Franklin to Bill Gates—A Ranking of the Richest Americans, Past and Present*, 270-273. Secaucus, N.J. : Carol Pub. Group, 1996.

PULLMAN, GEORGE MORTIMER

Burnley, James. "George M. Pullman: The Pullman Car Pioneer." In *Millionaires and Kings of Enterprise; The Marvellous Careers of Some Americans Who by Pluck, Foresight, And Energy Have Made Themselves Masters in the Fields of Industry and Finance*, 133-145. Philadelphia, Penn.: J. B. Lippincott, 1901.

Davis, William. "George Mortimer Pullman, 1831-1897: The Sleeping Car King." In *The Innovators: The Essential Guide to Business Thinkers, Achievers and Entrepreneurs*, 304-306. New York, N.Y.: AMACOM, 1987.

"George Mortimer Pullman." In *A Dozen Roads to Success: Being Graphic Sketches of Twelve of the Most Prominent Business Men of America, And Showing How They Became Millionaires, 136-149. Philadelphia, Penn.: Girard Pub. Co., 1894.*

Klepper, Michael M., and Robert Gunther. "George M. Pullman (1831-1897): A Sleeping Giant." In *The Wealthy 100 : From Benjamin Franklin to Bill Gates—A Ranking of the Richest Americans, Past and Present*, 220-223. Secaucus, N.J. : Carol Pub. Group, 1996.

QUEENY, EDGAR M.

Farrar, Larston D. "Edgar M. Queeny." In *America's Fifty Foremost Business Leaders,* ed. B. C. Forbes, 361-370. New York, N.Y.: B.C. Forbes, 1948.

QURESHEY, SAFI U.

Kingston, Brett. "Qureshey, Wong, And Yuen of AST Research, Inc." In *The Dynamos: Who Are They Anyway?*, 113-117. New York, N.Y: Wiley, 1987.

Aronoff, Craig E., and John L. Ward. "Safi U. Qureshey; Thomas C. K. Yuen." In *Contemporary Entrepreneurs*, 402-407. Detroit, Mich.: Omnigraphics, Inc., 1992.

RAINWATER, RICHARD

Train, John. "Richard Rainwater: Ring the Changes." In *Money Masters of Our Time*, 65-80. New York, N.Y.: HarperBusiness, 2000.

RALSTON, DONALD

Cleary, David Powers. "Ralston Purina Foods & Feeds; Find the Right Foundations and Build on Them." In *Great American Brands: The Success Formulas That Made Them Famous*, 239-245. New York, N.Y: Fairchild Publications, 1981.

RALSTON, WILLIAM H.

Cleary, David Powers. "Ralston Purina Foods & Feeds; Find the Right Foundations and Build on Them." In *Great American Brands: The Success Formulas That Made Them Famous*, 239-245. New York, N.Y: Fairchild Publications, 1981.

RAMO, SIMON

"Making Technology Serves Society: Simon Ramo." In *Lessons of Leadership: 21 Executives Speak Out on Creating, Developing and Managing Success*. Presented by the editors of Nation's Business, 144-154. Garden City, N.Y.: Doubleday, 1968.

RAND, A. BARRY

Clarke, Caroline V. "A. Barry Rand: Chairman and CEO, The Avis Group." In *Take a Lesson: Today's Black Achievers and How They Made It and What They Learned Along the Way,* 161-172. New York, N.Y.: Wiley, 2001.

RAND, AYN

Landrum, Gene N. "Ayn Rand—Macro-Oriented Intuitor." In *Profiles of Female Genius: Thirteen Creative Women Who Changed the World,* 298-310. Amherst, N.Y.: Prometheus Books, 1994.

RAND, JAMES H.

Shannon, Homer H. "James H. Rand." In *America's Fifty Foremost Business Leaders,* ed. B. C. Forbes, 371-380. New York, N.Y.: B.C. Forbes, 1948.

RANDOLPH, OCTAVIA PORTER

Welles, Edward O. "Educating Octavia; Or, A Crash Course in the Art of Starting Up." In *Anatomy of a Start-Up: Why Some New Businesses Succeed and Others Fail: 27 Real-Life Case Studies,* ed. Elizabeth K. Longsworth, 150-159. Boston, Mass.: Inc. Publishing, 1991.

RASCHKE, LINDA BRADFORD

Herera, Sue. "Linda Bradford Raschke: LBR Group." In *Women of the Street: Making It on Wall Street—The World's Toughest Business,* 163-182. New York, N.Y.: Wiley, 1997.

RATHBONE, MONROE JACKSON

"Deciding the Tough Ones: Monroe Jackson Rathbone." In *Lessons of Leadership: 21 Executives Speak Out on Creating, Developing and Managing Success.* Presented by the editors of Nation's Business, 187-201. Garden City, N.Y.: Doubleday, 1968.

RAVEIS, WILLIAM

Levitt, Mortimer. "William Raveis: 'Scratch an Entrepreneur and You Will Find an Ego'." In *How to Start Your Own Business Without Losing*

Your Shirt; Secrets of Seventeen Successful Entrepreneurs, 157-163. New York, N.Y: Atheneum, 1988.

RAVKIND, EDNA

Rich-McCoy, Lois. "A Pregnant Pattern: Edna Ravkind and Elsie Frankfurt Pollock." In *Millionairess: Self-Made Women of America*, 96-126. New York, N.Y.: Harper & Row, 1978.

REDSTONE, SUMMNER MURRAY

Kadlec, Daniel J. "Summner Redstone: The Vision Thing." In *Masters of the Universe; Winning Strategies of America's Greatest Deal Makers*, 247-274. New York, N.Y.: HarperBusiness, 1999.

Klepper, Michael M., and Robert Gunther. "Sumner Murray Redstone (1923-): The Viceroy of Viacom." In *The Wealthy 100 : From Benjamin Franklin to Bill Gates—A Ranking of the Richest Americans, Past and Present*, 297-299. Secaucus, N.J. : Carol Pub. Group, 1996.

REID, TOM

Murphy, Linda. "Tom Reid: Photo Craft." In *Computer Entrepreneurs: People Who Built Successful Businesses Around Computers*, 49-54. San Diego, Calif.: Computer Publishing Enterprises, 1990.

REIMER, KAREN

White, Jane. "Karen Reimer of Honeywell, Inc.: Just Don't Call Her 'Honey'." In *A Few Good Women: Breaking the Barriers to Top Management*, 39-51. Englewood Cliffs, N.J.: Prentice Hall, 1992.

REINHARD, KEITH

Millman, Nancy. In *Emperors of Adland; Inside the Advertising Revolution*, 57-64. New York, N.Y.: Warner Books, 1988.

REINSCH, J. LEONARD

Uris, Auren. "J. Leonard Reinsch—Service in the Air." In *The Executive Breakthrough; 21 Roads to the Top*, 85-96. Garden City, N.Y.: Doubleday, 1967.

RENSHAW, LISA G.

Liberman, Gail, and Alan Lavine. "Lisa G. Renshaw: Living in Parking Garage Pays Off." In *Rags to Riches: Motivating Stories of How Ordinary People Achieved Extraordinary Wealth!*, 117-139. Chicago, Ill.: Dearborn, 2000.

RENTSCHLER, GORDON S.

Shankland, Elmer M. "Gordon S. Rentschler." In *America's Fifty Foremost Business Leaders*, ed. B. C. Forbes, 477-483. New York, N.Y.: B.C. Forbes, 1948.

REYNOLDS, ANGELO

Koppel, Robert. "Momma Said There'd Be Days Like This: Angelo Reynolds." In *Bulls, Bears, And Millionaires: War Stories of Trading Life*, 188-197. Chicago, Ill.: Dearborn Financial Publishers, 1997.

REYNOLDS FAMILY

Cleary, David Powers. "Camel Cigarettes; Don't Look for Premiums or Coupons..." In *Great American Brands: The Success Formulas That Made Them Famous*, 40-52. New York, N.Y: Fairchild Publications, 1981.

Pottker, Jan. "Citizens for a SmokeFree America: A Breath of Fresh Heir, Patrick Reynolds, Founding President" In *Born to Power: Heirs to America's Leading Businesses*, 444-448. New York, N.Y.: Barron's, 1992.

REYNOLDS, RICHARD SAMUEL JR.

"Being an Innovator: Richard Samuel Reynolds." In *Lessons of Leadership:*

21 Executives Speak Out on Creating, Developing and Managing Success. Presented by the editors of Nation's Business, 132-143. Garden City, N.Y.: Doubleday, 1968.

RHODE, NAOMI

Rhode, Naomi. "Saying 'Yes' to Living." In *Success Secrets: How Eighteen Everyday Women Became Fortune Builders and Famous Speakers*, 65-80. Glendora, Calif.: Royal CBS Publishing, 1978.

RICE, ALVIS

Mitchell, Niki Butler. "A Kinder, Gentler Way Out of Debt: Alvis Rice, President, D & R Recovery." In *The New Color of Success: Twenty Young Black Millionaires Tell You How They're Making it*, 211-223. Rocklin, Calif.: Prima Publishing, 2000.

RICE, JOE

Kadlec, Daniel J. "Joe Rice: LBOs with a Twist." In *Masters of the Universe; Winning Strategies of America's Greatest Deal Makers*, 191-246. New York, N.Y.: HarperBusiness, 1999.

RICE, JOYCE

Aronoff, Craig E., and John L. Ward. "Joyce Rice; Ted Rice." In *Contemporary Entrepreneurs*, 408-413. Detroit, Mich.: Omnigraphics, Inc., 1992.

RICE, TED

Aronoff, Craig E., and John L. Ward. "Joyce Rice; Ted Rice." In *Contemporary Entrepreneurs*, 408-413. Detroit, Mich.: Omnigraphics, Inc., 1992.

RICE, THEIS

Brokaw, Leslie. "Play by Play; When Is a Great Product Not a Great Business? Maybe, Just Maybe, In the Case of SportsBand Network." In *Anatomy of a Start-Up: Why Some New Businesses Succeed and*

Others Fail: 27 Real-Life Case Studies, ed. Elizabeth K. Longsworth, 328-338. Boston, Mass.: Inc. Publishing, 1991.

RICH, JEAN

Rich-McCoy, Lois. "The Flying 'R': Jean Rich." In *Millionairess: Self-Made Women of America*, 152-168. New York, N.Y.: Harper & Row, 1978.

RICHARDS, WILLIAM J.

Shook, Robert L. "William J. Richards." In *The Entrepreneurs: Twelve Who Took Risks and Succeeded*, 81-91. New York, N.Y: Harper & Row, 1980.

RICHARDSON, EARL

"Household Horsepower: Earl Richardson and George Hughes, Designers of First Successful Irons and Stoves, Were Fathers of Today's $6 Billion Household Appliance Industry." In *The Pioneers of American Industry*. By the Editors of News Front and Year, 175-177. Maplewood, N.J.: C.S. Hammond, 1964.

RICKENBACKER, EDWARD V.

Furcolowe, Charles. "Edward V. Rickenbacker." In *America's Fifty Foremost Business Leaders,* ed. B. C. Forbes, 381-390. New York, N.Y.: B.C. Forbes, 1948.

Lewis, W. David "A Man Born Out of Season: Edward V. Rickenbacker, Eastern Airlines, and the Civil Aeronautics Board." In *Airline Executives and Federal Regulation: Case Studies in American Enterprise from the Airmail Era to the Dawn of the Jet Age*, ed. W. David Lewis, 242-292. Columbus, Ohio: Ohio State University Press, 2000.

RIDDER FAMILY

Cose, Ellis. "The Chains: Gannett and Knight-Ridder." In *The Press*, 281-356. New York, N.Y.: Morrow, 1989.

RILEY, WALTER

Aronoff, Craig E., and John L. Ward. "Walter Riley." In *Contemporary Entrepreneurs*, 414-419. Detroit, Mich.: Omnigraphics, Inc., 1992.

RISCH, TOM

"Tom Risch,The August West System." In *Profiles in Success: How Six Entrepreneurs Have Prospered in a Tough Business Environment*, 26-35. By the editors of *Managing*. New York, N.Y.: HBJ Newsletters, 1981.

RITCHIE, DENNIS

Slater, Robert. "Dennis Ritchie and Kenneth Thompson: Creators of UNIX." In *Portraits in Silicon*, 272-283. Cambridge, Mass.: MIT Press, 1987.

RITZ, SANDRA

Ritz, Sandra. "A Strong Sense of Porpoise." In *How I Became a Nurse Entrepreneur: Tales from 50 Nurses in Business*, 71-86. Petaluma, Calif.: National Nurses in Business Association, 1991.

RIVENDELL, CAROL

Alexander, Shoshana. "Carol Rivendell & Martha Lindt: Wild Women Adventures, Sebastopol, California." In *Women's Ventures, Women's Visions: 29 Inspiring Stories From Women Who Started Their Own Businesses*, 186-192. Freedom, Calif.: The Crossing Press, 1997.

ROACH, ALFRED J.

Fucini, Joseph J., and Suzy Fucini. "Alfred J. Roach, TII Industries, Inc.: 'There are Still So Many New Ideas to Be Tried'." In *Experience Inc.; Men and Women Who Founded Famous Companies After the Age of 40*, 30-36. New York, N.Y: Free Press, 1987.

ROACH, JOHN

Stoddard, William Osborn. "John Roach—Genius." In *Men of Business*, 75-93. New York, N.Y.: Scribner's Sons, 1893. 317 p.

ROBBINS, ALAN E.

Brown, Paul B. "Plastics!; Alan Robbins Is Betting Everything He Owns That the World Will Pay More for Picnic Tables, Mailbox Posts, And Speed Bumps If They're Made from Recycled Plastics." In *Anatomy of a Start-Up: Why Some New Businesses Succeed and Others Fail: 27 Real-Life Case Studies,* ed. Elizabeth K. Longsworth, 217-225. Boston, Mass.: Inc. Publishing, 1991.

ROBBINS, JOHN

Pottker, Jan. "The EarthSave Foundation: Rain Forest Ripple, John Robbins, Founder—Heir to Baskin-Robbins." In *Born to Power: Heirs to America's Leading Businesses*, 452-455. New York, N.Y.: Barron's, 1992.

ROBERT, ELISABETH B.

Mikaelian, A. "Elisabeth B. Robert." In *Women Who Mean Business: Success Stories of Women Over Forty*, 310-314. New York, N.Y.: William Morrow & Co., 1999.

ROBERTS, GEORGE

Gross, Daniel, and the Editors of Forbes Magazine. "Kohlberg Kravis Roberts & Co. and the Leveraged Buyout." In *Forbes Greatest Business Stories of All Time*, 314-333. New York, N.Y.: Wiley, 1996.

ROBERTS, MARSHALL OWEN

Stoddard, William Osborn. "Marshall Owen Roberts—Dash." In *Men of Business*, 229-245. New York, N.Y.: Scribner's Sons, 1893. 317 p.

ROBERTS, XAVIER

Shook, Robert L. "BabyLand General." In *Why Didn't I Think of That*, 126-145. New York, N.Y.: New American Library, 1982.

ROBERTSON, JULIAN

Train, John. "Julian Robertson: The Queen Bee." In *Money Masters of Our Time*, 156-170. New York, N.Y.: HarperBusiness, 2000.

ROBINSON, JAMES D. III

Shook, Robert L. "James D. Robinson III: American Express Corporation." In *The Chief Executive Officers: Men Who Run Big Business in America*, 183-202. New York, N.Y.: Harper & Row, 1981.

ROCHE, JOYCE M.

Clarke, Caroline V. "Joyce M. Roche: Former President, Carson Products." In *Take a Lesson: Today's Black Achievers and How They Made It and What They Learned Along the Way*, 183-192. New York, N.Y.: Wiley, 2001.

ROCKEFELLER, JOHN D.

Brands, H. W. "The Monopoly Esthetic: John D. Rockefeller." In *Masters of Enterprise: Giants of American Business from John Jacob Astor and J.P. Morgan to Bill Gates and Oprah Winfrey*, 80-94. New York, N.Y.: Free Press, 1999.

Burnley, James. "John D. Rockefeller: The Oil King." In *Millionaires and Kings of Enterprise; The Marvellous Careers of Some Americans Who by Pluck, Foresight, And Energy Have Made Themselves Masters in the Fields of Industry and Finance*, 17-29. Philadelphia, Penn.: J. B. Lippincott, 1901.

Diamond, Sigmond. "John D. Rockefeller." In *The Reputation of the American Businessman*, 107-141. Cambridge, Mass.: Harvard University Press, 1955.

Fanning, Leonard M. "John D. Rockefeller." In *Titans of Business*, 75-106. Philadelphia, Penn.: Lippincott, 1964. 240 p.

Gross, Daniel, and the Editors of Forbes Magazine. "John D. Rockefeller and the Modern Corporation." In *Forbes Greatest Business Stories of All Time*, 40-57. New York, N.Y.: Wiley, 1996.

"He Brought Order to Troubled Oil: Rockefeller Ended Industry Chaos." In *The 50 Great Pioneers of American Industry*. By the Editors of News Front and Year, 88-90. Maplewood, N.J.: C.S. Hammond, 1964.

Heilbroner, Robert L. "The Grand Acquisitor." In *Great Stories of American Businessmen*, From *American Heritage, The Magazine of History*, 170-181. New York, N.Y.: American Heritage Publishing Co., 1954.

"John D. Rockefeller." In *A Dozen Roads to Success: Being Graphic Sketches of Twelve of the Most Prominent Business Men of America, And Showing How They Became Millionaires, 32-44. Philadelphia, Penn.: Girard Pub. Co., 1894.*

Klepper, Michael M., and Robert Gunther. "John D. Rockefeller (1839-1937): The Oil King." In *The Wealthy 100 : From Benjamin Franklin to Bill Gates—A Ranking of the Richest Americans, Past and Present*, 2-8. Secaucus, N.J. : Carol Pub. Group, 1996.

McSherry, Ronald T. "John D. Rockefeller: The Man Who Struck Oil." In *Nine American Self-Made Men and Their Secrets to Success*, 16-24. Denver, Colo.: U.S.A. Publishing, 1983.

Means, Howard B. "John D. Rockefeller: Organizing the Octopus." In *Money & Power: The History of Business*, 145-163. New York, N.Y.: Wiley, 2001.

ROCKEFELLER, NELSON A.

Williams, A. Wyn. "Nelson A. Rockefeller." In *America's Fifty Foremost Business Leaders,* ed. B. C. Forbes, 391-400. New York, N.Y.: B.C. Forbes, 1948.

RODDICK, ANITA

Davis, William. "Anita Roddick, b. 1942: 'Common Sense Sells'." In *The Innovators: The Essential Guide to Business Thinkers, Achievers and Entrepreneurs*, 314-317. New York, N.Y.: AMACOM, 1987.

Mariotti, Steve, and Mike Caslin. "Anita Roddick, The Body Shop, Inc.: Business As a Force for Social Change." In *The Very Very Rich: How They Got That Way and How You Can, Too!*, 81-90. Franklin Lakes, NJ: Career Press, 2000.

RODGERS, FRAN SUSSNER

Ericksen, Gregory K. "Fran Sussner Rodgers: Work/Family Directions, 'I Think About Reality'." In *What's Luck Got to Do with It; Twelve Entrepreneurs Reveal the Secrets Behind Their Success*, 119-138. New York, N.Y.: Wiley, 1997.

RODGERS, THURMAN JOHN

Aronoff, Craig E., and John L. Ward. "Thurman John Rodgers." In *Contemporary Entrepreneurs*, 420-425. Detroit, Mich.: Omnigraphics, Inc., 1992.

Jager, Rama Dev, and Rafael Ortiz. "T. J. Rodgers: Cypress Semiconductor; The Importance of Vision, According to the General." In *In the Company of Giants: Candid Conversations with the Visionaries of the Digital World*, 27-43. New York, N.Y.: McGraw-Hill, 1997.

RODRIGUEZ, BONDDY A.

Suarez, Ruth. "Bonddy A. Rodriguez: Cambridge Technologies, 'Kick Your Way to the Top'." In *Superstar Entrepreneurs of Small and Large Businesses Reveal Their Secrets*, 56. Piscataway, N.J.: Research and Education Association, 1998.

RODRIGUEZ, JUAN "CHI CHI"

Liberman, Gail, and Alan Lavine. "Juan 'Chi Chi' Rodriguez: Golfs His Way to Millions." In *Rags to Riches: Motivating Stories of How Ordinary*

People Achieved Extraordinary Wealth!, 13-27. Chicago, Ill.: Dearborn, 2000.

ROGERS, HENRY HUTTLESTON

Klepper, Michael M., and Robert Gunther. "Henry Huttleston Rogers (1840-1909): From Whale Oil to Standard Oil." In *The Wealthy 100 : From Benjamin Franklin to Bill Gates—A Ranking of the Richest Americans, Past and Present*, 95-97. Secaucus, N.J. : Carol Pub. Group, 1996.

ROGERS, JIM

Train, John. "Jim Rogers: Far Out." In *Money Masters of Our Time*, 171-190. New York, N.Y.: HarperBusiness, 2000.

Train, John. "Jim Rogers: Top-Down Investor." In *The New Money Masters : Winning Investment Strategies of Soros, Lynch, Steinhardt, Rogers, Neff, Wanger, Michaelis, Carret*, 1-30. New York, N.Y.: Harper & Row, 1989.

ROSENBERG, ARTHUR

Roberts, Edward B. "Arthur Rosenberg and Tyco Laboratories, Inc." In *Entrepreneurs in High Technology: Lessons from MIT and Beyond*, 13-16. New York: Oxford University Press, 1991.

ROSENBERG, LARRY

Koppel, Robert. "Trading Suits Him: Larry Rosenberg." In *Bulls, Bears, And Millionaires: War Stories of Trading Life*, 56-67. Chicago, Ill.: Dearborn Financial Publishers, 1997.

ROSENBERG, WILLIAM

Cahill, Timothy Patrick. "The Bill Rosenberg Story." In *Profiles in the American Dream: The Real-Life Stories of the Struggles of American Entrepreneurs* , 79-104. Hanover, Mass.: Christopher Publishing Company, 1994.

Shook, Carrie, and Robert L. Shook. "Dunkin' Donuts: Dollars from Doughnuts." In *Franchising: The Business Strategy That Changed the World*, 49-72. Englewood Cliffs, NJ: Prentice Hall, 1993.

Uris, Auren. "William Rosenberg—Do Not Underestimate the Doughnut." In *The Executive Breakthrough; 21 Roads to the Top*, 343-356. Garden City, N.Y.: Doubleday, 1967.

ROSENWALD, JULIUS

Klepper, Michael M., and Robert Gunther. "Julius Rosenwald (1862-1932): A Mail-Order Fortune." In *The Wealthy 100 : From Benjamin Franklin to Bill Gates—A Ranking of the Richest Americans, Past and Present*, 197-201. Secaucus, N.J. : Carol Pub. Group, 1996.

ROSSI, ANTHONY T.

Fucini, Joseph J., and Suzy Fucini. "Anthony T. Rossi, Tropicana Juice: 'Control—That Is the Most Important Thing'." In *Experience Inc.; Men and Women Who Founded Famous Companies After the Age of 40*, 137-180. New York, N.Y: Free Press, 1987.

ROSSO, JULEE

Levitt, Mortimer. "Julee Rosso and Sheila Lukins: Gourmet Takeout, Palatable at Any Price." In *How to Start Your Own Business Without Losing Your Shirt; Secrets of Seventeen Successful Entrepreneurs*, 188-194. New York, N.Y: Atheneum, 1988.

ROUSE, CHARLES BROADWAY

Burnley, James. "Charles Broadway Rouse: The Blind Millionaire." In *Millionaires and Kings of Enterprise; The Marvellous Careers of Some Americans Who by Pluck, Foresight, And Energy Have Made Themselves Masters in the Fields of Industry and Finance*, 313-321. Philadelphia, Penn.: J. B. Lippincott, 1901.

ROUSE, JAMES W.

Meyer, Michael. "The Spiritualist." In *The Alexander Complex: The Dreams That Drive the Great Businessmen*, 105-156. New York, N.Y.: Times Books, 1989.

Silver, A. David. "James W. Rouse." In *Entrepreneurial Megabucks: The 100 Greatest Entrepreneurs of the Last 25 Years*, 374-378. New York, N.Y.: Wiley, 1985.

ROWLAND, PLEASANT

Ericksen, Gregory K. "Pleasant T. Rowland: Pleasant Company, 'I Want to Answer to Girls'." In *What's Luck Got to Do with It; Twelve Entrepreneurs Reveal the Secrets Behind Their Success*, 163-180. New York, N.Y.: Wiley, 1997.

"Pleasant Rowland: Founder and President, Pleasant Company." In *Forbes Great Minds of Business*, ed. Gretchen Morgenson, 121-156. New York, N.Y.: Wiley, 1997. 228 p.

RUETHLING, ANN

Alexander, Shoshana. "Ann Ruethling: Chinaberry Book Service, Spring Valley, California." In *Women's Ventures, Women's Visions: 29 Inspiring Stories From Women Who Started Their Own Businesses*, 43-48. Freedom, Calif.: The Crossing Press, 1997.

RUFF, HOWARD

King, Norman. "Howard Ruff." In *The Money Messiah$*, 148-180. New York, N.Y.: Coward-McCann, 1983.

RUSSELL, HERMAN J.

Dingle, Derek T. "Herman J. Russell: H. J. Russell & Company, 'The Builder'." In *Black Enterprise Titans of the B.E. 100s: Black CEOs Who Redefined and Conquered American Business*, 155-172. New York, N.Y.: Wiley, 1999.

RUSSELL, RICHARD

King, Norman. "Richard Russell." In *The Money Messiah$*, 202-204. New York, N.Y.: Coward-McCann, 1983.

RYAN, THOMAS FORTUNE

Klepper, Michael M., and Robert Gunther. "Thomas Fortune Ryan (1851-1928): New York Transit King." In *The Wealthy 100 : From Benjamin Franklin to Bill Gates—A Ranking of the Richest Americans, Past and Present,* 169-172. Secaucus, N.J. : Carol Pub. Group, 1996.

SAGE, RUSSELL

Klepper, Michael M., and Robert Gunther. "Russell Sage (1816-1906): Market Manipulator." In *The Wealthy 100 : From Benjamin Franklin to Bill Gates—A Ranking of the Richest Americans, Past and Present,* 81-84. Secaucus, N.J. : Carol Pub. Group, 1996.

SALLE, JIM

Gray, Bob, ed. "A Record Supply of Nostalgia." In *How Entrepreneurs Make Business Profits: A Study of Personal Success Stories From Cordovan Business Journals,* 128-131. Houston, Tex.: Cordovan Press, 1982.

SALOMON, GARY

Suarez, Ruth. "Gary Salomon: Fastsigns, 'Exceeding Expectations'." In *Superstar Entrepreneurs of Small and Large Businesses Reveal Their Secrets,* 15-19. Piscataway, N.J.: Research and Education Association, 1998.

SALZMAN, JEFF

Kingston, Brett. "James Calano and Jeff Salzman of Careertrack." In *The Dynamos: Who Are They Anyway?,* 97-100. New York, N.Y: Wiley, 1987.

SAMPLE, MARGARET MARONICK

Mikaelian, A. "Margaret Maronick Sample." In *Women Who Mean Business: Success Stories of Women Over Forty*, 190-194. New York, N.Y.: William Morrow & Co., 1999.

SANDERS, JEROME

Wallace, Robert L. "Jerome Sanders, Eliot Powell, Robert 'Bob' Wallace: Founders, The SDGG Holding Company, Inc., Summit, New Jersey." In *Black Wealth: Your Road to Small Business Success*, 175-184. New York, N.Y.: Wiley, 2000.

SANDERS, W. JEREMIAH, III

Silver, A. David. "W. Jeremiah Sanders, III." In *Entrepreneurial Megabucks: The 100 Greatest Entrepreneurs of the Last 25 Years*, 379-383. New York, N.Y.: Wiley, 1985.

SANDNER, JACK

Koppel, Robert. "Chairman Jack: Jack Sandner." In *Bulls, Bears, And Millionaires: War Stories of Trading Life*, 8-15. Chicago, Ill.: Dearborn Financial Publishers, 1997.

SANDS, FRED

Gray, Bob, ed. "Thriving in a Tough Market." In *How Entrepreneurs Make Business Profits: A Study of Personal Success Stories From Cordovan Business Journals*, 32-37. Houston, Tex.: Cordovan Press, 1982.

SANFORD, RICHARD D.

Aronoff, Craig E., and John L. Ward. "Richard D. Sanford." In *Contemporary Entrepreneurs*, 426-431. Detroit, Mich.: Omnigraphics, Inc., 1992.

SANTINI FAMILY

Buchholz, Barbara B., and Margaret Crane. "The 7 Santini Brothers, Bronx, NY." In *Corporate Blood Lines: The Future of the Family Firm*, 92-110. New York, N.Y: Carol Publishing Group, 1989.

SARNO, SAM A.

Fucini, Joseph J., and Suzy Fucini. "Sam A. Sarno, Seven Oaks International: 'The Market Was Wide Open—You Could Not Help But Make Money'." In *Experience Inc.; Men and Women Who Founded Famous Companies After the Age of 40*, 119-125. New York, N.Y: Free Press, 1987.

SARNOFF, DAVID

Brands, H. W. "Emperor of the Air: David Sarnoff." In *Masters of Enterprise: Giants of American Business from John Jacob Astor and J.P. Morgan to Bill Gates and Oprah Winfrey*, 168-181. New York, N.Y.: Free Press, 1999.

Cleary, David Powers. "RCA TV/Radio/Stereo; It Is the Use to Which the New Invention Is Put, And Not the Invention Itself, That Determines Its Value to Society." In *Great American Brands: The Success Formulas That Made Them Famous*, 246-255. New York, N.Y: Fairchild Publications, 1981.

"Envisioning the Future: General David Sarnoff." In *Lessons of Leadership: 21 Executives Speak Out on Creating, Developing and Managing Success*. Presented by the editors of Nation's Business, 70-82. Garden City, N.Y.: Doubleday, 1968.

Gross, Daniel, and the Editors of Forbes Magazine. "David Sarnoff, RCA, And the Rise of Broadcasting." In *Forbes Greatest Business Stories of All Time*, 106-120. New York, N.Y.: Wiley, 1996.

Westbrook, Francis Jr. "David Sarnoff." In *America's Fifty Foremost Business Leaders,* ed. B. C. Forbes, 401-412. New York, N.Y.: B.C. Forbes, 1948.

SAUNDERS, ELLEN ANN

Woodard, Michael D. "Sumanco, Inc.—Ellen Ann Saunders." In *Black Entrepreneurs in America: Stories of Struggle and Success*, 60-70. New Brunswick, N.J.: Rutgers University Press, 1977.

SAUNDERS, ROBERT

Kao, John J. "Robert Michael Companies (A)." In *The Entrepreneur*, 110-124. Englewood Cliffs, New Jersey: Prentice Hall, 1991.

SAWYER, DOBORAH M.

Mitchell, Niki Butler. "Cleaning Up the World: Deborah M. Sawyer, President and CEO Environmental Design International, Inc." In *The New Color of Success: Twenty Young Black Millionaires Tell You How They're Making it*, 119-130. Rocklin, Calif.: Prima Publishing, 2000.

SCANDONE, JOSEPH

Solomon, Stephen D. "Head of the Class; Will Parents Pay More for Day Care If the Centers are Positioned As Schools?" In *Anatomy of a Start-Up: Why Some New Businesses Succeed and Others Fail: 27 Real-Life Case Studies,* ed. Elizabeth K. Longsworth, 86-95. Boston, Mass.: Inc. Publishing, 1991.

SCARBOROUGH, CHERRY

"Cherry Scarborough." In *Women Achievers: A Series of Dialogues from the Womanagement Process*, 27-40. New York, N.Y.: American Telephone and Telegraph Co., 1997.

SCHAAK, RICHARD

Pine, Carol, and Susan Mundale. "Richard Schaak; The Battler." In *Self-Made: The Stories of 12 Minnesota Entrepreneurs*, 127-143. Minneapolis, Minn.: Dorn Books, 1982.

SCHAEFFER, JAN

Lassen, Ali. "Jan Schaeffer: Partner, JJS Signs." In *The Secret of Their Success: Women Entrepreneurs Reveal How They Made It*, 133-138. Carlsbad, Calif.: Ali Lassen Success System, 1990.

SCHAFER, ROBIN ANN

Mikaelian, A. "Robin Ann Schafer, L.M.T., N.C.T.M.B." In *Women Who Mean Business: Success Stories of Women Over Forty*, 6-10. New York, N.Y.: William Morrow & Co., 1999.

SCHAFFNER, JOSEPH

Cleary, David Powers. "Hart Schaffner & Marx Suits; The Clothes a Man Wears Are to Some Extent a True Index of His Character and Taste, But They Are Also an Influence Upon His Character and Taste." In *Great American Brands: The Success Formulas That Made Them Famous*, 158-165. New York, N.Y: Fairchild Publications, 1981.

SCHEERLE, PATRICIA KATHLEEN

"Expanding Nursing Frontiers." In *How I Became a Nurse Entrepreneur: Tales from 50 Nurses in Business*, 19-24. Petaluma, Calif.: National Nurses in Business Association, 1991.

SCHJELDAHL, G. T.

Pine, Carol, and Susan Mundale. "G. T. Schjeldahl; A Life of Pure Events." In *Self-Made: The Stories of 12 Minnesota Entrepreneurs*, 69-84. Minneapolis, Minn.: Dorn Books, 1982.

SCHNEIDER, BARBARA TOME

Mikaelian, A. "Barbara Tome Schneider." In *Women Who Mean Business: Success Stories of Women Over Forty*, 127-131. New York, N.Y.: William Morrow & Co., 1999.

SCHNEIDER, CAROL FRANCES

Schneider, Carol Frances. "Alive—And So Are You!" In *Success Secrets: How Eighteen Everyday Women Became Fortune Builders and Famous Speakers*, 251-262. Glendora, Calif.: Royal CBS Publishing, 1978.

SCHNEIDER, RALPH E.

Fucini, Joseph J., and Suzy Fucini. "Ralph E. Schneider, Diners Club: 'I Had a Good Idea and Worked Hard, But I Was Very Lucky, Too'." In *Experience Inc.; Men and Women Who Founded Famous Companies After the Age of 40*, 96-101. New York, N.Y: Free Press, 1987.

SCHOEN, DOUG

Gardner, Ralph. "Doug Schoen." In *Young, Gifted, and Rich: The Secrets of America's Most Successful Entrepreneurs*, 157-170. New York, N.Y.: Wallaby Books, 1984.

SCHRADER, WILLIAM

Ericksen, Gregory K. "William Schrader—PSINet 'Shaping the Internet—and the World'." In *Net Entrepreneurs Only : 10 Entrepreneurs Tell the Stories of Their Success*, 141-160. New York : John Wiley, 2000.

SCHRAM, EMIL

Hillyer, William Hurd. "Emil Schram." In *America's Fifty Foremost Business Leaders,* ed. B. C. Forbes, 413-420. New York, N.Y.: B.C. Forbes, 1948.

SCHROCK, ALTA

Dueck, Jack. "Alta Schrock: A Pragmatic Visionary." In *Entrepreneurs in the Faith Community: Profiles of Mennonites in Business*, ed. Calvin W. Redekop, and Benjamin W. Redekop, 59-79. Scottdale, Penn.: Herald Press, 1996.

SCHROCK, ROD

Price, Christopher. "Rod Schrock—AltaVista 'From Big Business to Net Start-Up'." In *The Internet Entrepreneurs: Business Rules Are Good: Break Them*, 130-140. London, Eng.: FT.com, 2000.

SCHULTZ, HARRY

King, Norman. "Harry Schultz." In *The Money Messiah$*, 184-185. New York, N.Y.: Coward-McCann, 1983.

SCHULTZ, HOWARD

Koehn, Nancy F. "Howard Schultz and Starbucks Coffee Company." In *Brand New: How Entrepreneurs Earned Consumers' Trust from Wedgwood to Dell*, 203-256. Boston, Mass.: Harvard Business School Press, 2001.

SCHULTZ, RICHARD D.

Shook, Robert L. "Richard D. Schultz." In *The Entrepreneurs: Twelve Who Took Risks and Succeeded*, 127-137. New York, N.Y: Harper & Row, 1980.

SCHULTZE, RICHARD M.

Ericksen, Gregory K. "Richard M. Schultze: Best Buy Co., Inc., 'The Right Strategy at the Right Time'." In *What's Luck Got to Do with It; Twelve Entrepreneurs Reveal the Secrets Behind Their Success*, 197-213. New York, N.Y.: Wiley, 1997.

SCHWAB, CHARLES M.

Burnley, James. "Charles M. Schwab: America's New Steel King." In *Millionaires and Kings of Enterprise; The Marvellous Careers of Some Americans Who by Pluck, Foresight, And Energy Have Made Themselves Masters in the Fields of Industry and Finance*, 50-63. Philadelphia, Penn.: J. B. Lippincott, 1901.

Garraty, John A. "When the Headlines Said, 'Charlie Schwab Breaks the Bank'." In *Great Stories of American Businessmen, From American Heritage, The Magazine of History,* 268-273. New York, N.Y.: American Heritage Publishing Co., 1954.

SCHWAN, MARVIN

Pine, Carol, and Susan Mundale. "Marvin Schwan; The Emperor of Ice Cream." In *Self-Made: The Stories of 12 Minnesota Entrepreneurs,* 57-67. Minneapolis, Minn.: Dorn Books, 1982.

SCHWARTZ, DAVE

Shook, Robert L. "Rent-a-Wreck." In *Why Didn't I Think of That,* 104-125. New York, N.Y.: New American Library, 1982.

SCOVILLE, RICK

Gray, Bob, ed. "A Whiz in Fizzling Water." In *How Entrepreneurs Make Business Profits: A Study of Personal Success Stories From Cordovan Business Journals,* 45-49. Houston, Tex.: Cordovan Press, 1982.

SCRIBHIBHADH, PAUL

Tsang, Cheryl D. "Paul Scribhibhadh: 'The Diplomat,' 1987-1997." In *Microsoft First Generation: The Success Secrets of the Visionaries Who Launched a Technology Empire,* 195-212. New York, N.Y.: Wiley, 2000.

SCRUSHY, RICHARD M.

Aronoff, Craig E., and John L. Ward. "Richard M. Scrushy." In *Contemporary Entrepreneurs,* 432-439. Detroit, Mich.: Omnigraphics, Inc., 1992.

SCURRY, PAMELA

Taylor, Russel R. "Pamela Scurry: 'I Think It Is Okay to Want It All'." In *Exceptional Entrepreneurial Women*, 87-92. New York, N.Y: Quorum Books, 1988.

THE SEARS FAMILY

Klein Frederick C. "The Sears." In *American Dynasties Today*, 45-70. Homewood, Ill.: Dow Jones-Irwin, 1990.

Klepper, Michael M., and Robert Gunther. "Richard Warren Sears (1863-1914): A Mail-Order Fortune." In *The Wealthy 100 : From Benjamin Franklin to Bill Gates—A Ranking of the Richest Americans, Past and Present*, 197-201. Secaucus, N.J. : Carol Pub. Group, 1996.

"Mail Order Magician: Richard Warren Sears, Founder of the $4 Billion Sears, Roebuck Mail Order Empire, Wrote Catalogs That Talked Hard-Headed Buyers' Language." In *The 50 Great Pioneers of American Industry*. By the Editors of News Front and Year, 110-113. Maplewood, N.J.: C.S. Hammond, 1964.

Wren, Daniel A., and Ronald G. Greenwood. "Richard W. Sears." In *Management Innovators: The People and Ideas That Have Shaped Modern Business*, 58-68. New York, N.Y.: Oxford University Press, 1998.

SEELBINDER, G. ARTHUR

Aronoff, Craig E., and John L. Ward. "G. Arthur Seelbinder." In *Contemporary Entrepreneurs*, 440-444. Detroit, Mich.: Omnigraphics, Inc., 1992.

SEIBERLING, FRANK A.

Cleary, David Powers. "Goodyear Tires; It is Harder to Stay Ahead Than to Get Ahead." In *Great American Brands: The Success Formulas That Made Them Famous*, 128-148. New York, N.Y: Fairchild Publications, 1981.

SEIFF, KEN

Suarez, Ruth. "Ken Seiff: Pivot Rules, 'The Rules Have Changed'." In *Superstar Entrepreneurs of Small and Large Businesses Reveal Their Secrets*. 215-219. Piscataway, N.J.: Research and Education Association, 1998.

SELFRIDGE, HARRY GORDON

Davis, William. "Harry Gordon Selfridge, 1858-1947: Mile a Minute Harry." In *The Innovators: The Essential Guide to Business Thinkers, Achievers and Entrepreneurs*, 340-342. New York, N.Y.: AMACOM, 1987.

SERRA, JACK

Elfstrand, Rhonda. "Jack Serra: Omega Communications, Inc." In *The Story Behind the Success: Learning From Pittsburgh Professionals*, 218-236. Pittsburgh, Penn.: Steel Publishing Partners, 1996.

SEYBOLD, SARAH A.

Seybold, Sarah A. "Flight of the Dove." In *How I Became a Nurse Entrepreneur: Tales from 50 Nurses in Business*, 13-17. Petaluma, Calif.: National Nurses in Business Association, 1991.

SHAKARIAN, DAVID B.

Gray, Bob, ed. "Feasting on the Health Fad." In *How Entrepreneurs Make Business Profits: A Study of Personal Success Stories From Cordovan Business Journals*, 27-31. Houston, Tex.: Cordovan Press, 1982.

Silver, A. David. "David B. Shakarian." In *Entrepreneurial Megabucks: The 100 Greatest Entrepreneurs of the Last 25 Years*, 384-386. New York, N.Y.: Wiley, 1985.

SHAMES, KARILEE HALO

Shames, Karilee Halo. "The Path with a Heart." In *How I Became a Nurse Entrepreneur: Tales from 50 Nurses in Business*, 25-35. Petaluma, Calif.: National Nurses in Business Association, 1991.

SHANKS, A. THOMAS

Koppel, Robert. "Learn to Learn: A. Thomas Shanks." In *Bulls, Bears, And Millionaires: War Stories of Trading Life*, 129-138. Chicago, Ill.: Dearborn Financial Publishers, 1997.

SHAPIRO, IRVING S.

Shook, Robert L. "Irving S. Shapiro: E. I. du Pont de Nemours & Company." In *The Chief Executive Officers: Men Who Run Big Business in America*, New York, N.Y.: Harper & Row, 1981.

SHARP, NANCY J.

"Promoting Political Action." In *How I Became a Nurse Entrepreneur: Tales from 50 Nurses in Business*, 239-242. Petaluma, Calif.: National Nurses in Business Association, 1991.

SHAUGHNESSY, KATHLEEN

Lassen, Ali. "Kathleen Shaughnessy: Consultant, Jean-Paul Sands Perfumes and Regional Consultant for Leads Club." In *The Secret of Their Success: Women Entrepreneurs Reveal How They Made It*, 57-64. Carlsbad, Calif.: Ali Lassen Success System, 1990.

SHAW, JANE E.

Enkelis, Liane, and Karen Olsen. "Jane E. Shaw: President & Chief Operating Officer, Alza Corporation." In *On Our Own Terms: Portraits of Women Business Leaders* , 72-81. San Francisco, Calif.: Berrett-Koehler, 1995.

SHAW, JOANNE

Ericksen, Gregory K. "JoAnne Shaw—The Coffee Beanery, Ltd., 'The Best Coffee in the World and Service with a Smile'." In *Women Entrepreneurs Only: Twelve Women Entrepreneurs Tell The Stories of Their Success*, 151-171. New York, N.Y.: Wiley, 1999.

SHAW, PETER

Murphy, Linda. "Peter Shaw: Advanced Graphics Engineering." In *Computer Entrepreneurs: People Who Built Successful Businesses Around Computers*, 23-30. San Diego, Calif.: Computer Publishing Enterprises, 1990.

SHEARER, WILLIAM

Woodard, Michael D. "KGFJ Radio—William Shearer." In *Black Entrepreneurs in America: Stories of Struggle and Success*, 171-183. New Brunswick, N.J.: Rutgers University Press, 1997.

SHEETS, MARY ELLEN

Ericksen, Gregory K. "Mary Ellen Sheets—Two Men and a Truck, 'Owning a Business Is Like Owning the Greatest Toy in the World'." In *Women Entrepreneurs Only: Twelve Women Entrepreneurs Tell The Stories of Their Success*, New York, N.Y.: Wiley, 1999.

SHENK, JACOB A.

Redekop, Calvin W. "Jacob A. Shenk: Business Was Servant to the Church." In *Entrepreneurs in the Faith Community: Profiles of Mennonites in Business*, ed. Calvin W. Redekop, and Benjamin W. Redekop, 18-36 . Scottdale, Penn.: Herald Press, 1996.

SHENSON, HOWARD L.

Gray, Bob, ed. "How to Make More with Less." In *How Entrepreneurs Make Business Profits: A Study of Personal Success Stories From Cordovan Business Journals*, 1-6. Houston, Tex.: Cordovan Press, 1982.

SHERMAN, KEN

"Ken and Larry Sherman, Cambridge Research and Development Corporation." In *Profiles in Success: How Six Entrepreneurs Have Prospered in a Tough Business Environment*, 5-14. By the editors of *Managing*. New York, N.Y.: HBJ Newsletters, 1981.

SHERMAN, LARRY

"Ken and Larry Sherman, Cambridge Research and Development Corporation." In *Profiles in Success: How Six Entrepreneurs Have Prospered in a Tough Business Environment*, 5-14. By the editors of *Managing*. New York, N.Y.: HBJ Newsletters, 1981.

SHERMAN, NATE

Shook, Carrie, and Robert L. Shook. "Midas International Corporation: Franchising a Golden Opportunity." In *Franchising: The Business Strategy That Changed the World*, 115-137. Englewood Cliffs, NJ: Prentice Hall, 1993.

SHERWIN, HENRY ALDEN

Cleary, David Powers. "Sherwin-Williams Paints—Not Just to Produce Paints, But to Contribute to Brighter, More Colorful Living." In *Great American Brands: The Success Formulas That Made Them Famous*, 256-260. New York, N.Y: Fairchild Publications, 1981.

SHIMA, GEORGE

Hata, Don, and Nadine Hata. "George Shima: 'The Potato King of California'." In *Business Entrepreneurs in the West*, ed. Ted C. Hinckley, 55-63. Manhattan, Kans.: Sunflower University Press, 1986.

SHIPLEY, WALTER V.

Wendel, Charles B. "Creating a Unified Corporate Focus: Walter V. Shipley, Chairman & CEO, Chase Manhattan Bank." In *The New Financiers*, 239-258. Chicago, Ill.: Irwin Professional Pub., 1996.

SHIVERS, JANE EDWARDS

Mikaelian, A. "Jane Edwards Shivers." In *Women Who Mean Business: Success Stories of Women Over Forty*, 69-73. New York, N.Y.: William Morrow & Co., 1999.

SHOCKLEY, WILLIAM

Slater, Robert. "William Shockley: Co-Inventor of the Transistor." In *Portraits in Silicon*, 140-151. Cambridge, Mass.: MIT Press, 1987.

SHOEN FAMILY

Pottker, Jan. "U-Haul International, Inc.: 'Mr. Chairman, I Am Your Father'." In *Born to Power: Heirs to America's Leading Businesses*, 340-349. New York, N.Y.: Barron's, 1992.

Silver, A. David. "Leonard Samuel Shoen." In *Entrepreneurial Megabucks: The 100 Greatest Entrepreneurs of the Last 25 Years*, 387-390. New York, N.Y.: Wiley, 1985.

SHOLES, CHRISTOPHER LATHAM

"The Fabulous Writing Machine: Christopher Sholes and the Remington Company Revolutionized U.S. Business Life with the First Practical Typewriter." In *The 50 Great Pioneers of American Industry*. By the Editors of News Front and Year, 98-101. Maplewood, N.J.: C.S. Hammond, 1964.

SHUFLATA, MARYRUTH

Lassen, Ali. "Maryruth Shaflata: Professional Photographer." In *The Secret of Their Success: Women Entrepreneurs Reveal How They Made It*, 77-80. Carlsbad, Calif.: Ali Lassen Success System, 1990.

SHUGART, ALAN F.

Aronoff, Craig E., and John L. Ward. "Alan F. Shugart." In *Contemporary Entrepreneurs*, 445-450. Detroit, Mich.: Omnigraphics, Inc., 1992.

SIEBERT, MURIEL

Herera, Sue. "Muriel Siebert: Muriel Siebert & Company." In *Women of the Street: Making It on Wall Street—The World's Toughest Business*, 83-98. New York, N.Y.: Wiley, 1997.

Taylor, Russel R. "Muriel Siebert; Rebel of Wall Street." In *Exceptional Entrepreneurial Women*, 59-64. New York, N.Y: Quorum Books, 1988.

SIEGEL, MORRIS J. "MO"

Shook, Robert L. "Celestial Seasonings." In *Why Didn't I Think of That*, 164-181. New York, N.Y.: New American Library, 1982.

Silver, A. David. "Morris J. Siegel." In *Entrepreneurial Megabucks: The 100 Greatest Entrepreneurs of the Last 25 Years*, 391-393. New York, N.Y.: Wiley, 1985.

SIKORA, ROBERT F.

Silver, A. David. "Robert F. Sikora." In *Entrepreneurial Megabucks: The 100 Greatest Entrepreneurs of the Last 25 Years*, 394-396. New York, N.Y.: Wiley, 1985.

SILVER, MARJORIE

Enkelis, Liane, and Karen Olsen. "Marjorie Silver: President, Pinsly Railroad Company." In *On Our Own Terms: Portraits of Women Business Leaders* , 134-143. San Francisco, Calif.: Berrett-Koehler, 1995.

SILVER, SPENCE

Nayak, P. Ranganath, and John M. Ketteringham. "3M's Post-It Notepads 'Never Mind, I'll Do It Myself'." In *Breakthroughs!*, 35-56. San Diego, Calif.: Pfeiffer & Company, 1994.

SILVERMAN, HENRY

Kadlec, Daniel J. "Henry Silverman: Agent of Change." In *Masters of the Universe; Winning Strategies of America's Greatest Deal Makers*, 219-246. New York, N.Y.: HarperBusiness, 1999.

SILVERMAN, TOM

Posner Bruce G. "Good Vibrations; A New Recording Studio Stakes Its Pitch on Service, But Will Its Customers Care?" In *Anatomy of a Start-Up: Why Some New Businesses Succeed and Others Fail: 27 Real-Life Case Studies,* ed. Elizabeth K. Longsworth, 46-55. Boston, Mass.: Inc. Publishing, 1991.

SILVERS, LAURIE

Mikaelian, A. "Laurie Silvers." In *Women Who Mean Business: Success Stories of Women Over Forty*, 60-63. New York, N.Y.: William Morrow & Co., 1999.

SIMMONS, JAKE

Mariotti, Steve, and Lorraine Mooney. "Jake Simmons Jr.: A Unique Kind of Oil Tycoon." In *Entrepreneurs in Profile*, 28-33. London: National Foundation for Teaching Entrepreneurship, 1991.

SIMMONS, RUSSELL

Dingle, Derek T. "Russell Simmons: Rush Communications and Affiliated Companies, 'The Hip-Hopreneur'." In *Black Enterprise Titans of the B.E. 100s: Black CEOs Who Redefined and Conquered American Business*, 73-92. New York, N.Y.: Wiley, 1999.

Mariotti, Steve, and Mike Caslin. "Russell Simmons, Rush Communications, Inc.: Marketing Urban Culture to Mainstream USA." In *The Very Very Rich: How They Got That Way and How You Can, Too!*, 91-96. Franklin Lakes, NJ: Career Press, 2000.

SIMMONS, ZALMON G.

Cleary, David Powers. "Simmons Beautyrest Mattresses; Bedding is Dull and Unappreciated. In Fact, No One Even Sees It; It's Usually Covered with Sheets." In *Great American Brands: The Success Formulas That Made Them Famous*, 261-268. New York, N.Y: Fairchild Publications, 1981.

SIMON, ALAN

Suarez, Ruth. "Alan Simon: On Location Education, 'Education in Entertainment'." In *Superstar Entrepreneurs of Small and Large Businesses Reveal Their Secrets*. 249-253. Piscataway, N.J.: Research and Education Association, 1998.

SIMON, TAMI

Alexander, Shoshana. "Tami Simon: Sounds True Catalog, Boulder, Colorado." In *Women's Ventures, Women's Visions: 29 Inspiring Stories From Women Who Started Their Own Businesses*, 146-152. Freedom, Calif.: The Crossing Press, 1997.

SIMPLOT, JACK R.

Gilder, George. "A Patch of Sand." In *The Spirit of Enterprise*, 23-41. New York, N.Y: Simon and Schuster, 1984.

MacPhee, William. "J. R. 'Jack' Simplot of J. R. Simplot Company." In *Rare Breed: The Entrepreneur, An American Culture*, 117-130. Chicago, Ill.: Probus Publishing Company, 1987.

Silver, A. David. "Jack R. Simplot." In *Entrepreneurial Megabucks: The 100 Greatest Entrepreneurs of the Last 25 Years*, 397-400. New York, N.Y.: Wiley, 1985.

SINCLAIR, JAMES E.

King, Norman. "James E. Sinclair." In *The Money Messiah$*, 186-187. New York, N.Y.: Coward-McCann, 1983.

SINGER, ISAAC MERRITT

Cleary, David Powers. "Singer Sewing Machines; If the Purchase Price is a Problem, Why Not Let Her Buy the Machine with Monthly Rental Fees?" In *Great American Brands: The Success Formulas That Made Them Famous*, 269-279. New York, N.Y: Fairchild Publications, 1981.

Davis, William. "Isaac Merritt Singer, 1811-1875: Inventor of the First Practical Sewing Machine." In *The Innovators: The Essential Guide to Business Thinkers, Achievers and Entrepreneurs*, 353-355. New York, N.Y.: AMACOM, 1987.

"He Kept the World 'In Stitches': Singer's Global Empire Spans 67 Nations, Has Sold Over 100 Million Sewing Machines." In *The 50 Great Pioneers of American Industry*. By the Editors of News Front and Year, 34-37. Maplewood, N.J.: C.S. Hammond, 1964.

Lyon, Peter. "Isaac Singer and His Wonderful Sewing Machine." In *Great Stories of American Businessmen*, From *American Heritage, The Magazine of History*, 146-157. New York, N.Y.: American Heritage Publishing Co., 1954.

SINGLETON, HENRY E.

Silver, A. David. "Henry E. Singleton." In *Entrepreneurial Megabucks: The 100 Greatest Entrepreneurs of the Last 25 Years*, 401-402. New York, N.Y.: Wiley, 1985.

SINGLETON, WILLIAM DEAN

Coleridge, Nicholas. "Cut and Slash in the Lone Star State: Dean Singleton's Survival Journalism." In *Paper Tigers: The Latest, Greatest Newspaper Tycoons*, 133-154. New York, N.Y.: Carol Publishing Group, 1994.

SIX, ROBERT F.

Gorn, Michael H. "Robert F. Six: Continental Giant." In *Airline Executives and Federal Regulation: Case Studies in American Enterprise from the Airmail Era to the Dawn of the Jet Age*, ed. W. David Lewis, 169-212. Columbus, Ohio: Ohio State University Press, 2000.

SKEES, JANET

Mikaelian, A. "Janet Skees." In *Women Who Mean Business: Success Stories of Women Over Forty*, 118-122. New York, N.Y.: William Morrow & Co., 1999.

SLATER, SAMUEL

"He Put Cotton on the Map: Samuel Slater Sparked the U.S. Industrial Revolution with His Invention of the First Mechanical Cotton Mill." In *The 50 Great Pioneers of American Industry*. By the Editors of News Front and Year, 8-10. Maplewood, N.J.: C.S. Hammond, 1964.

Klepper, Michael M., and Robert Gunther. "Samuel Slater (1768-1835): Industrial Spy." In *The Wealthy 100 : From Benjamin Franklin to Bill Gates—A Ranking of the Richest Americans, Past and Present*, 288-290. Secaucus, N.J. : Carol Pub. Group, 1996.

Welles, Arnold. "Father of Our Factory System." In *Great Stories of American Businessmen*, From *American Heritage, The Magazine of History*, 50-58. New York, N.Y.: American Heritage Publishing Co., 1954.

SLOAN, ALFRED P.

Brands, H. W. "Organization Man: Alfred Sloan." In *Masters of Enterprise: Giants of American Business from John Jacob Astor and J.P. Morgan to Bill Gates and Oprah Winfrey*, 107-119. New York, N.Y.: Free Press, 1999.

Fanning, Leonard M. "Alfred P. Sloan Jr." In *Titans of Business*, 207-235. Philadelphia, Penn.: Lippincott, 1964. 240 p.

Davis, William. "Alfred P. Sloan, 1875-1966: 'The Greatest Genius Ever in the Auto Business." In *The Innovators: The Essential Guide to Business Thinkers, Achievers and Entrepreneurs*, 356-360. New York, N.Y.: AMACOM, 1987.

Livesay, Harold C. "The Organization Man: Alfred P. Sloan." In *American Made: Men Who Shaped the American Economy*, 212-239. Boston, Mass.: Little, Brown, 1979.

Wren, Daniel A., and Ronald G. Greenwood. "Alfred P. Sloan Jr." In *Management Innovators: The People and Ideas That Have Shaped Modern Business*, 158-163. New York, N.Y.: Oxford University Press, 1998.

SLOAN, C. DIANNE

Mikaelian, A. "C. Dianne Sloan." In *Women Who Mean Business: Success Stories of Women Over Forty*, 141-145. New York, N.Y.: William Morrow & Co., 1999.

SLOANE, DEAN

Levitt, Mortimer. "Dean Sloane: Delivering Sophisticated Health Care in a Profitable New Way." In *How to Start Your Own Business Without Losing Your Shirt; Secrets of Seventeen Successful Entrepreneurs*, 97-103. New York, N.Y: Atheneum, 1988.

SLOVER, JAMES

"Optimal Employee Health Through Screening." In *How I Became a Nurse Entrepreneur: Tales from 50 Nurses in Business*, 185-190. Petaluma, Calif.: National Nurses in Business Association, 1991.

SMITH, BOB

Buchholz, Barbara B., and Margaret Crane. "Smith Farms, Chula, MO." In *Corporate Blood Lines: The Future of the Family Firm*, 127-144. New York, N.Y: Carol Publishing Group, 1989.

SMITH, BRUTON

Farnham, Alan. "Bruton Smith: Cofounder of the Charlotte Motor Speedway, 'Negativity? That's Not the Way to Make Any Money'." In *Forbes Great Success Stories: Twelve Tales of*

Victory Wrested from Defeat, 168-185. New York, N.Y.: Wiley, 2000.

SMITH, CLARENCE O.

Dingle, Derek T. "Clarence O. Smith: Essence Communications, Inc., 'The Salesman'." In *Black Enterprise Titans of the B.E. 100s: Black CEOs Who Redefined and Conquered American Business*, 51-72. New York, N.Y.: Wiley, 1999.

SMITH, CYRUS ROWLETT

Bilstein, Roger E. "C. R. Smith: An American Original." In *Airline Executives and Federal Regulation: Case Studies in American Enterprise from the Airmail Era to the Dawn of the Jet Age*, ed. W. David Lewis, 83-124. Columbus, Ohio: Ohio State University Press, 2000.

"Riding High in a New Era: C. R. Smith." In *Lessons of Leadership: 21 Executives Speak Out on Creating, Developing and Managing Success*. Presented by the editors of Nation's Business, 111-122. Garden City, N.Y.: Doubleday, 1968.

SMITH, DAVID M.

Gray, Bob, ed. "Waste Not, Want Not." In *How Entrepreneurs Make Business Profits: A Study of Personal Success Stories From Cordovan Business Journals*, 83-89. Houston, Tex.: Cordovan Press, 1982.

SMITH, FREDERICK W.

Davis, William. "Frederick Smith, b. 1944: Mover of 'High-Priority, Time-Sensitive' Goods." In *The Innovators: The Essential Guide to Business Thinkers, Achievers and Entrepreneurs*, 361-365. New York, N.Y.: AMACOM, 1987.

"Fred Smith: Founder and CEO, Federal Express Corporation." In *Forbes Great Minds of Business*, ed. Gretchen Morgenson, 35-72. New York, N.Y.: Wiley, 1997. 228 p.

Landrum, Gene N. "Fred Smith—Charismatic." In *Profiles of Genius: Thirteen Creative Men Who Changed the World*, 86-95. Buffalo, N.Y.: Prometheus Books, 1993.

Nayak, P. Ranganath, and John M. Ketteringham. "Federal Express: The Knights on the Last White Horse." In *Breakthroughs!*, 307-336. San Diego, Calif.: Pfeiffer & Company, 1994.

Silver, A. David. "Frederick W. Smith." In *Entrepreneurial Megabucks: The 100 Greatest Entrepreneurs of the Last 25 Years*, 403-406. New York, N.Y.: Wiley, 1985.

Sobel, Robert, and David B. Sicilia. "Fred Smith and Federal Express." In *The Entrepreneurs: An American Adventure*, 42-48. Boston, Mass.: Houghton Mifflin Company, 1986.

SMITH, GERALD

MacPhee, William. "Gerald Smith of Allied Bankshares." In *Rare Breed: The Entrepreneur, An American Culture*, 133-141. Chicago, Ill.: Probus Publishing Company, 1987.

SNODDY, ANTHONY

Woodard, Michael D. "Exemplar Manufacturing, Inc.—Anthony Snoddy." In *Black Entrepreneurs in America: Stories of Struggle and Success*, 142-154. New Brunswick, N.J.: Rutgers University Press, 1997.

SOLOMON, DAVID

Kingston, Brett. "David Solomon of Solomon Equities." In *The Dynamos: Who Are They Anyway?*, 145-151. New York, N.Y.: Wiley, 1987.

SOLOMON, JODI F.

Mikaelian, A. "Jodi F. Solomon." In *Women Who Mean Business: Success Stories of Women Over Forty*, 146-150. New York, N.Y.: William Morrow & Co., 1999.

SONTHEIMER, CARL G.

Fucini, Joseph J., and Suzy Fucini. "Carl G. Sontheimer, Cuisinart, Inc.: 'If You Aren't Passionate—Don't Even Bother'." In *Experience Inc.; Men and Women Who Founded Famous Companies After the Age of 40*, 215-220. New York, N.Y: Free Press, 1987.

SOROS, GEORGE

Smith, Roy C. "The World's Greatest Investor." In *Wealth Creators: The Rise of Today's Rich and Super-Rich*, 166-176. New York, N.Y.: Truman Talley, 2001.

Train, John. "George Soros: Macro Games." In *Money Masters of Our Time*, 191-217. New York, N.Y.: HarperBusiness, 2000.

Train, John. "George Soros: Global Speculator." In *The New Money Masters : Winning Investment Strategies of Soros, Lynch, Steinhardt, Rogers, Neff, Wanger, Michaelis, Carret*, 67-96. New York, N.Y.: Harper & Row, 1989.

SPALDING, ALBERT GOODWILL

Cleary, David Powers. "Spalding Sporting Goods; Spalding Has Gone into the Baseball Business." In *Great American Brands: The Success Formulas That Made Them Famous*, 280-286. New York, N.Y: Fairchild Publications, 1981.

SPALLA, LUCIAN

Gray, Bob, ed. "Starting From Base Zero." In *How Entrepreneurs Make Business Profits: A Study of Personal Success Stories From Cordovan Business Journals*, 38-44. Houston, Tex.: Cordovan Press, 1982.

SPEER, ROY M.

Aronoff, Craig E., and John L. Ward. "Roy M. Speer." In *Contemporary Entrepreneurs*, 451-457. Detroit, Mich.: Omnigraphics, Inc., 1992.

Fucini, Joseph J., and Suzy Fucini. "Lowell W. Paxson, Roy M. Speer, Home Shopping Network, Inc.: 'We Knew We Were on a Rocket'." In *Experience Inc.; Men and Women Who Founded Famous Companies After the Age of 40*, 89-95. New York, N.Y: Free Press, 1987.

SPENCER, MARY KAY

Mikaelian, A. "Mary Kay Spencer." In *Women Who Mean Business: Success Stories of Women Over Forty*, 132-135. New York, N.Y.: William Morrow & Co., 1999.

SPRECKELS, CLAUS

Burnley, James. "Havemeyer and Spreckels: The Sugar Kings of America." In *Millionaires and Kings of Enterprise; The Marvellous Careers of Some Americans Who by Pluck, Foresight, And Energy Have Made Themselves Masters in the Fields of Industry and Finance*, 212-223. Philadelphia, Penn.: J. B. Lippincott, 1901.

"Claus Spreckels." In *A Dozen Roads to Success: Being Graphic Sketches of Twelve of the Most Prominent Business Men of America, And Showing How They Became Millionaires*, 118-133. Philadelphia, Penn.: Girard Pub. Co., 1894.

Klepper, Michael M., and Robert Gunther. "Claus Speckels (1828-1908): Sweet Success." In *The Wealthy 100 : From Benjamin Franklin to Bill Gates—A Ranking of the Richest Americans, Past and Present*, 153-155. Secaucus, N.J. : Carol Pub. Group, 1996.

SQUIBB, EDWARD ROBINSON

"Billion Dollar By-product: Impurities, Adulteration of Mid-19th Century Drugs Outraged Young Navy Surgeon Squibb; Unintended Result of Lifelong Campaign Was Modern Pharmaceutical Industry, Vast Enterprise Still Bearing His Name." In *The 50 Great Pioneers of American Industry*. By the Editors of News Front and Year, 38-41. Maplewood, N.J.: C.S. Hammond, 1964.

STACK, JACK

Ericksen, Gregory K. "Jack Stack: Springfield Remanufacturing Corp., 'Business Is a Way of Creating Opportunity'." In *What's Luck Got to Do with It; Twelve Entrepreneurs Reveal the Secrets Behind Their Success*, 99-117. New York, N.Y.: Wiley, 1997.

STAFFORD, EARL

Farnham, Alan. "Earl Stafford: Founder of Universal Systems & Technology (UNITECH), A Leader in Net-Based Training Systems, 'Bloody, But Unbowed'." In *Forbes Great Success Stories: Twelve Tales of Victory Wrested from Defeat*, 186-205. New York, N.Y.: Wiley, 2000.

STANFIELD, JANICE M.

Stanfield, Janice M. "It Is Not the Critic Who Counts." In *How I Became a Nurse Entrepreneur: Tales from 50 Nurses in Business*, 307-313. Petaluma, Calif.: National Nurses in Business Association, 1991.

STANFORD, LELAND

"Leland Stanford." In *A Dozen Roads to Success: Being Graphic Sketches of Twelve of the Most Prominent Business Men of America, And Showing How They Became Millionaires*, 74-88. *Philadelphia, Penn.: Girard Pub. Co., 1894.*

Lewis, Oscar. "Stanford: 'It Is Pleasant to Be Rich...'." In *The Big Four; The Story of Huntington, Stanford, Hopkins, and Crocker, And of the Building of the Central Pacific*, 156-210. New York, N.Y.: A.A. Knopf, 1938.

Stoddard, William Osborn. "Leland Stanford—Councillor." In *Men of Business*, 295-317. New York, N.Y.: Scribner's Sons, 1893. 317 p.

STANLEY FAMILY

Carlova, John. "The Stanleys and Their Steamer." In *Great Stories of American Businessmen*, From *American Heritage, The Magazine of*

History, 326-334. New York, N.Y.: American Heritage Publishing Co., 1954.

STASH, SANDRA M.

Mikaelian, A. "Sandra M. Stash." In *Women Who Mean Business: Success Stories of Women Over Forty,* 185-189. New York, N.Y.: William Morrow & Co., 1999.

STATA, RAYMOND

Silver, A. David. "Raymond Stata." In *Entrepreneurial Megabucks: The 100 Greatest Entrepreneurs of the Last 25 Years,* 407-412. New York, N.Y.: Wiley, 1985.

STATLER, ELLSWORTH MILTON

"The Customer Is Always Right: E.M. Statler Believed in Fussless Comfort, Bath in Every Room, He Pioneered Hotel Standardization and Today's $2.7 Billion-A-Year Hotel Industry." In *The 50 Great Pioneers of American Industry.* By the Editors of News Front and Year, 138-140. Maplewood, N.J.: C.S. Hammond, 1964.

STEELE, GARY

Kingston, Brett. "Gary Steele of Molecular Devices Corporation." In *The Dynamos: Who Are They Anyway?,* 137-142. New York, N.Y.: Wiley, 1987.

STEELE, RUSSELL

Tsang, Cheryl D. "Russell Steele: 'The Musician,' 1986-1994." In *Microsoft First Generation: The Success Secrets of the Visionaries Who Launched a Technology Empire,* 213-226. New York, N.Y.: Wiley, 2000.

STEIGERWALDT, DONNA WOLF

Pottker, Jan. "Jockey International, Inc.: Holding the Reins." In *Born to Power: Heirs to America's Leading Businesses*, 196-200. New York, N.Y.: Barron's, 1992.

STEIN, AVY

Kingston, Brett. "Avy Stein of Regent Corporation." In *The Dynamos: Who Are They Anyway?*, 65-74. New York, N.Y.: Wiley, 1987.

STEIN, KAROL

"Hemodialysis Company Rises to the Top." In *How I Became a Nurse Entrepreneur: Tales from 50 Nurses in Business*, 43-46. Petaluma, Calif.: National Nurses in Business Association, 1991.

STEIN, MARSHALL

Koppel, Robert. "A View From the Bridge: Marshall Stein." In *Bulls, Bears, And Millionaires: War Stories of Trading Life*, 96-105. Chicago, Ill.: Dearborn Financial Publishers, 1997.

STEINEM, GLORIA

Landrum, Gene N. "Gloria Steinem—Rebellious Social Conscience." In *Profiles of Female Genius: Thirteen Creative Women Who Changed the World*, 312-329. Amherst, N.Y.: Prometheus Books, 1994.

STEINHARDT, MICHAEL

Train, John. "Michael Steinhardt: Strategic Trader." In *The New Money Masters : Winning Investment Strategies of Soros, Lynch, Steinhardt, Rogers, Neff, Wanger, Michaelis, Carret*, 31-49. New York, N.Y.: Harper & Row, 1989.

Train, John. "Michael Steinhardt: Strategic Trader." In *Money Masters of Our Time*, 227-243. New York, N.Y.: HarperBusiness, 2000.

STEMBERG, THOMAS G.

Aronoff, Craig E., and John L. Ward. "Thomas G. Stemberg." In *Contemporary Entrepreneurs*, 458-462. Detroit, Mich.: Omnigraphics, Inc., 1992.

STERN, BONNIE

Mikaelian, A. "Bonnie Stern." In *Women Who Mean Business: Success Stories of Women Over Forty*, 340-344. New York, N.Y.: William Morrow & Co., 1999.

STEWART, ALEXANDER TURNEY

Klepper, Michael M., and Robert Gunther. "Alexander Turney Stewart (1803-1876): The Merchant Prince." In *The Wealthy 100 : From Benjamin Franklin to Bill Gates—A Ranking of the Richest Americans, Past and Present*, 34-37. Secaucus, N.J. : Carol Pub. Group, 1996.

Stoddard, William Osborn. "Alexander Turney Stewart—Perception." In *Men of Business*, 182-196. New York, N.Y.: Scribner's Sons, 1893. 317 p.

Wren, Daniel A., and Ronald G. Greenwood. "Alexander T. Stewart." In *Management Innovators: The People and Ideas That Have Shaped Modern Business*, 51-58. New York, N.Y.: Oxford University Press, 1998.

STEWART, SARAH

"Healing the Healers." In *How I Became a Nurse Entrepreneur: Tales from 50 Nurses in Business*, 107-111. Petaluma, Calif.: National Nurses in Business Association, 1991.

STILLMAN, JAMES

Klepper, Michael M., and Robert Gunther. "James Stillman (1850-1918): The Invisible Hand." In *The Wealthy 100 : From Benjamin Franklin to*

Bill Gates—A Ranking of the Richest Americans, Past and Present,
250-252. Secaucus, N.J. : Carol Pub. Group, 1996.

STODDARD, BRANDON

Hillkirk, John, and Gary Jacobson. "Brandon Stoddard: The Thin Man Behind
'Roseane'." In *Grit, Guts, And Genius: True Tales of Megasuccess:
Who Made Them Happen and How They Did It*, 38-47. Boston,
Mass.: Houghton Mifflin, 1990.

STOMBAUGH, DAVE

Elfstrand, Rhonda. "Dave Stombaugh, CPA: Stenger, Bies, And Company,
Inc." In *The Story Behind the Success: Learning From Pittsburgh
Professionals*, 238-248. Pittsburgh, Penn.: Steel Publishing Partners,
1996.

STONE, JULIE

Herera, Sue. "Julie Stone: Senior Investment Management Consultant, Smith
Barney." In *Women of the Street: Making It on Wall Street—The
World's Toughest Business*, 183-196. New York, N.Y.: Wiley, 1997.

STONE, W. CLEMENT

Gunther, Max, "W. Clement Stone: Four Hundred Million Dollars." In *The
Very, Very Rich and How They Got That Way*, ed. Max Gunther, 30-
40. Chicago, Ill.: The Playboy Press, 1972.

Mariotti, Steve, and Lorraine Mooney. "Clement Stone: The Power of Positive
Thinking." In *Entrepreneurs in Profile*, 40-42. London: National
Foundation for Teaching Entrepreneurship, 1991.

Shook, Robert L. "W. Clement Stone." In *The Entrepreneurs: Twelve Who
Took Risks and Succeeded*, 19-39. New York, N.Y: Harper & Row,
1980.

STOPPER, ED

Murphy, Linda. "Jack Dunning & Ed Stopper: ComputorEdge." In *Computer Entrepreneurs: People Who Built Successful Businesses Around Computers*, 101-110. San Diego, Calif.: Computer Publishing Enterprises, 1990.

STOVALL, JIM

Farnham, Alan. "Jim Stovall: CoCreator of the Narrative Television Network, 'I Was More Scared Than I'd Ever Been in My Life'." In *Forbes Great Success Stories: Twelve Tales of Victory Wrested from Defeat*, 206-225. New York, N.Y.: Wiley, 2000.

STOVER, W. ROBERT

Oster, Merrill J. "Exceptionally Ordinary." In *The Entrepreneur's Creed: The Principles & Passions of 20 Successful Entrepreneurs*, 46-55. Nashville, Tenn.: Broadman & Holman Publishers, 2001.

STOWE, SIBRENA

Mitchell, Niki Butler. "Class Act: Sibrena Stowe, President and CEO, Stowe Communications, Inc." In *The New Color of Success: Twenty Young Black Millionaires Tell You How They're Making it*, 225-237. Rocklin, Calif.: Prima Publishing, 2000.

STRADLEY, CAROLYN J.

Aronoff, Craig E., and John L. Ward. "Carolyn J. Stradley." In *Contemporary Entrepreneurs*, 463-469. Detroit, Mich.: Omnigraphics, Inc., 1992.

STRATTON, W.S.

Burnley, James. "W. S. Stratton: The Colorado Gold King." In **Millionaires and Kings of Enterprise; The Marvellous Careers of Some Americans Who by Pluck, Foresight, And Energy Have Made Themselves Masters in the Fields of Industry and Finance**, 200-211. Philadelphia, Penn.: J. B. Lippincott, 1901.

STRAUSBERG, JENNIFER

Koppel, Mara. "The Matchmaker From Minsk—Jennifer Strausberg." In *Women of the Pits: Shattering the Glass Ceiling in Financial Markets*, 73-80. Chicago, Ill.: Dearborn Financial Publishers, 1998.

STRAUSS, LEVI

Cleary, David Powers. "Levi's Jeans: The Cowboy's Tailor." In *Great American Brands: The Success Formulas That Made Them Famous*, 211-216. New York, N.Y: Fairchild Publications, 1981.

STROUD FAMILY

Pottker, Jan. "Milliken & Co., Inc.: Unraveling the Family Shares." In *Born to Power: Heirs to America's Leading Businesses*, 384-389. New York, N.Y.: Barron's, 1992.

STUTZ, GERALDINE

Taylor, Russel R. "Geraldine Stutz; She Bought the Store." In *Exceptional Entrepreneurial Women*, 33-39. New York, N.Y: Quorum Books, 1988.

SUGARMAN, JOSEPH

Shook, Robert L. "Joseph Sugarman." In *The Entrepreneurs: Twelve Who Took Risks and Succeeded*, 115-125. New York, N.Y: Harper & Row, 1980.

SULLIVAN, LOUIS H.

Davis, William. "Louis H. Sullivan, 1856-1924: Father of Modern Architecture." In *The Innovators: The Essential Guide to Business Thinkers, Achievers and Entrepreneurs*, 369-372. New York, N.Y.: AMACOM, 1987.

SULZBERGER, ARTHUR OCHS

Coleridge, Nicholas. "All the Cash That's Fit to Print: The Sulzbergers and the New York Times." In *Paper Tigers: The Latest, Greatest Newspaper Tycoons*, 30-73. New York, N.Y.: Carol Publishing Group, 1994.

Cose, Ellis. "The Cathedral: The New York Times." In *The Press*, 185-279. New York, N.Y.: Morrow, 1989.

Levinson, Harry, and Stuart Rosenthal. "Arthur O. Sulzberger." In *CEO: Corporate Leadership in Action*, 219-258. New York, N.Y.: Basic Books, 1984.

SUNDBACK, GIDEON

Davis, William. "Gideon Sundback, 1880-1949, Developer of the Zip Fastener." In *The Innovators: The Essential Guide to Business Thinkers, Achievers and Entrepreneurs*, 372-374. New York, N.Y.: AMACOM, 1987.

SUTTON, PERCY E.

Dingle, Derek T. "Percy E. Sutton: Inner City Broadcasting Corporation, 'The Politician'." In *Black Enterprise Titans of the B.E. 100s: Black CEOs Who Redefined and Conquered American Business*, 193-212. New York, N.Y.: Wiley, 1999.

SWANSON, ROBERT A.

Meyer, Michael. "The Builder." In *The Alexander Complex: The Dreams That Drive the Great Businessmen*, 157-193. New York, N.Y.: Times Books, 1989.

Silver, A. David. "Robert A. Swanson; Herbert W. Boyer." In *Entrepreneurial Megabucks: The 100 Greatest Entrepreneurs of the Last 25 Years*, 413-416. New York, N.Y.: Wiley, 1985.

SWEENEY, ANNE

Pestrak, Debra. "Anne Sweeney: President, Disney/ABC Networks and President, Disney Channel." In *Playing with the Big Boys: Success Stories of the Most Powerful Women in Business*, 33-46. Carlsbad, CA: SUN Publications, 2001.

SWERSKY, PHYLLIS

White, Jane. "Phyllis Swersky of AICorp, Inc.: So Much for 'The Mommy Track'." In *A Few Good Women: Breaking the Barriers to Top Management*, 151-157. Englewood Cliffs, N.J.: Prentice Hall, 1992.

SWIFT, GUSTAVUS F.

Darby, Edwin. "Swift." In *The Fortune Builders*, 155-165. Garden City, N.Y.: Doubleday and Company, Inc., 1986.

"How to Build a Business: Gustavus Swift, At 16, Borrowed $25 from his Father, Bought and Butchered a Heifer, When He Died 58 Years Later His Meat-Packing Firm Was World's Largest, With Yearly Sales Today over $2.5 Billion." In *The 50 Great Pioneers of American Industry*. By the Editors of News Front and Year, 91-94. Maplewood, N.J.: C.S. Hammond, 1964.

SZABO, EVA

Elfstrand, Rhonda. "Eva Szabo: European Skin Care." In *The Story Behind the Success: Learning From Pittsburgh Professionals*, 250-262. Pittsburgh, Penn.: Steel Publishing Partners, 1996.

TAGGARES, KATHY

Enkelis, Liane, and Karen Olsen. "Kathy Taggares: President, K.T.'s Kitchens." In *On Our Own Terms: Portraits of Women Business Leaders* , 28-39. San Francisco, Calif.: Berrett-Koehler, 1995.

TANDON, SIRJANG LAL

Gray, Bob, ed. "Filling a Niche in Computers." In *How Entrepreneurs Make Business Profits: A Study of Personal Success Stories From Cordovan Business Journals*, 50-56. Houston, Tex.: Cordovan Press, 1982.

Silver, A. David. "Sirjang Lal Tandon." In *Entrepreneurial Megabucks: The 100 Greatest Entrepreneurs of the Last 25 Years*, 417-419. New York, N.Y.: Wiley, 1985.

TANDY, CHARLES

Silver, A. David. "Charles Tandy." In *Entrepreneurial Megabucks: The 100 Greatest Entrepreneurs of the Last 25 Years*, 420-422. New York, N.Y.: Wiley, 1985.

TAPLAN, JOHN E.

Taplan, John E. "The Education of an Inventor." In *The Power of Boldness: Ten Master Builders of American Industry Tell Their Success Stories*, ed. Elkan Blout, 23-40. Washington, D.C.: Joseph Henry Press, 1996.

TAUB, FRANK

Silver, A. David. "Henry Taub; Frank Lautenberg; Joseph Taub." In *Entrepreneurial Megabucks: The 100 Greatest Entrepreneurs of the Last 25 Years*, 423-425. New York, N.Y.: Wiley, 1985.

TAUB, JOSEPH

Silver, A. David. "Henry Taub; Frank Lautenberg; Joseph Taub." In *Entrepreneurial Megabucks: The 100 Greatest Entrepreneurs of the Last 25 Years*, 423-425. New York, N.Y.: Wiley, 1985.

TAUGHER, ROSEMARY

Lassen, Ali. "Rosemary Taugher: Owner, Anacapa Financial Services." In *The Secret of Their Success: Women Entrepreneurs Reveal How*

They Made It, 197-202. Carlsbad, Calif.: Ali Lassen Success System, 1990.

TAUSCHER, WILLIAM Y.

Silver, A. David. "William Y. Tauscher." In *Entrepreneurial Megabucks: The 100 Greatest Entrepreneurs of the Last 25 Years*, 426-428. New York, N.Y.: Wiley, 1985.

TAYLOR, CAROLYN J.

Taylor, Carolyn J. "The Seed of the Entrepreneurial Spirit." In *How I Became a Nurse Entrepreneur: Tales from 50 Nurses in Business*, 199-202. Petaluma, Calif.: National Nurses in Business Association, 1991.

TAYLOR, FREDERICK WINSLOW

McSherry, Ronald T. "Frederick Winslow Taylor: The Founder of Industrial Efficiency." In *Nine American Self-Made Men and Their Secrets to Success*, 40-45. Denver, Colo.: U.S.A. Publishing, 1983.

"Management Man: Frederick W. Taylor Showed Industry That 'There's a Best Way to Do Everything'." In *The 50 Great Pioneers of American Industry*. By the Editors of News Front and Year, 127-129. Maplewood, N.J.: C.S. Hammond, 1964.

Wren, Daniel A., and Ronald G. Greenwood. "Frederick W. Taylor." In *Management Innovators: The People and Ideas That Have Shaped Modern Business*, 134-140. New York, N.Y.: Oxford University Press, 1998.

TAYLOR, MOSES

Klepper, Michael M., and Robert Gunther. "Moses Taylor (1806-1882): City Banker." In *The Wealthy 100 : From Benjamin Franklin to Bill Gates—A Ranking of the Richest Americans, Past and Present*, 78-80. Secaucus, N.J. : Carol Pub. Group, 1996.

TAYLOR, ROBERT R.

Davis, William. "Robert R. Taylor, b. 1935: Creator of Fads." In *The Innovators: The Essential Guide to Business Thinkers, Achievers and Entrepreneurs*, 374-378. New York, N.Y.: AMACOM, 1987.

TEMPELSMAN, LEON

Pottker, Jan. "Lazare Kaplan International, Inc.: A Family Is Forever." In *Born to Power: Heirs to America's Leading Businesses*, 80-97. New York, N.Y.: Barron's, 1992.

TEMPLETON, JOHN

King, Norman. "John M. Templeton." In *The Money Messiah$*, 88-117. New York, N.Y.: Coward-McCann, 1983.

Train, John. "John Templeton: Search Many Markets." In *Money Masters of Our Time*, 52-64. New York, N.Y.: HarperBusiness, 2000.

Train, John. "John Templeton: To Everything There Is a Season." In *The Money Masters*, 158-177. New York, N.Y.: Harper & Row, 1980.

TERRELL, FREDERICK O.

Clarke, Caroline V. "Frederick O. Terrell: Managing Partner and CEO, Provender Capital Group, LLC." In *Take a Lesson: Today's Black Achievers and How They Made It and What They Learned Along the Way*, 201-212. New York, N.Y.: Wiley, 2001.

TERRY, ELLEN

Alexander, Shoshana. "Ellen Terry, Realtors, Dallas, Texas." In *Women's Ventures, Women's Visions: 29 Inspiring Stories From Women Who Started Their Own Businesses*, 206-214. Freedom, Calif.: The Crossing Press, 1997.

THAW, WILLIAM

Klepper, Michael M., and Robert Gunther. "William Thaw (1818-1889): Father of the Trial of the Century." In *The Wealthy 100 : From Benjamin Franklin to Bill Gates—A Ranking of the Richest Americans, Past and Present,* 256-258. Secaucus, N.J. : Carol Pub. Group, 1996.

THAYER, KELLY

Suarez, Ruth. "Kelly Thayer: Clear Image, 'Playing Hardball'." In *Superstar Entrepreneurs of Small and Large Businesses Reveal Their Secrets,* 137-143. Piscataway, N.J.: Research and Education Association, 1998.

THIESSENS, JAY

Liberman, Gail, and Alan Lavine. "Jay Thiessens: Despite Illiteracy, Builds $5 Million-A-Year Business." In *Rags to Riches: Motivating Stories of How Ordinary People Achieved Extraordinary Wealth!,* 28-40. Chicago, Ill.: Dearborn, 2000.

THOMAS, BRANDY M.

Mitchell, Niki Butler. "Conquering the Internet: Christopher D. Young, President and CEO; Brandy M. Thomas, Chairman and CEO, Cyveillance." In *The New Color of Success: Twenty Young Black Millionaires Tell You How They're Making it,* 169-182. Rocklin, Calif.: Prima Publishing, 2000.

THOMAS, PHILIP

"All Aboard! Philip Thomas Founded Baltimore and Ohio, First U.S. Railroad, Opened the Way to the Middle West." In *The 50 Great Pioneers of American Industry.* By the Editors of News Front and Year, 11-13. Maplewood, N.J.: C.S. Hammond, 1964.

THOMAS, WENDY

Pottker, Jan. "Wendy's International, Inc.: Dave's Deluxe Daughter." In *Born to Power: Heirs to America's Leading Businesses*, 254-259. New York, N.Y.: Barron's, 1992.

THOMPSON, CHARLES

Gross, Daniel, and the Editors of Forbes Magazine. "The Turnaround at Harley-Davidson." In *Forbes Greatest Business Stories of All Time*, 298-312. New York, N.Y.: Wiley, 1996.

THOMPSON, DAVID W.

Aronoff, Craig E., and John L. Ward. "David W. Thompson." In *Contemporary Entrepreneurs*, 471-477. Detroit, Mich.: Omnigraphics, Inc., 1992.

THOMPSON-DRAPER, CHERYL L.

Mikaelian, A. "Cheryl L. Thompson-Draper." In *Women Who Mean Business: Success Stories of Women Over Forty*, 296-300. New York, N.Y.: William Morrow & Co., 1999.

THOMPSON, JOE C. JR.

Shook, Carrie, and Robert L. Shook. "The Southland Corporation: Franchising Convenience Around the World." In *Franchising: The Business Strategy That Changed the World*, 225-252. Englewood Cliffs, NJ: Prentice Hall, 1993.

THOMPSON, KENNETH

Slater, Robert. "Dennis Ritchie and Kenneth Thompson: Creators of UNIX." In *Portraits in Silicon*, 272-283. Cambridge, Mass.: MIT Press, 1987.

THOMPSON, MACRO

Murphy, Linda. "Macro Thompson: Doctor Design." In *Computer Entrepreneurs: People Who Built Successful Businesses Around*

Computers, 31-38. San Diego, Calif.: Computer Publishing Enterprises, 1990.

THOMPSON, MAURICE C. "TOMMY"

"Maurice C. 'Tommy' Thompson, Smokenders." In *Profiles in Success: How Six Entrepreneurs Have Prospered in a Tough Business Environment*, 16-25. By the editors of *Managing*. New York, N.Y.: HBJ Newsletters, 1981.

THOMPSON, RICHARD C.

Thompson, Richard C. "A Marketing Approach to the Nursing Crisis." In *How I Became a Nurse Entrepreneur: Tales from 50 Nurses in Business*, 91-97. Petaluma, Calif.: National Nurses in Business Association, 1991.

THORNDIKE, ISRAEL

Klepper, Michael M., and Robert Gunther. "Israel Thorndike (1755-1832): Massachusetts Privateer." In *The Wealthy 100 : From Benjamin Franklin to Bill Gates—A Ranking of the Richest Americans, Past and Present*, 186-187. Secaucus, N.J. : Carol Pub. Group, 1996.

THORNTON, TEX

Sobel, Robert. "Tex Thornton: The Illusionist." In *The Rise and Fall of the Conglomerate Kings*, 47-76. New York, N.Y.: Stein and Day, 1984.

TIDBALL, RICK

Elfstrand, Rhonda. "Ron O'Dowd, CFP, Rick Tidball, CFP: Oakwood Financial Group." In *The Story Behind the Success: Learning From Pittsburgh Professionals*, 202-216. Pittsburgh, Penn.: Steel Publishing Partners, 1996.

TIFFANY, CHARLES LEWIS

"Charles Lewis Tiffany." In *A Dozen Roads to Success: Being Graphic Sketches of Twelve of the Most Prominent Business Men of America,*

And Showing How They Became Millionaires, 172-198. Philadelphia, Penn.: Girard Pub. Co., 1894.

Klepper, Michael M., and Robert Gunther. "Charles L. Tiffany (1812-1902): A Real Gem." In *The Wealthy 100 : From Benjamin Franklin to Bill Gates—A Ranking of the Richest Americans, Past and Present,* 166-168. Secaucus, N.J. : Carol Pub. Group, 1996.

Stoddard, William Osborn. "Charles Louis Tiffany—Taste." In *Men of Business,* 53-74. New York, N.Y.: Scribner's Sons, 1893. 317 p.

TISCH, LARRY

Train, John. "Larry Tisch: The Pragmatist." In *The Money Masters,* 178-186. New York, N.Y.: Harper & Row, 1980.

TOD, G. ROBERT

Kao, John J. "Managing Entrepreneurship at the CML Group." In *The Entrepreneur,* 155-163. Englewood Cliffs, New Jersey: Prentice Hall, 1991.

TOMER, HERMAN

Elfstrand, Rhonda. "Frank Jakovac, Herman Tomer: Gateway Archives, Inc." In *The Story Behind the Success: Learning From Pittsburgh Professionals,* 128-148. Pittsburgh, Penn.: Steel Publishing Partners, 1996.

TOMSON, MICHAEL

Aronoff, Craig E., and John L. Ward. "Joel Cooper; Michael Tomson." In *Contemporary Entrepreneurs,* 114-118. Detroit, Mich.: Omnigraphics, Inc., 1992.

TORAÑO, MARIA ELENA

Suarez, Ruth. "Maria Elena Toraño: META, 'A Woman of All Trades'." In *Superstar Entrepreneurs of Small and Large Businesses Reveal Their*

Secrets, 57-61. Piscataway, N.J.: Research and Education Association, 1998.

TOTINO, ROSE

Pile, Robert B. "Rose Totino: The Pizza Lady from Minneapolis." In *Top Entrepreneurs and Their Businesses*, 129-137. Minneapolis, Minn.: The Oliver Press, Inc., 1993.

Pine, Carol, and Susan Mundale. "Rose Totino; Big Business in the Kitchen." In *Self-Made: The Stories of 12 Minnesota Entrepreneurs*, 145-159. Minneapolis, Minn.: Dorn Books, 1982.

Taylor, Russel R. "Rose Totino; The Loving Queen of Pizza." In *Exceptional Entrepreneurial Women*, 93-102. New York, N.Y: Quorum Books, 1988.

TREYBIG, JAMES G.

Silver, A. David. "James G. Treybig." In *Entrepreneurial Megabucks: The 100 Greatest Entrepreneurs of the Last 25 Years*, 429-431. New York, N.Y.: Wiley, 1985.

TRIPPE, JUAN TERRY

Davis, William. "Juan Terry Trippe, 1899-1981: Emperor of the Air." In *The Innovators: The Essential Guide to Business Thinkers, Achievers and Entrepreneurs*, 383-386. New York, N.Y.: AMACOM, 1987.

TRUMP, DONALD

Farnham, Alan. "Donald Trump: Chairman of the Trump Organization, 'Fight Back, Always Fight Back Until You Win'." In *Forbes Great Success Stories: Twelve Tales of Victory Wrested from Defeat*, 124-147. New York, N.Y.: Wiley, 2000.

TUCHLER, ANDREW

Suarez, Ruth. "Andrew Tuchler: Ultimate Parking, Inc., 'Quality Service'." In *Superstar Entrepreneurs of Small and Large Businesses Reveal Their*

Secrets, 103-107. Piscataway, N.J.: Research and Education Association, 1998.

TULLY, DANIEL P.

Wendel, Charles B. "Reflections on Transforming a Company: Daniel P. Tully, Chairman & CEO, Merrill Lynch & Co., Inc." In *The New Financiers*, 259-282. Chicago, Ill.: Irwin Professional Pub., 1996.

TURNER, GLENN W.

Thompson, Thomas. "Glenn Turner: One-Hundred Million Dollars." In *The Very, Very Rich and How They Got That Way*, ed. Max Gunther, 231-242. Chicago, Ill.: The Playboy Press, 1972.

TURNER, MAXINE

Mikaelian, A. "Maxine Turner." In *Women Who Mean Business: Success Stories of Women Over Forty*, 301-304. New York, N.Y.: William Morrow & Co., 1999.

TURNER, TED

Brands, H. W. "The World in Real Time: Ted Turner." In *Masters of Enterprise: Giants of American Business from John Jacob Astor and J.P. Morgan to Bill Gates and Oprah Winfrey*, 275-291. New York, N.Y.: Free Press, 1999.

Davis, William. "Ted Turner, b. 1938: The Maverick Idealist." In *The Innovators: The Essential Guide to Business Thinkers, Achievers and Entrepreneurs*, 386-389. New York, N.Y.: AMACOM, 1987.

Kao, John J. "Ted Turner (A)." In *The Entrepreneur*, 62-68. Englewood Cliffs, New Jersey: Prentice Hall, 1991.

Landrum, Gene N. "Ted Turner—Risk-Taking." In *Profiles of Genius: Thirteen Creative Men Who Changed the World*, 213-229. Buffalo, N.Y.: Prometheus Books, 1993.

Meyer, Michael. "Glory." In *The Alexander Complex: The Dreams That Drive the Great Businessmen*, 195-234. New York, N.Y.: Times Books, 1989.

Silver, A. David. "Robert Edward Turner III." In *Entrepreneurial Megabucks: The 100 Greatest Entrepreneurs of the Last 25 Years*, 432-434. New York, N.Y.: Wiley, 1985.

TUSHINSKY, JOSEPH S.

Fucini, Joseph J., and Suzy Fucini. "Joseph S. Tushinsky, Superscope, Inc.: 'I Knew That the Sony Tape Recorder Couldn't Miss This Country'." In *Experience Inc.; Men and Women Who Founded Famous Companies After the Age of 40*, 37-42. New York, N.Y: Free Press, 1987

TYSON, DON

MacPhee, William. "Don Tyson of Tyson Foods, Inc." In *Rare Breed: The Entrepreneur, An American Culture*, 145-161. Chicago, Ill.: Probus Publishing Company, 1987.

UELTSCHI, ALBERT L.

Silver, A. David. "Albert L. Ueltschi." In *Entrepreneurial Megabucks: The 100 Greatest Entrepreneurs of the Last 25 Years*, 435-437. New York, N.Y.: Wiley, 1985.

UIBLE, DAVID

Suarez, Ruth. "David Uible: Rosegate Technology Group, 'An Accidental Invitation by the Department of Commerce'." In *Superstar Entrepreneurs of Small and Large Businesses Reveal Their Secrets*, 63-67. Piscataway, N.J.: Research and Education Association, 1998.

UNGAR, WILLIAM

Ericksen, Gregory K. "William Ungar: National Envelope Corp., 'Decisions That Project Into the Near Future'." In *What's Luck Got to Do with It;*

Twelve Entrepreneurs Reveal the Secrets Behind Their Success, 215-231. New York, N.Y.: Wiley, 1997.

VAIL, THEODORE N.

"Long Lines Lifetime: Theodore N. Vail's Faith and Flair Made Long Distance Telephone Practical Reality, Built Up AT&T 'Empire'." In *The 50 Great Pioneers of American Industry*. By the Editors of News Front and Year, 106-109. Maplewood, N.J.: C.S. Hammond, 1964.

Sobel, Robert. "Theodore N. Vail: The Subtle Serendipist." In *The Entrepreneurs: Explorations Within the American Business Tradition*, 195-246. New York, N.Y.: Weybright and Talley, 1974.

VAN ANDEL, JAY

Uris, Auren. "Jay Van Andel and Richard De Vos—Prospecting on the Doorstep." In *The Executive Breakthrough; 21 Roads to the Top*, 381-394. Garden City, N.Y.: Doubleday, 1967.

VAN RENSSELAER, STEPHEN

Klepper, Michael M., and Robert Gunther. "Stephen Van Rensselaer (1764-1839): The Last Patroon." In *The Wealthy 100 : From Benjamin Franklin to Bill Gates—A Ranking of the Richest Americans, Past and Present*, 46-48. Secaucus, N.J. : Carol Pub. Group, 1996.

VANDERBILT, CORNELIUS

Brands, H. W. "The Warrior: Cornelius Vanderbilt." In *Masters of Enterprise: Giants of American Business from John Jacob Astor and J.P. Morgan to Bill Gates and Oprah Winfrey*, 12-25. New York, N.Y.: Free Press, 1999.

Burnley, James. "Kings of Finance and Fortune: The Astors and Vanderbilts." In *Millionaires and Kings of Enterprise; The Marvellous Careers of Some Americans Who by Pluck, Foresight, And Energy Have Made Themselves Masters in the Fields of Industry and Finance*, 490-508. Philadelphia, Penn.: J. B. Lippincott, 1901.

Clark, Frank. "The Commodore Left Two Sons." In *Great Stories of American Businessmen*, From *American Heritage, The Magazine of History,* 199-229. New York, N.Y.: American Heritage Publishing Co., 1954.

Diamond, Sigmond. "Cornelius Vanderbilt." In *The Reputation of the American Businessman*, 53-78 Cambridge, Mass.: Harvard University Press, 1955.

Klepper, Michael M., and Robert Gunther. "Cornelius Vanderbilt (1794-1877): A Captain of Enterprise." In *The Wealthy 100 : From Benjamin Franklin to Bill Gates—A Ranking of the Richest Americans, Past and Present,* 9-17 . Secaucus, N.J. : Carol Pub. Group, 1996.

Stoddard, William Osborn. "Cornelius Vanderbilt—Competition." In *Men of Business*, 31-52. New York, N.Y.: Scribner's Sons, 1893. 317 p.

VERNON, LILLIAN

Landrum, Gene N. "Lilian Vernon—Internally Empowered Entrepreneur." In *Profiles of Female Genius: Thirteen Creative Women Who Changed the World,* 346-358. Amherst, N.Y.: Prometheus Books, 1994.

Pottker, Jan. "Lillian Vernon Corporation: 'Mother Is Genius'." In *Born to Power: Heirs to America's Leading Businesses*, 204-219. New York, N.Y.: Barron's, 1992.

Taylor, Russel R. "Lillian Vernon Katz: Queen Mother of Mail Order." In *Exceptional Entrepreneurial Women*, 19-24. New York, N.Y: Quorum Books, 1988.

VILLAFANA, MANUEL

Pine, Carol, and Susan Mundale. "Manuel Villafana." In *Self-Made: The Stories of 12 Minnesota Entrepreneurs*, 161-172. Minneapolis, Minn.: Dorn Books, 1982.

VINING, EARLENE

Vining, Earlene. "Dream Big Dreams And—Make Them Live!" In *Success Secrets: How Eighteen Everyday Women Became Fortune Builders and Famous Speakers*, 43-64. Glendora, Calif.: Royal CBS Publishing, 1978.

VINTON, WILL

Hillkirk, John, and Gary Jacobson. "California Raisins": 'Oh, I Heard It Through the Grapevine'." In *Grit, Guts, And Genius: True Tales of Megasuccess: Who Made Them Happen and How They Did It*, 24-32. Boston, Mass.: Houghton Mifflin, 1990.

VOLKER, PAUL

"Paul Volker: Former Chairman, Federal Reserve Board." In *Forbes Great Minds of Business*, ed. Gretchen Morgenson, 157-200. New York, N.Y.: Wiley, 1997. 228 p.

VOLLUM, HOWARD

Silver, A. David. "Howard Vollum." In *Entrepreneurial Megabucks: The 100 Greatest Entrepreneurs of the Last 25 Years*, 438-439. New York, N.Y.: Wiley, 1985.

VONFROLIO, LAURA GASPARIS

Vonfrolio, Laura Gasparis. "The Sky's the Limit." In *How I Became a Nurse Entrepreneur: Tales from 50 Nurses in Business*, 1-5. Petaluma, Calif.: National Nurses in Business Association, 1991.

WACHNER, LINDA JOY

Landrum, Gene N. "Linda Wachner—'Type A' Workaholic." In *Profiles of Female Genius: Thirteen Creative Women Who Changed the World*, 360-372. Amherst, N.Y.: Prometheus Books, 1994.

WADE, MARION

Shook, Carrie, and Robert L. Shook. "ServiceMaster: The Masters of Service, Serving the Master." In *Franchising: The Business Strategy That Changed the World*, 197-224. Englewood Cliffs, NJ: Prentice Hall, 1993.

WAGNER, RALPH

Train, John. "Ralph Wagner: Small Metaphors." In *The New Money Masters : Winning Investment Strategies of Soros, Lynch, Steinhardt, Rogers, Neff, Wanger, Michaelis, Carret*, 152-170. New York, N.Y.: Harper & Row, 1989.

WAGNER, TODD

Ericksen, Gregory K. "Mark Cuban & Todd Wagner—Yahoo Broadcast 'Every Business in the World Is a Potential Customer'." In *Net Entrepreneurs Only : 10 Entrepreneurs Tell the Stories of Their Success*, 185-206. New York : John Wiley, 2000.

WAITE, DON

Elfstrand, Rhonda. "Don and Kathy Waite: Flex Source, Inc., Pirate Diamond Club." In *The Story Behind the Success: Learning From Pittsburgh Professionals*, 264-278. Pittsburgh, Penn.: Steel Publishing Partners, 1996.

WAITE, KATHY

Elfstrand, Rhonda. "Don and Kathy Waite: Flex Source, Inc., Pirate Diamond Club." In *The Story Behind the Success: Learning From Pittsburgh Professionals*, 264-278. Pittsburgh, Penn.: Steel Publishing Partners, 1996.

WAITT, TED

Ericksen, Gregory K. "Ted Waitt: Gateway 2000, 'Keep Things Simple'." In *What's Luck Got to Do with It; Twelve Entrepreneurs Reveal the Secrets Behind Their Success*, 1-17. New York, N.Y.: Wiley, 1997.

WALKER, ALFREDA

Walker, Alfreda. "Turning Points." In *How I Became a Nurse Entrepreneur: Tales from 50 Nurses in Business*, 287-289. Petaluma, Calif.: National Nurses in Business Association, 1991.

WALKER, C. J. "MADAM"

Forbes, Malcolm S. "Madame C. J. Walker, 'Creator of a New Standard of Black Beauty'." In *Women Who Made a Difference*, 299-301. New York, N.Y.: Simon & Schuster, 1990.

Jeffrey, Laura S. "Madam C. J. Walker: African-American Entrepreneur." In *Great American Businesswomen*, 16-26. Springfield, N.J.: Enslow Publishers, Inc., 1996.

Mariotti, Steve, and Lorraine Mooney. "Madam Walker: A Revolutionary for Black Beauty and Hygiene." In *Entrepreneurs in Profile*, 2-4. London: National Foundation for Teaching Entrepreneurship, 1991.

Mariotti, Steve, and Mike Caslin. "Madame C. J. Walker: The First African American Millionaire." In *The Very Very Rich: How They Got That Way and How You Can, Too!*, 97-100. Franklin Lakes, NJ: Career Press, 2000.

WALKER, JAY S.

Ericksen, Gregory K. "Jay S. Walker—Priceline.com 'Name Your Own Price'." In *Net Entrepreneurs Only : 10 Entrepreneurs Tell the Stories of Their Success*, 1-20. New York : John Wiley, 2000.

Price, Christopher. "Jay Walker—Priceline 'Storming the Barricades of Commerce'." In *The Internet Entrepreneurs: Business Rules Are Good: Break Them*, 34-49. London, Eng.: FT.com, 2000.

WALKER, JUDY

Liberman, Gail, and Alan Lavine. "Judy Walker: From Abject Poverty to Detroit Real Estate Wealth." In *Rags to Riches: Motivating Stories of How Ordinary People Achieved Extraordinary Wealth!*, 54-65.

Chicago, Ill.: Dearborn, 2000.

WALKER, MAGGIE L.

Jeffrey, Laura S. "Maggie L. Walker: First Female Banker." In *Great American Businesswomen*, 8-16. Springfield, N.J.: Enslow Publishers, Inc., 1996.

WALLACE, ROBERT (BOB)

Wallace, Robert L. "Jerome Sanders, Eliot Powell, Robert (Bob) Wallace: Founders, The SDGG Holding Company, Inc., Summit, New Jersey." In *Black Wealth: Your Road to Small Business Success*, 175-184. New York, N.Y.: Wiley, 2000.

WALTERS, DOTTIE

Walters, Dottie. "What Do You Say to an Audience of 14,000." In *Success Secrets: How Eighteen Everyday Women Became Fortune Builders and Famous Speakers*, 1-12. Glendora, Calif.: Royal CBS Publishing, 1978.

WALTERS, KATE

Walters, Kate. "From Dream to Reality Through Caring." In *How I Became a Nurse Entrepreneur: Tales from 50 Nurses in Business*, 299-307. Petaluma, Calif.: National Nurses in Business Association, 1991.

WALTON FAMILY

Brands, H. W. "Bentonville, U.S.A.: Sam Walton." In *Masters of Enterprise: Giants of American Business from John Jacob Astor and J.P. Morgan to Bill Gates and Oprah Winfrey*, 223-234. New York, N.Y.: Free Press, 1999.

Gross, Daniel, and the Editors of Forbes Magazine. "Sam Walton, Wal-Mart, And the Discounting of America." In *Forbes Greatest Business Stories of All Time*, 266-283. New York, N.Y.: Wiley, 1996.

Klepper, Michael M., and Robert Gunther. "Sam Moore Walton (1918-1992): The Wizard of Wal-Mart." In *The Wealthy 100 : From Benjamin Franklin to Bill Gates—A Ranking of the Richest Americans, Past and Present*, 65-69. Secaucus, N.J. : Carol Pub. Group, 1996.

Mariotti, Steve, and Mike Caslin. "Sam Walton, Wal-Mart: Master of Motivation." In *The Very Very Rich: How They Got That Way and How You Can, Too!*, 101-108. Franklin Lakes, NJ: Career Press, 2000.

Pile, Robert B. "Sam Walton: Discounting to Riches." In *Top Entrepreneurs and Their Businesses*, 110-127. Minneapolis, Minn.: The Oliver Press, Inc., 1993.

Pottker, Jan. "Wal-Mart Stores, Inc.: Caretakers of $22 Billion." In *Born to Power: Heirs to America's Leading Businesses*, 306-313. New York, N.Y.: Barron's, 1992.

Silver, A. David. "Sam Moore Walton." In *Entrepreneurial Megabucks: The 100 Greatest Entrepreneurs of the Last 25 Years*, 440-441. New York, N.Y.: Wiley, 1985.

WANAMAKER, JOHN

Burnley, James. "John Wanamaker: The Department Store King." In *Millionaires and Kings of Enterprise; The Marvellous Careers of Some Americans Who by Pluck, Foresight, And Energy Have Made Themselves Masters in the Fields of Industry and Finance*, 430-440. Philadelphia, Penn.: J. B. Lippincott, 1901.

McSherry, Ronald T. "John Wanamaker: The Grand Old Storekeeper." In *Nine American Self-Made Men and Their Secrets to Success*, 47-51. Denver, Colo.: U.S.A. Publishing, 1983.

Sobel, Robert. "John Wanamaker: The Triumph of Content Over Form." In *The Entrepreneurs: Explorations Within the American Business Tradition*, 73-109. New York, N.Y.: Weybright and Talley, 1974.

WANG, AN

Silver, A. David. "An Wang." In *Entrepreneurial Megabucks: The 100 Greatest Entrepreneurs of the Last 25 Years*, 442-443. New York, N.Y.: Wiley, 1985.

WANG, BEN C.

Gray, Bob, ed. "Three Computer Challenges." In *How Entrepreneurs Make Business Profits: A Study of Personal Success Stories From Cordovan Business Journals*, 57-63. Houston, Tex.: Cordovan Press, 1982.

WANG, CHARLES

Jager, Rama Dev, and Rafael Ortiz. "Charles Wang: Computer Associates; Managin', New Yawk Style." In *In the Company of Giants: Candid Conversations with the Visionaries of the Digital World*, 127-142. New York, N.Y.: McGraw-Hill, 1997.

WANGER, RALPH

Train, John. "Ralph Wanger: Zebras and Other Small Metaphors." In *Money Masters of Our Time*, 244-259. New York, N.Y.: HarperBusiness, 2000.

WARD, LLOYD D.

Clarke, Caroline V. "Lloyd D. Ward: Former Chairman and CEO, Maytag Corporation." In *Take a Lesson: Today's Black Achievers and How They Made It and What They Learned Along the Way*, 213-221. New York, N.Y.: Wiley, 2001.

WARE, LINDSEY

Murphy, Linda. "Janathin Miller & Lindsey Ware: Access Research Corporation." In *Computer Entrepreneurs: People Who Built Successful Businesses Around Computers*, 71-79. San Diego, Calif.: Computer Publishing Enterprises, 1990.

WARHOL, ANDY

Davis, William. "Andy Warhol, 1928-1987: 'America's Most Famous Artist'." In *The Innovators: The Essential Guide to Business Thinkers, Achievers and Entrepreneurs*, 390-392. New York, N.Y.: AMACOM, 1987.

WARNER, MARVIN

Adams, James Ring. "The Friends of Marvin Warner." In *The Big Fix: Inside the S&L Scandal: How an Unholy Alliance of Politics and Money Destroyed America's Banking System*, 145-165. New York, N.Y: Wiley, 1990.

WARNOCK, JOHN

Jager, Rama Dev, and Rafael Ortiz. "John Warnock/Charles Geschke: Adobe Systems; On Partnership." In *In the Company of Giants: Candid Conversations with the Visionaries of the Digital World*, 99-113. New York, N.Y.: McGraw-Hill, 1997.

WARREN, RENÉE E.

Harris, Wendy Beech. "Renée E. Warren and Kristen N. Poe, Noelle-Elaine Media Consultants: PR's Dynamic Duo." In *Against All Odds: Ten Entrepreneurs Who Followed Their Hearts and Found Success*, 181-201. New York, N.Y.: Wiley, 2001.

WARREN, SYLVIA

Alexander, Shoshana. "Sylvia Warren: Warren International, Oakland, California." In *Women's Ventures, Women's Visions: 29 Inspiring Stories From Women Who Started Their Own Businesses*, 193-198. Freedom, Calif.: The Crossing Press, 1997.

WASHINGTON, ALONZO

Harris, Wendy Beech. "Alonzo Washington, Omega 7 Inc.: A King of Black Comics." In *Against All Odds: Ten Entrepreneurs Who Followed Their Hearts and Found Success*, 93-112. New York, N.Y.: Wiley,

2001.

WATANABE-GERDES, PAMELA

Mikaelian, A. "Pamela Watanabe-Gerdes." In *Women Who Mean Business: Success Stories of Women Over Forty*, 195-199. New York, N.Y.: William Morrow & Co., 1999.

WATSON, THOMAS J. SR.

Bell, Laurence. "Thomas J. Watson." In *America's Fifty Foremost Business Leaders,* ed. B. C. Forbes, 421-430. New York, N.Y.: B.C. Forbes, 1948.

Brands, H. W. "Think—And Sell: Thomas J. Watson." In *Masters of Enterprise: Giants of American Business from John Jacob Astor and J.P. Morgan to Bill Gates and Oprah Winfrey*, 120-133. New York, N.Y.: Free Press, 1999.

Davis, William. "Thomas Watson Sr., 1874-1956: Autocrat of Computing." In *The Innovators: The Essential Guide to Business Thinkers, Achievers and Entrepreneurs*, 393-396. New York, N.Y.: AMACOM, 1987.

Slater, Robert. "Thomas J. Watson Sr.: Founder of IBM." In *Portraits in Silicon*, 102-111. Cambridge, Mass.: MIT Press, 1987.

WATSON, THOMAS J. JR.

Levinson, Harry, and Stuart Rosenthal. "Thomas J. Watson Jr." In *CEO: Corporate Leadership in Action*, 178-218. New York, N.Y: Basic Books, 1984.

WEATHERBY, ROY

MacPhee, William. "Roy Weatherby of Weatherby (Firearms), Inc." In *Rare Breed: The Entrepreneur, An American Culture*, 165-185. Chicago, Ill.: Probus Publishing Company, 1987.

WEATHERLY, MIKE

Levitt, Mortimer. "Mike Weatherly: Carving Out a Fortune with the Swiss Army Knife." In *How to Start Your Own Business Without Losing Your Shirt; Secrets of Seventeen Successful Entrepreneurs*, 120-132. New York, N.Y: Atheneum, 1988.

WEBER, CLAUDETTE

Suarez, Ruth. "Claudette Weber: Brero Construction, 'Building Success'." In *Superstar Entrepreneurs of Small and Large Businesses Reveal Their Secrets*, 77-82. Piscataway, N.J.: Research and Education Association, 1998.

WEIGHTMAN, WILLIAM

Klepper, Michael M., and Robert Gunther. "William Weightman (1813-1904): Rx for Riches." In *The Wealthy 100 : From Benjamin Franklin to Bill Gates—A Ranking of the Richest Americans, Past and Present*, 75-77. Secaucus, N.J. : Carol Pub. Group, 1996.

WEILL, SANFORD I.

Kadlec, Daniel J. "Sandy Weill: Another Year, Another Office." In *Masters of the Universe; Winning Strategies of America's Greatest Deal Makers*, 71-100. New York, N.Y.: HarperBusiness, 1999.

Silver, A. David. "Sanford I. Weill." In *Entrepreneurial Megabucks: The 100 Greatest Entrepreneurs of the Last 25 Years*, 444-446. New York, N.Y.: Wiley, 1985.

Smith, Roy C. "Reloading Sandy." In *Wealth Creators: The Rise of Today's Rich and Super-Rich*, 220-230. New York, N.Y.: Truman Talley, 2001.

Wendel, Charles B. "Building a Brand Name: Sanford I. Weill, Chairman & CEO, The Travelers Group." In *The New Financiers*, 283-302. Chicago, Ill.: Irwin Professional Pub., 1996.

WEINBERG, SIDNEY J.

"Balancing Ability with Humility: Sidney J. Weinberg." In *Lessons of Leadership: 21 Executives Speak Out on Creating, Developing and Managing Success*. Presented by the editors of Nation's Business, 32-43. Garden City, N.Y.: Doubleday, 1968.

WEINMANN, DENNIS

Koppel, Robert. "Hook, Line, And Sinker: Dennis Weinmann." In *Bulls, Bears, And Millionaires: War Stories of Trading Life*, 75-86. Chicago, Ill.: Dearborn Financial Publishers, 1997.

WEINSTEIN, STANLEY

King, Norman. "Stanley Weinstein." In *The Money Messiah$*, 205-206. New York, N.Y.: Coward-McCann, 1983.

WENDT, GARY C.

Wendel, Charles B. "Encouraging Entrepreneurialism Within a Financial Services Giant: Gary C. Wendt, Chairman & CEO, GE Capital Corporation." In *The New Financiers*, 303-332. Chicago, Ill.: Irwin Professional Pub., 1996.

WERNICK, MARVIN

Shook, Robert L. "The Mood Ring." In *Why Didn't I Think of That*, 38-49. New York, N.Y.: New American Library, 1982.

WESTENDORF, SARA

White, Jane. "Sara Westendorf of Hewlett-Packard: Getting the Password to the Men's Club." In *A Few Good Women: Breaking the Barriers to Top Management*, 97-111. Englewood Cliffs, N.J.: Prentice Hall, 1992.

WESTINGHOUSE, GEORGE

Burnley, James. "George Westinghouse: The Inventor of the Air-Brake." In *Millionaires and Kings of Enterprise; The Marvellous Careers of*

Some Americans Who by Pluck, Foresight, And Energy Have Made Themselves Masters in the Fields of Industry and Finance, 122-132. Philadelphia, Penn.: J. B. Lippincott, 1901.

"He Electrified Industry: Westinghouse's AC Transformer Made Economic Distribution of Electric Power Possible." In *The 50 Great Pioneers of American Industry*. By the Editors of News Front and Year, 123-126. Maplewood, N.J.: C.S. Hammond, 1964.

WETTHER, KAREN L.

Wetther, Karen L. "A Good Sign." In *How I Became a Nurse Entrepreneur: Tales from 50 Nurses in Business*, 47-55. Petaluma, Calif.: National Nurses in Business Association, 1991.

WEYERHAEUSER, FREDERICK

De Lorme, Roland L. "Rational Management Takes to the Woods: Frederick Weyerhaeuser and the Pacific Northwest Wood Products Industry." In *Business Entrepreneurs in the West*, ed. Ted C. Hinckley, 39-43. Manhattan, Kans.: Sunflower University Press, 1986.

Klepper, Michael M., and Robert Gunther. "Frederick Weyerhaeuser (1834-1914): Lumber Baron." In *The Wealthy 100 : From Benjamin Franklin to Bill Gates—A Ranking of the Richest Americans, Past and Present*, 38-40. Secaucus, N.J. : Carol Pub. Group, 1996.

WHITE, DOROTHY J.

Ericksen, Gregory K. "Dorothy J. White—Miracle Services, Inc., 'If You Do a Good Job, Someone Will Notice'." In *Women Entrepreneurs Only: Twelve Women Entrepreneurs Tell The Stories of Their Success*, 131-149. New York, N.Y.: Wiley, 1999.

WHITE, TOMMI A.

Mikaelian, A. "Tommi A. White." In *Women Who Mean Business: Success Stories of Women Over Forty*, 156-160. New York, N.Y.: William Morrow & Co., 1999.

WHITNEY, ELI

Livesay, Harold C. "The Artist of His Country: Eli Whitney. " In *American Made: Men Who Shaped the American Economy*, 19-50. Boston, Mass.: Little, Brown, 1979.

Wren, Daniel A., and Ronald G. Greenwood. "Eli Whitney." In *Management Innovators: The People and Ideas That Have Shaped Modern Business*, 10-16. New York, N.Y.: Oxford University Press, 1998.

WHITNEY, WILLIAM COLLINS

Burnley, James. "William Collins Whitney: Traction Magnate and Politician." In *Millionaires and Kings of Enterprise; The Marvellous Careers of Some Americans Who by Pluck, Foresight, And Energy Have Made Themselves Masters in the Fields of Industry and Finance*, 271-284. Philadelphia, Penn.: J. B. Lippincott, 1901.

Klepper, Michael M., and Robert Gunther. "William Collins Whitney (1841-1904): A Gentleman Bandit." In *The Wealthy 100 : From Benjamin Franklin to Bill Gates—A Ranking of the Richest Americans, Past and Present*, 253-255. Secaucus, N.J. : Carol Pub. Group, 1996.

WHITTLE, CHRISTOPHER

Silver, A. David. "Philip Moffitt; Christopher Whittle." In *Entrepreneurial Megabucks: The 100 Greatest Entrepreneurs of the Last 25 Years*, 317-319. New York, N.Y.: Wiley, 1985.

WICK, GAIL

Wick, Gail. "The Evolution of a Nurse Entrepreneur." In *How I Became a Nurse Entrepreneur: Tales from 50 Nurses in Business*, 121-124. Petaluma, Calif.: National Nurses in Business Association, 1991.

WIDENER, PETER ARRELL

Klepper, Michael M., and Robert Gunther. "Peter A. Widener (1834-1915): A Streetcar Named Success." In *The Wealthy 100 : From Benjamin*

Franklin to Bill Gates—A Ranking of the Richest Americans, Past and Present, 117-119. Secaucus, N.J. : Carol Pub. Group, 1996.

WILLIAMS, CHRISTOPHER J.

Wallace, Robert L. "Christopher J. Williams: President and CEO, The Williams Capital Group, L.P." In *Black Wealth: Your Road to Small Business Success*, 166-174. New York, N.Y.: Wiley, 2000.

WILLIAMS, EDWARD PORTER

Cleary, David Powers. "Sherwin-Williams Paints—Not Just to Produce Paints, But to Contribute to Brighter, More Colorful Living." In *Great American Brands: The Success Formulas That Made Them Famous*, 256-260. New York, N.Y: Fairchild Publications, 1981.

WILLIAMS, ELLA

Woodard, Michael D. "AEGIR Systems—Ella Williams." In *Black Entrepreneurs in America: Stories of Struggle and Success*, 158-171. New Brunswick, N.J.: Rutgers University Press, 1997.

WILLIAMS, GRETCHEN MINYARD

Enkelis, Liane, and Karen Olsen. "Liz Minyard & Gretchen Minyard Williams: Co-Chairmen of the Board, Minyard Foods Stores, Inc." In *On Our Own Terms: Portraits of Women Business Leaders* , 102-111. San Francisco, Calif.: Berrett-Koehler, 1995.

WILLIAMS, TERRIE

Clarke, Caroline V. "Terrie Williams: CEO, The Terrie Williams Agency." In *Take a Lesson: Today's Black Achievers and How They Made It and What They Learned Along the Way*, 255-263. New York, N.Y.: Wiley, 2001.

WILLIAMS, VERONICA ANN

Mikaelian, A. "Veronica Ann Williams." In *Women Who Mean Business: Success Stories of Women Over Forty*, 210-214. New York, N.Y.: William Morrow & Co., 1999.

WILLIS, BEVERLY

Rich-McCoy, Lois. "An Understatement of Herself: Beverly Willis." In *Millionairess: Self-Made Women of America*, 169-188. New York, N.Y.: Harper & Row, 1978.

WILSON, CHARLES E. (G.E.)

Shannon, Homer H. "Charles E. Wilson." In *America's Fifty Foremost Business Leaders,* ed. B. C. Forbes, 431-438. New York, N.Y.: B.C. Forbes, 1948.

WILSON, CHARLES E. (G.M.)

Finlay, Bob. "Charles E. Wilson." In *America's Fifty Foremost Business Leaders,* ed. B. C. Forbes, 439-450. New York, N.Y.: B.C. Forbes, 1948.

WILSON, CHARLES KEMMONS

Shook, Carrie, and Robert L. Shook. "Holiday Inn, Worldwide: Nobody Understands the Trials and Travails of Franchisees Like Holiday Inn." In *Franchising: The Business Strategy That Changed the World*, 93-114. Englewood Cliffs, NJ: Prentice Hall, 1993.

Silver, A. David. "Charles Kemmons Wilson." In *Entrepreneurial Megabucks: The 100 Greatest Entrepreneurs of the Last 25 Years*, 447-449. New York, N.Y.: Wiley, 1985.

WILSON, DOUG

Kingston, Brett. "Doug Wilson of Doug Wilson Studios." In *The Dynamos: Who Are They Anyway?*, 199-205. New York, N.Y.: Wiley, 1987.

WILSON, GARY

Kadlec, Daniel J. "Gary Wilson: Other People's Money." In *Masters of the Universe; Winning Strategies of America's Greatest Deal Makers*, 133-160. New York, N.Y.: HarperBusiness, 1999.

WILSON, JOSEPH

Gross, Daniel, and the Editors of Forbes Magazine. "Betting the Company: Joseph Wilson and the Xerox 914." In *Forbes Greatest Business Stories of All Time*, 194-211. New York, N.Y.: Wiley, 1996.

WILSON, ROBERT

Train, John. "Robert Wilson: Pumping Up the Tulips." In *The Money Masters*, 187-206. New York, N.Y.: Harper & Row, 1980.

Train, John. "Robert Wilson: Without a Rope." In *Money Masters of Our Time*, 260-273. New York, N.Y.: HarperBusiness, 2000.

WINBLAD, ANN

Zientara, Marguerite. "Ann Winblad: Creating Something Out of Thin Air." In *Women, Technology & Power: Ten Stars and the History They Made*, 72-77. New York, N.Y.: AMACOM, American Management Association, 1987.

Zientara, Marguerite. "Ann Winblad: 'Lucky Stumbling'." In *Women, Technology & Power: Ten Stars and the History They Made*, 83-89. New York, N.Y.: AMACOM, American Management Association, 1987.

Zientara, Marguerite. "Ann Winblad: Money, Fame, And a New Start." In *Women, Technology & Power: Ten Stars and the History They Made*, 219-225. New York, N.Y.: AMACOM, American Management Association, 1987.

WINFREY, OPRAH

Brands, H. W. "The Celebrity As Entrepreneur." In *Masters of Enterprise: Giants of American Business from John Jacob Astor and J.P. Morgan to Bill Gates and Oprah Winfrey*, 292-302. New York, N.Y.: Free Press, 1999.

Jeffrey, Laura S. "Oprah Winfrey: If She Can Make It…" In *Great American Businesswomen*, 82-91. Springfield, N.J.: Enslow Publishers, Inc., 1996.

Landrum, Gene N. "Oprah Winfrey—Persuasive Charismatic." In *Profiles of Female Genius: Thirteen Creative Women Who Changed the World*, 374-391. Amherst, N.Y.: Prometheus Books, 1994.

Mariotti, Steve, and Mike Caslin. "Oprah Winfrey: Harpo, Inc." In *The Very Very Rich: How They Got That Way and How You Can, Too!*, 109-115. Franklin Lakes, NJ: Career Press, 2000.

WINTER, EVELYN

Lyons, Mary. "Evelyn Winter: Evelyn Winter Fine Art, Artist, 'Doing What is You'." In *Maine's Achieving Women: Conversations with Entrepreneurs*, 95-104. Old Orchard Beach, ME: Lilac River Press, 1999.

WINTER, LYNN

Alexander, Shoshana. "Lynn Winter: Lynn's Paradise Café, Louisville, Kentucky." In *Women's Ventures, Women's Visions: 29 Inspiring Stories From Women Who Started Their Own Businesses*, 11-19. Freedom, Calif.: The Crossing Press, 1997.

WINTERS, JAMES W. II

Mitchell, Niki Butler. "He's Got the Power: James W. Winters II, CEO, United Energy, Inc." In *The New Color of Success: Twenty Young Black Millionaires Tell You How They're Making it*, 199-209. Rocklin, Calif.: Prima Publishing, 2000.

WISE, RANDY

Posner, Bruce G. "Seeing Red; He Who laughs last, Laughs Best—So Randy Wise Doesn't Mind the Inevitable Reaction When He Tells People About His Contact Lenses for Chickens. That's Right, For Chickens." In *Anatomy of a Start-Up: Why Some New Businesses Succeed and Others Fail: 27 Real-Life Case Studies,* ed. Elizabeth K. Longsworth, 253-262. Boston, Mass.: Inc. Publishing, 1991.

WOLFSON, LOUIS

Sobel, Robert. "Louis Wolfson—The Junkman." In *Dangerous Dreamers: The Financial Innovators from Charles Merrill to Michael Milken*, 9-22. New York, N.Y.: Wiley, 1993.

WONG, ALBERT

Kingston, Brett. "Qureshey, Wong, And Yuen of AST Research, Inc." In *The Dynamos: Who Are They Anyway?*, 113-117. New York, N.Y: Wiley, 1987.

WOOD, FORREST

MacPhee, William. "Forrest and Nina Wood of Ranger Boats." In *Rare Breed: The Entrepreneur, An American Culture*, 189+. Chicago, Ill.: Probus Publishing Company, 1987.

WOOD, NINA

MacPhee, William. "Forrest and Nina Wood of Ranger Boats." In *Rare Breed: The Entrepreneur, An American Culture*, 189+. Chicago, Ill.: Probus Publishing Company, 1987.

WOOD, REX

Uris, Auren. "Rex Wood—Showroom in the Parlor." In *The Executive Breakthrough; 21 Roads to the Top*, 187-204. Garden City, N.Y.: Doubleday, 1967.

WOOD, ROBERT E.

Bell, Laurence. "Robert E. Wood." In *America's Fifty Foremost Business Leaders,* ed. B. C. Forbes, 451-458. New York, N.Y.: B.C. Forbes, 1948.

"Profiting from Foresight: General Robert E. Wood." In *Lessons of Leadership: 21 Executives Speak Out on Creating, Developing and Managing Success.* Presented by the editors of Nation's Business, 99-110. Garden City, N.Y.: Doubleday, 1968.

Polos, Nicholas. "Marshall Field—The 'Merchant Prince'—And Robert E. Wood—The 'soldier Merchant'." In *Business Entrepreneurs in the West,* ed. Ted C. Hinckley, 28-38. Manhattan, Kans.: Sunflower University Press, 1986.

WOODRUFF, ROBERT W.

Bell, Laurence. "Robert W. Woodruff." In *America's Fifty Foremost Business Leaders,* ed. B. C. Forbes, 459-468. New York, N.Y.: B.C. Forbes, 1948.

Brands, H. W. "The Real Thing: Robert Woodruff." In *Masters of Enterprise: Giants of American Business from John Jacob Astor and J.P. Morgan to Bill Gates and Oprah Winfrey*, 195-210. New York, N.Y.: Free Press, 1999.

Means, Howard B. "Robert Woodruff: The Brand's the Thing." In *Money & Power: The History of Business*, 185-203. New York, N.Y.: Wiley, 2001.

WOODS, EMILY GINADER

Pottker, Jan. "J. Crew Group, Inc.: Merchant of Lifestyle." In *Born to Power: Heirs to America's Leading Businesses*, 270-276. New York, N.Y.: Barron's, 1992.

WOODS, HERBERT

Harris, Wendy Beech. "Sylvia and Herbert Woods, Sylvia's Restaurant: The Queen and King of Soul Food." In *Against All Odds: Ten Entrepreneurs Who Followed Their Hearts and Found Success,* 1-19. New York, N.Y.: Wiley, 2001.

WOODS, SYLVIA

Harris, Wendy Beech. "Sylvia and Herbert Woods, Sylvia's Restaurant: The Queen and King of Soul Food." In *Against All Odds: Ten Entrepreneurs Who Followed Their Hearts and Found Success*, 1-19. New York, N.Y.: Wiley, 2001.

WOOLWORTH, FRANK W.

"King of the Five-And-Dime: Nickels and Dimes Added Up to a Multi-Million-Dollar Merchandising Empire for Frank W. Woolworth." In *The 50 Great Pioneers of American Industry.* By the Editors of News Front and Year, 84-87. Maplewood, N.J.: C.S. Hammond, 1964.

Klepper, Michael M., and Robert Gunther. "Frank W. Woolworth (1852-1919): Nickeled and Dimed His Way to Wealth." In *The Wealthy 100 : From Benjamin Franklin to Bill Gates—A Ranking of the Richest Americans, Past and Present,* 281-283. Secaucus, N.J. : Carol Pub. Group, 1996.

McSherry, Ronald T. "Frank W. Woolworth: Nothing Over Ten Cents." In *Nine American Self-Made Men and Their Secrets to Success,* 1-10. Denver, Colo.: U.S.A. Publishing, 1983.

WOOTEN, PATTY

Wooten, Patty. "How I Became a Humor Consultant." In *How I Became a Nurse Entrepreneur: Tales from 50 Nurses in Business,* 233-238. Petaluma, Calif.: National Nurses in Business Association, 1991.

WORTH, RICHARD S.

Brown, Paul B. "Cookie Monsters; R.W. Frookies Inc. Is Betting Its All-Natural Product Can Grab Shelf Space Now Occupied by Such Classics As Oreo, Fig Newtons, and Mallomars." In *Anatomy of a Start-Up: Why Some New Businesses Succeed and Others Fail: 27 Real-Life Case Studies,* ed. Elizabeth K. Longsworth, 123-131. Boston, Mass.: Inc. Publishing, 1991.

WOZNIAK, STEVE

Mariotti, Steve, and Lorraine Mooney. "Steve Wozniak: Trailblazer of the Computer Era." In *Entrepreneurs in Profile,* 128-131. London: National Foundation for Teaching Entrepreneurship, 1991.

Mariotti, Steve, and Mike Caslin. "Steve Wozniak & Steve Jobs: Apple Computers." In *The Very Very Rich: How They Got That Way and How You Can, Too!,* 117-125. Franklin Lakes, NJ: Career Press, 2000.

Silver, A. David. "Steven P. Jobs; Steven Wozniak." In *Entrepreneurial Megabucks: The 100 Greatest Entrepreneurs of the Last 25 Years,* 250-253. New York, N.Y.: Wiley, 1985.

WRENN, JOYCE

Zientara, Marguerite. "Joyce Wrenn: Making Every Minute Count." In *Women, Technology & Power: Ten Stars and the History They Made,* 56-62. New York, N.Y.: AMACOM, American Management Association, 1987.

Zientara, Marguerite. "Joyce Wrenn: Making the Elephant Dance." In *Women, Technology & Power: Ten Stars and the History They Made,* 141-147. New York, N.Y.: AMACOM, American Management Association, 1987.

Zientara, Marguerite. "Joyce Wrenn: Sailing into a Storm." In *Women, Technology & Power: Ten Stars and the History They Made,* 183-186. New York, N.Y.: AMACOM, American Management Association, 1987.

WRIGHT, DEBORAH C.

Clarke, Caroline V. "Deborah C. Wright: President and CEO, Carver Federal Savings Bank." In *Take a Lesson: Today's Black Achievers and How They Made It and What They Learned Along the Way*, 265-275. New York, N.Y.: Wiley, 2001.

WRIGHT, HARRY

"Baseball's First Pro: Harry Wright and the Cincinnati Red Stockings of 1869 Started Baseball on the Road to Big Time." In *The 50 Great Pioneers of American Industry*. By the Editors of News Front and Year, 59-63. Maplewood, N.J.: C.S. Hammond, 1964.

WRIGHT, MIKE A.

"Solving Problems by Organized Action: M. A. Wright." In *Lessons of Leadership: 21 Executives Speak Out on Creating, Developing and Managing Success*. Presented by the editors of Nation's Business, 226-236. Garden City, N.Y.: Doubleday, 1968.

WRIGLEY, WILLIAM JR.

Cleary, David Powers. "Wrigley's Chewing Gum; Restraint in Regard to Immediate Profits." In *Great American Brands: The Success Formulas That Made Them Famous*, 287-294. New York, N.Y: Fairchild Publications, 1981.

Klepper, Michael M., and Robert Gunther. "William Wrigley Jr. (1861-1932): Double the Flavor, Double the Fortune." In *The Wealthy 100 : From Benjamin Franklin to Bill Gates—A Ranking of the Richest Americans, Past and Present*, 333-335. Secaucus, N.J. : Carol Pub. Group, 1996.

WRISTON, WALTER B.

Levinson, Harry, and Stuart Rosenthal. "Walter B. Wriston." In *CEO: Corporate Leadership in Action*, 56-95. New York, N.Y: Basic Books, 1984.

WYLIE, JANET C.

Mikaelian, A. "Janet C. Wylie." In *Women Who Mean Business: Success Stories of Women Over Forty*, 315-319. New York, N.Y.: William Morrow & Co., 1999.

THE WYNNE FAMILY

Sheehy, Sandy. "The Wynnes: Dynasty III." In *Texas Big Rich; Exploits, Eccentricities, And Fabulous Fortunes Won and Lost*, 174-183. New York, N.Y.: Morrow, 1990.

WYNNE, PATRICE

Alexander, Shoshana. "Patrice Wynne: GAIA Bookstore and Community Center, Berkeley, California." In *Women's Ventures, Women's Visions: 29 Inspiring Stories From Women Who Started Their Own Businesses*, 167-174. Freedom, Calif.: The Crossing Press, 1997.

WYRSCH, ANN MARIE

Wyrsch, Ann Marie. "Recovery/Discovery: Conception to Now." In *How I Became a Nurse Entrepreneur: Tales from 50 Nurses in Business*, 249-254. Petaluma, Calif.: National Nurses in Business Association, 1991.

WYRWAS, MARGARET E.

Mikaelian, A. "Margaret E. Wyrwas." In *Women Who Mean Business: Success Stories of Women Over Forty*, 219-223. New York, N.Y.: William Morrow & Co., 1999.

WYSE, LOIS

Taylor, Russel R. "Lois Wyse; She Writes Books on the Side." In *Exceptional Entrepreneurial Women*, 13-17. New York, N.Y: Quorum Books, 1988.

YANG, JERRY

Mariotti, Steve, and Mike Caslin. "Jerry Yang: Yahoo!" In *The Very Very Rich: How They Got That Way and How You Can, Too!*, 127-130. Franklin Lakes, NJ: Career Press, 2000.

Price, Christopher. "Jerry Yang—Yahoo! 'Size Matters'." In *The Internet Entrepreneurs: Business Rules Are Good: Break Them*, 18-33. London, Eng.: FT.com, 2000.

YANG, MEI PING

Herera, Sue. "Mei Ping Yang: Vice President and Proprietory Trader, Goldman Sachs." In *Women of the Street: Making It on Wall Street— The World's Toughest Business*, 35-46. New York, N.Y.: Wiley, 1997.

Koppel, Mara. "A Women for All Seasons—Mei Ping Yang." In *Women of the Pits: Shattering the Glass Ceiling in Financial Markets*, 129-140. Chicago, Ill.: Dearborn Financial Publishers, 1998.

YATES, JEAN

Gardner, Ralph. "Jean Yates." In *Young, Gifted, and Rich: The Secrets of America's Most Successful Entrepreneurs*, 143-155. New York, N.Y.: Wallaby Books, 1984.

YATES, LUCINDA

Lyons, Mary. "Lucinda Yates: Designs by Lucinda, President, 'Changing the World One Pin at a Time'." In *Maine's Achieving Women: Conversations with Entrepreneurs*, 19-28. Old Orchard Beach, ME: Lilac River Press, 1999.

YEE, MIN

Tsang, Cheryl D. "Min Yee 'Min', 1985-1992." In *Microsoft First Generation: The Success Secrets of the Visionaries Who Launched a Technology Empire*, 149-178. New York, N.Y.: Wiley, 2000.

YERKES, CHARLES TYSON

Burnley, James. "Charles Tyson Terkes: The American Street Railway King." In *Millionaires and Kings of Enterprise; The Marvellous Careers of Some Americans Who by Pluck, Foresight, And Energy Have Made Themselves Masters in the Fields of Industry and Finance*, 64-78. Philadelphia, Penn.: J. B. Lippincott, 1901.

YILK, NANCY

Lassen, Ali. "Nancy Yilk: Founder, Corporate Solutions." In *The Secret of Their Success: Women Entrepreneurs Reveal How They Made It*, 215-220. Carlsbad, Calif.: Ali Lassen Success System, 1990.

YOUNG, AMIE

Lassen, Ali. "Amie Young: Financial Planner, S. G. Zimmerman and Associates." In *The Secret of Their Success: Women Entrepreneurs Reveal How They Made It*, 67-74. Carlsbad, Calif.: Ali Lassen Success System, 1990.

YOUNG, CHRISTOPHER D.

Mitchell, Niki Butler. "Conquering the Internet: Christopher D. Young, President and CEO; Brandy M. Thomas, Chairman and CEO, Cyveillance." In *The New Color of Success: Twenty Young Black Millionaires Tell You How They're Making it*, 169-182. Rocklin, Calif.: Prima Publishing, 2000.

YOUNG, ROBERT R.

Hillyer, William Hurd. "Robert R. Young." In *America's Fifty Foremost Business Leaders,* ed. B. C. Forbes, 469-476. New York, N.Y.: B.C. Forbes, 1948.

YUEN, THOMAS

Kingston, Brett. "Qureshey, Wong, And Yuen of AST Research, Inc." In *The Dynamos: Who Are They Anyway?*, 113-117. New York, N.Y: Wiley, 1987.

Aronoff, Craig E., and John L. Ward. "Safi U. Qureshey; Thomas C. K. Yuen." In *Contemporary Entrepreneurs*, 402-407. Detroit, Mich.: Omnigraphics, Inc., 1992.

ZAGURY, CAROL S.

"Consulting Services Through PHA." In *How I Became a Nurse Entrepreneur: Tales from 50 Nurses in Business*, 143-150. Petaluma, Calif.: National Nurses in Business Association, 1991.

ZEISS, BEVERLY J.

Zeiss, Beverly J. "The Courage to Take the First Step." In *How I Became a Nurse Entrepreneur: Tales from 50 Nurses in Business*, 99-106. Petaluma, Calif.: National Nurses in Business Association, 1991.

ZIMMERMAN, JAN

Murphy, Linda. "Jan Zimmerman and Sandra Hutchins." In *Computer Entrepreneurs: People Who Built Successful Businesses Around Computers*, 13-22. San Diego, Calif.: Computer Publishing Enterprises, 1990.

ZORAN, LADICORBIC

Agins, Teri. "Outside of the Box: Zoran." In *The End of Fashion: The Mass Marketing of the Clothing Business*, 247-274. New York, N.Y.: William Morrow, 1999.

ZWEIG, MARTIN

King, Norman. "Martin Zweig." In *The Money Messiah$*, 196-198. New York, N.Y.: Coward-McCann, 1983.

APPENDIX

COLLECTED WORKS

Adams, James Ring. *The Big Fix: Inside the S&L Scandal: How an Unholy Alliance of Politics and Money Destroyed America's Banking System.* New York, N.Y.: Wiley, 1990. 308 p.

Agins, Teri. *The End of Fashion: The Mass Marketing of the Clothing Business.* New York, N.Y.: William Morrow, 1999. 320 p.

Airline Executives and Federal Regulation: Case Studies in American Enterprise from the Airmail Era to the Dawn of the Jet Age, ed. W. David Lewis. Columbus, Ohio: Ohio State University Press, 2000. 379 p.

Alexander, Shoshana. *Women's Ventures, Women's Visions: 29 Inspiring Stories From Women Who Started Their Own Businesses.* Freedom, Calif.: The Crossing Press, 1997. 217 p.

American Dynasties Today. By the editors of the Wall Street Journal. Homewood, Ill.: Dow Jones-Irwin, 1980. 281 p.

Aronoff, Craig E., and John L. Ward. *Contemporary Entrepreneurs.* Detroit, Mich.: Omnigraphics, Inc., 1992. 488 p.

Auletta, Ken. *The Highwaymen; Warriors of the Information Superhighway.* New York, N.Y.: Random House, 1997. 346 p.

Blout, Elkan. *The Power of Boldness: Ten Master Builders of American Industry Tell Their Success Stories*. Washington, D.C.: Joseph Henry Press, 1996. 214 p.

Brands, H. W. *Masters of Enterprise: Giants of American Business from John Jacob Astor and J.P. Morgan to Bill Gates and Oprah Winfrey*. New York, N.Y.: Free Press, 1999. 354 p.

Buchholz, Barbara B., and Margaret Crane. *Corporate Bloodlines: The Future of the Family Firm*. New York, N.Y.: Carol Publishing Group, 1989. 290 p.

Bunley, James. *Millionaires and Kings of Enterprise; The Marvellous Careers of Some Americans Who by Pluck, Foresight, And Energy Have Made Themselves Masters in the Fields of Industry and Finance*. Philadelphia, Penn.: J. B. Lippincott, 1901. 512 p.

Business Entrepreneurs in the West, ed. Ted C. Hinckley. Manhattan, Kans.: Sunflower University Press, 1986. 120 p.

Cahill, Timothy Patrick. *Profiles in the American Dream: The Real-Life Stories of the Struggles of American Entrepreneurs*. Hanover, Mass.: Christopher Publishing House, 1994. 143 p.

Clarke, Caroline V. *Take a Lesson: Today's Black Achievers and How They Made It and What They Learned Along the Way*. New York, N.Y.: Wiley, 2001. 283 p.

Cleary, David Powers. *Great American Brands: The Success Formulas That Made Them Famous*. New York, N.Y.: Morrow, 1989. 380 p.

Coleridge, Nicholas. *Paper Tigers: The Latest, Greatest Newspaper Tycoons*. New York, N.Y.: Carol Publishing Group, 1994. 592 p.

Cose, Ellis. *The Press*. New York, N.Y.: Morrow, 1989. 380 p.

Darby, Edwin. *The Fortune Builders*. Garden City, N.Y.: Doublweday, 1986. 276 p.

Davis, William. *The Innovators: The Essential Guide to Business Thinkers, Achievers and Entrepreneurs*. New York, N.Y.: AMACOM, 1987. 408 p.

Diamond, Sigmond. *The Reputation of the American Businessman*. Cambridge, Mass.: Harvard University Press, 1955. 209 p.

Dingle, Derek T. *Black Enterprise Titans of the B.E. 100s: Black CEOs Who Redefined and Conquered American Business*. New York, N.Y.: Wiley, 1999. 238 p.

A Dozen Roads to Success: Being Graphic Sketches of Twelve of the Most Prominent Business Men of America, And Showing How They Became Millionaires. Philadelphia, Penn.: Girard Pub. Co., 1894. 198 p.

Elfstrand, Rhonda. *The Story Behind the Success: Learning From Pittsburgh Professionals*. Pittsburgh, Penn.: Steel Publishing Partners, 1996. 283 p.

Enkelis, Liane, and Karen Olsen. *On Our Own Terms: Portraits of Women Business Leaders*. San Francisco, Calif.: Berrett-Koehler, 1995. 154 p.

Ericksen, Gregory K. *Net Entrepreneurs Only : 10 Entrepreneurs Tell the Stories of Their Success*. New York : John Wiley, 2000. 207 P.

Ericksen, Gregory K. *What's Luck Got to Do With It; Twelve Entrepreneurs Reveal the Secrets Behind Their Success*. New York, N.Y.: Wiley, 1997. 231 p.

Ericksen, Gregory K. *Women Entrepreneurs Only: Twelve Women Entrepreneurs Tell The Stories of Their Success*. New York, N.Y.: Wiley, 1999. 259 p.

Erlich, Judith Ramsey. *The New Crowd: The Changing of the Jewish Guard on Wall Street*. Boston, Mass.: Little Brown, 1989. 444 p.

Fanning, Leonard M. *Titans of Business*. Philadelphia, Penn.: Lippincott, 1964. 240 p.

Farnham, Alan. *Forbes Great Success Stories: Twelve Tales of Victory Wrested from Defeat.* New York, N.Y.: Wiley, 2000. 271 p.

The 50 Great Pioneers of American Industry; The Stories of Rockefeller, Swift, Edison, Woolworth, Squibb, Procter, Sears, Otis, Singer, Carrier, and 40 Other Business Leaders and Courageous Innovators Whose Activities Founded Major Industries and Shaped Today's Economy. By the Editors of News Front and Year. Maplewood, N.J.: C.S. Hammond, 1964. 207 p.

Folsom, Burton W. *Empire Builders: How Michigan Entrepreneurs Helped Make America Great.* Traverse City, Mich.: Rhodes & Easton, 1998. 205 p.

Forbes, B. C., ed. *America's Fifty Foremost Business Leaders.* New York, N.Y.: B.C. Forbes, 1948. 483 p.

Forbes, Malcolm S. *Women Who Made a Difference.* New York, N.Y.: Simon & Schuster, 1990. 320 p.

Fucini, Joseph J., and Suzi Fucini. *Experience, Inc.; Men and Women Who Founded Famous Companies After the Age of 40.* New York, N.Y.: Free Press, 1987. 244 p.

Gardner, Ralph. *Young, Gifted, and Rich: The Secrets of America's Most Successful Entrepreneurs.* New York, N.Y.: Wallaby Books, 1984. 207 p.

Gilder, George. *The Spirit of Enterprise.* New York, N.Y.: Simon and Schuster, 1984. 274 p.

Goldwasser, Thomas. *Family Pride; Profiles of Five of America's Best-Run Family Businesses.* New York, N.Y.: Dodd, Mead & Company, 1986.

Gray, Bob, ed. *How Entrepreneurs Make Business Profits: A Study of Personal Success Stories From Cordovan Business Journals.* Houston, Tex.: Cordovan Press, 1982. 173 p.

Great Stories of American Businessmen, From *American Heritage, The Magazine of History*. New York, N.Y.: American Heritage Publishing Co., 1954. 382 p.

Gross, Daniel, and the Editors of Forbes Magazine. *Forbes Greatest Business Stories of All Time*. New York, N.Y.: Wiley, 1996. 362 p.

Gunther, Max, ed. *The Very, Very Rich and How They Got That Way*. Chicago, Ill.: The Playboy Press, 1972. 311 p.

Harris, Wendy Beech. *Against All Odds: Ten Entrepreneurs Who Followed Their Hearts and Found Success*. New York, N.Y.: Wiley, 2001. 237 p.

Herera, Sue. *Women of the Street: Making It on Wall Street—The World's Toughest Business*. New York, N.Y.: Wiley, 1997. 208 p.

Hillkirk, John, and Gary Jacobson. *Grit, Guts, And Genius: True Tales of Megasuccess: Who Made Them Happen and How They Did It*. Boston, Mass.: Houghton Mifflin, 1990. 283 p.

How I Became a Nurse Entrepreneur: Tales From 50 Nurses in Business. Petaluma, Calif.: National Nurses in Business Association, 1991. 313 p.

Hughes, Jonathan. *The Vital Few: The Entrepreneur and American Economic Progress*. Expanded Edition, New York, N.Y.: Oxford University Press, 1986. 610 p.

Jager, Rama Dev, and Rafael Ortiz. *In the Company of Giants: Candid Conversations With the Visionaries of the Digital World*. New York, N.Y.: McGraw-Hill, 1997. 232 p.

Jeffrey, Laura S. *Great American Businesswomen*. Springfield, N.J.: Enslow Publishers, Inc., 1996. 112 p.

Kadlec, Daniel J. *Masters of the Universe; Winning Strategies of America's Greatest Deal Makers*. New York, N.Y.: HarperBusiness, 1999. 282 p.

Kao, John J. *The Entrepreneur*. Englewood Cliffs, N.J.: Prentice Hall, 1991. 207 p.

King, Norman. *The Money Messiah$*. New York, N.Y.: Coward-McCann, 1983. 221 p.

Kingstone, Brett. *The Dynamos: Who Are They Anyway?* New York, N.Y.: Wiley, 1987. 256 p.

Klepper, Michael M., and Robert Gunther. *The Wealthy 100 : From Benjamin Franklin to Bill Gates—A Ranking of the Richest Americans, Past and Present.* Secaucus, N.J. : Carol Pub. Group, 1996. 362 p.

Koehn, Nancy F. *Brand New: How Entrepreneurs Earned Consumers' Trust from Wedgwood to Dell.* Boston, Mass.: Harvard Business School Press, 2001. 469 p.

Koppel, Mara. *Women of the Pits: Shattering the Glass Ceiling in Financial Markets.* Chicago, Ill.: Dearborn Financial Publishers, 1998. 175 p.

Koppel, Robert. *Bulls, Bears, And Millionaires: War Stories of Trading Life.* Chicago, Ill.: Dearborn Financial Publishers, 1997. 209 p.

Landrum, Gene N. *Profiles of Female Genius: Thirteen Creative Women Who Changed the World.* Amherst, N.Y.: Prometheus Books, 1994. 437 P.

Landrum, Gene N. *Profiles of Genius: Thirteen Creative Men Who Changed the World.* Buffalo, N.Y.: Prometheus Books, 1993. 263 p.

Lassen, Ali. *The Secret of Their Success: Women Entrepreneurs Reveal How They Made It.* Carlsbad, Calif.: Ali Lassen Success System, 1990. 227 p.

Lessons of Leadership: 21 Executives Speak Out on Creating, Developing and Managing Success. Presented by the editors of Nation's Business. Garden City, N.Y.: Doubleday, 1968. 271 p.

Levinson, Harry, and Stuart Rosenthal. *CEO; Corporate Leadership in Action.* New York, N.Y.: Basic Books, 1984. 308 p.

Levitt, Mortimer. *How to Start Your Own Business Without Losing Your Shirt; Secrets of Seventeen Successful Entrepreneurs.* New York, N.Y.: Atheneum, 1988. 213 p.

Lewis, Oscar. *The Big Four; The Story of Huntington, Stanford, Hopkins, And Crocker, And of the Building of the Central Pacific.* New York, N.Y.: A.A. Knopf, 1938. 418 p.

Liberman, Gail, and Alan Lavine. *Rags to Riches: Motivating Stories of How Ordinary People Achieved Extraordinary Wealth!.* Chicago, Ill.: Dearborn, 2000. 228 p.

Livesay, Harold C. *American Made: Men Who Shaped the American Economy.* Boston, Mass.: Little, Brown, 1979. 310 p.

Longsworth, Elizabeth K., ed. *Anatomy of a Start-Up: Why Some New Businesses Succeed and Others Fail: 27 Real-Life Case Studies.* Boston, Mass.: Inc. Publishing, 1991. 432 p.

Lyons, Mary. *Maine's Achieving Women: Conversations with Entrepreneurs.* Old Orchard Beach, ME: Lilac River Press, 1999. 160 p.

MacPhee, William. *Rare Breed: The Entrepreneur, An American Culture.* Chicago, Ill.: Probusa Publishing Company, 1987. 224 p.

McSherry, Ronald T. *Nine American Self-Made Men and Their Secrets to Success.* Denver, Colo.: U.S.A. Publishing, 1983. 76 p.

Mariotti, Steve, and Mike Caslin. *The Very Very Rich: How They Got That Way and How You Can, Too!.* Franklin Lakes, NJ: Career Press, 2000. 153 p.

Mariotti, Steve, and Lorraine Mooney. *Entrepreneurs in Profile.* London: National Foundation for Teaching Entrepreneurship, 1991. 135 p.

Means, Howard B. *Money & Power: The History of Business.* New York, N.Y.: Wiley, 2001. 274 p.

Meyer, Michael. *The Alexander Complex; The Dreams That Drive the Great Businessmen.* New York, N.Y.: Times Books, 1989. 258 p.

Mikaelian, A. *Women Who Mean Business: Success Stories of Women Over Forty.* New York, N.Y.: William Morrow & Co., 1999. 353 p.

Millman, Nancy. *Emperors of Adland; Inside the Advertising Revolution.* New York, N.Y.: Warner Books, 1988. 225 p.

Mitchell, Niki Butler. *The New Color of Success: Twenty Young Black Millionaires Tell You How They're Making It.* Rocklin, Calif.: Prima Publishing, 2000. 268 p.

Morgenson, Gretchen, ed. *Forbes Great Minds of Business.* New York, N.Y.: Wiley, 1997. 228 p.

Mountfield, David. *The Railway Barons.* New York, N.Y.: Norton, 1979. 224 p.

Murphy, Linda. *Computer Entrepreneurs: People Who Built Successful Businesses Around Computers.* San Diego, Calif.: Computer Publishing Enterprises, 1990. 128 p.

Nayak, P. Ranganath, and John M. Ketteringham. *Breakthroughs!.* San Diego, Calif: Pfeiffer & Company, 1994. 428 p.

Oster, Merrill J. *The Entrepreneur's Creed: The Principles & Passions of 20 Successful Entrepreneurs.* Nashville, Tenn.: Broadman & Holman Publishers, 2001. 226 p.

Pestrak, Debra. *Playing with the Big Boys: Success Stories of the Most Powerful Women in Business.* Carlsbad, Calif.: SUN Publications, 2001. 250 p.

Pile, Robert B. *Top Entrepreneurs and Their Businesses.* Minneapolis, Minn.: The Oliver Press, 1993. 160 p.

Pine, Carol, and Susan Mundale. *Self-Made: The Stories of 12 Minnesota Entrepreneurs.* Minneapolis, Minn.: Dorn Books, 1982. 223 p.

Pottker, Jan. *Born to Power: Heirs to America's Leading Businesses*. New York, N.Y.: Barron's, 1992. 464 p.

Price, Christopher. *The Internet Entrepreneurs: Business Rules are Good: Break Them*. London, Eng.: FT.com, 2000. 195 p.

Profiles in Success: How Six Entrepreneurs Have Prospered in a Tough Business Environment. By the editors of *Managing*. New York, N.Y.: HBJ Newsletters, 1981. 63 p.

Redekop, Calvin W., and Benjamin W. Redekop, ed. *Entrepreneurs in the Faith Community: Profiles of Mennonites in Business*. Scottdale, Penn.: Herald Press, 1996. 268 p.

Rich-McCoy, Lois. *Millionairess: Self-Made Women of America*. New York, N.Y.: Harper & Row, 1978. 235 p.

Roberts, Edward B. *Entrepreneurs in High Technology: Lessons From MIT and Beyond*. New York, N.Y.: Oxford University Press, 1991. 385 p.

Sheehy, Sandy. *Texas Big Rich; Exploits, Eccentricities, and Fabulous Fortunes Won and Lost*. New York, N.Y.: Morrow, 1990. 415 p.

Shook, Carrie, and Robert L. Shook. *Franchising: The Business Strategy That Changed the World*, . Englewood Cliffs, NJ: Prentice Hall, 1993. 258 p.

Shook, Robert L. *The Entrepreneurs: Twelve Who Took Risks and Succeeded*. New York, N.Y.: Harper & Row, 1980. 181 p.

Shook, Robert L. *The Chief Executive Officers: Men Who Run Big Business in America*. New York, N.Y.: Harper & Row, 1981. 239 p.

Shook, Robert L. *Why Didn't I Think of That*. New York, N.Y.: New American Library, 1982. 188 p.

Silver, A. David. *Entrepreneurial Megabucks: The 100 Greatest Entrepreneurs of the Last 25 Years*. New York, N.Y.: Wiley, 1985. 467 p.

Slater, Robert. *Portraits in Silicon*. Cambridge, Mass.: MIT Press, 1987. 374 p.

Smith, Roy C. *Wealth Creators: The Rise of Today's Rich and Super-Rich*. New York, N.Y.: Truman Talley, 2001. 358 p.

Sobel, Robert. *Dangerous Dreamers: The Financial Innovators From Charles Merrill to Michael Milken*. New York, N.Y.: Wiley, 1993. 260 p.

Sobel, Robert. *The Entrepreneurs: Explorations Within the American Business Tradition*. New York, N.Y.: Weybright and Talley, 1974. 413 p.

Sobel, Robert. *The Rise and Fall of the Conglomerate Kings*. New York, N.Y.: Stein and Day, 1984. 240 p.

Sobel, Robert, and David B. Sicclia. *The Entrepreneurs: An American Adventure.* Boston, Mass.: Houghton Mifflin, 1986. 278 p.

Stevens, Mark. *Big Six: The Selling Out of America's Top Accounting Firms*. New York, N.Y.: Simon and Schuster, 1991. 352 p.

Stoddard, William Osborn. *Men of Business*. New York, N.Y.: Scribner's Sons, 1893. 317 p.

Suarez, Ruth. *Superstar Entrepreneurs of Small and Large Businesses Reveal Their Secrets*. Piscataway, N.J.: Research and Education Association, 1998. 253 p.

Success Secrets : How Eighteen Everyday Women Became Fortune Builders and Famous Speakers. Glendora, Calif.: Royal CBS Publishing, 1978. 276 p.

Taylor, Russel R. *Exceptional Entrepreneurial Women.* New York, N.Y.: Quorum Books, 1988. 178 p.

Train, John. *The Money Masters*. New York, N.Y.: Harper & Row, 1980. 296 p.

Train, John. *Money Masters of Our Time*. New York, N.Y.: HarperBusiness, 2000. 388 p.

Train, John. *The New Money Masters : Winning Investment Strategies of Soros, Lynch, Steinhardt, Rogers, Neff, Wanger, Michaelis, Carret*. New York, N.Y.: Harper & Row, 1989. 385 p.

Tsang, Cheryl D. *Microsoft First Generation: The Success Secrets of the Visionaries Who Launched a Technology Empire*. New York, N.Y.: Wiley, 2000. 254 p.

Uris, Auren. *The Executive Breakthrough; 21 Roads to the Top*. Garden City, N.Y.: Doubleday, 1967. 421 p.

Wallace, Robert L. *Black Wealth: Your Road to Small Business Success*. New York, N.Y.: Wiley, 2000. 285 p.

Wendel, Charles B. *The New Financiers*. Chicago, Ill.: Irwin Professional Pub., 1996. 342 p.

White, Jane. *A Few Good Women: Breaking the Barriers to Top Management*. Englewood Cliffs, N.J.: Prentice Hall, 1992. 229 p.

Women Achievers: A Series of Dialogues from the Womanagement Process. New York, N.Y.: American Telephone and Telegraph Co., 1997. 119 p.

Woodard, Michael D. *Black Entrepreneurs in America: Stories of Struggle and Success*. New Brunswick, N.J.: Rutgers University Press, 1997. 254 p.

Wren, Daniel A., and Ronald G. Greenwood. *Management Innovators: The People and Ideas That Have Shaped Modern Business*. New York, N.Y.: Oxford University Press, 1998. 254 p.

Zientara, Marguerite. *Women, Technology & Power: Ten Stars and the History They Made*. New York, N.Y.: AMACOM, American Management Association, 1987. 282 p.

INDEX BY CORPORATION